D0321015

1M

# Nobody's Child

DCPL0700007239

# Nobody's Child

## Cora Coleman

POOLBEG

Published 2007
by Poolbeg Press Ltd
123 Grange Hill, Baldoyle
Dublin 13, Ireland
E-mail: poolbeg@poolbeg.com
www.poolbeg.com

© Cora Coleman 2007

Copyright for typesetting, layout, design
© Poolbeg Press Ltd

The moral right of the author has been asserted.

1 3 5 7 9 10 8 6 4 2

A catalogue record for this book is available from the British Library.

ISBN 978-1-84223-312-2

All rights reserved. No part of this publication may be reproduced or transmitted in any form or by any means, electronic or mechanical, including photography, recording, or any information storage or retrieval system, without permission in writing from the publisher. The book is sold subject to the condition that it shall not, by way of trade or otherwise, be lent, resold or otherwise circulated without the publisher's prior consent in any form of binding or cover other than that in which it is published and without a similar condition, including this condition, being imposed on the subsequent purchaser.

Typeset by Patricia Hope in Sabon 11.5/15.5
Printed by
Litografia Rosés, S.A., Spain

## About the author

Cora Coleman was born in 1958 in Cobh, County Cork. She studied at University College Cork and received a BA Hons in Applied Psychology in 1979. She has lived abroad for many years, mainly in London and more recently in Dorset, where she lives with her son. She teaches English as a foreign language, has written and published poetry, paints and is a member of Wessex Astronomy, a local astronomical society.

# Acknowledgements

This book grew out of homework assignments set me by my counsellor Sue. She read the first drafts and encouraged me to continue. I would like to acknowledge my deep gratitude to her for this and for her help throughout our time working together.

*Note:* Most of the names and some of the details of people touched on in this memoir have been changed to preserve anonymity.

*For Luke and Christine*

# Part One

## Swill

In 1963, when I was five, I stood in our front room and looked out into the hall where my mother stood, crying. She was flanked by a policeman on one side and my father's mother, Cora, my namesake, on the other. Later that evening, after a hurried meal of scrambled eggs and toast, the policeman took us away – my mother and her five children: seven-year-old Grace, six-year-old Joseph, me, four-year-old Hannah, and Rose, who was just two. My grandmother was by turns threatening – "If you go, you needn't think you can come back!" – and pleading – "Please don't go, Kathleen, I'll make sure it never happens again". But my mother was in fear of her life so we made our way, in the police Morris Minor, to a convent in Midleton, a town about ten miles from our home in Cobh. She didn't take us to her family because they didn't want us. They'd never liked John, my father, and this turn-out was just too much. One of her sisters sent her five pounds and that was that.

The nuns ran a small refuge for people with nowhere else to go. It was a long red-brick annex at the side of the convent and contained dormitories, a refectory, wash rooms and a laundry. The toilets were outside, beyond the gardens. Our billet was an iron bed at the far end of a female dormitory, where all six of us slept together, some at the top and some at the bottom.

My mother's arms and shoulders were discoloured from extensive bruising. The bruises were black, blue, purple, yellow and green. The big inky splashes ran into each other so that there was hardly any healthy flesh visible. These bruises were an everyday sight to me but I knew they were shocking to others because a policeman, a doctor and the nuns had wanted to see them, after which there were hushed exclamations like "Dear God Almighty!" and "Sacred heart of Jesus!" and a lot of tutting.

We were the only children there and the dormitory was scary at first; cold and dark, with a high vaulted ceiling and Gothic windows. We girls wore liberty bodices, old-fashioned thermal vests and kept them on in bed. If we wanted to go to the toilet during the night, a nun accompanied us across the garden, her white habit flapping luminously in the dark. There were twenty beds in the room, in two rows of ten, occupied by a variety of women – old, destitute, disabled, alcoholic and mentally unwell – whose snores echoed around us during the night. The dormitory had a sort of ante-room with a stove which was lit at night. The women sat around it talking and sometimes laughing softly. When the fire was well away, the stove door was opened and our shadows were huge on the wall. When my mother was distracted, we dive-bombed under the beds and raced each other up and down the room, skating and slipping on the shiny linoleum. In the refectory every morning, there was porridge and boiled eggs and plates of bread and butter. The crockery was enamel and all around us people slurped cocoa or strong brown tea from white mugs with big blue spots.

It felt like a holiday – being away from home and getting sweets from strangers – but we still had to go to school and I was terrified because I didn't want to be separated from my mother. The school was just across the road and on the first day, between lessons, we huddled together in the playground, intimidated by the local children who closed in and shot blunt questions at us. "Where are ye from?" "Where's yer father?" "Why are ye staying with the nuns?" One of them reached out a fist and thumped me on the arm. This was a signal to the others and they began shuffling forward, fists clenched, until a girl in the crowd cried out in a voice as clear as a bell: "Leave them alone! Go on! Get away from them!" Bodies melted away and she stood there, older and taller, black curls blowing in the wind, smiling down at us. "Are ye all right?" she asked kindly. Then someone called her name and she ran off.

Hannah and I were together in Junior Infants but as soon as the classroom door closed and the lesson began, Hannah started crying and wouldn't stop. She thought our mother had left us and, considering the recent upheaval, I thought she might be right, so I started howling as well. The nun couldn't continue with the noise we were making so our mother was sent for, to show she hadn't abandoned us.

3

We were given a sweet each and, eyes riveted on our mother, we gradually quietened down. She stood in the hallway with the classroom door ajar, Rose asleep on her shoulder. Nuns passed up and down and enquired about her well-being. However, they can't have been too concerned because a few weeks later we were back at home with our father.

It happened like this. One Saturday we were told to tidy ourselves up and wait in the convent entrance for some visitors. My mother's face was like stone and my heart sank. Visitors. That could mean only two people: my father and his mother. Dutifully, we washed our hands and faces and stood inside the glass-panelled double doors. My mother was silent with her arms folded and then, inexorably, they arrived. But there were three, not two. Maude, my grand-aunt, had come as well. She'd been roped in because my mother liked her and might be persuaded by her to come home. My father was smiling in his Sunday best but my mother ignored him and went outside with the women. He stayed inside with us and it was like being with a sort of Santa Claus in a shirt and tie. He gave us sweets and seemed really glad to see us. He joked and played with us and let us tumble all over his good tweed overcoat.

I could see my mother through the glass doors. She was standing near the gate, crying and taking off her cardigan. Maude was shocked at the sight of her arms, which were still swollen and bruised. She shook her head incredulously and gasped: "Oh, Kathleen!"

My grandmother had no such sympathy. Her sole concern was to get us back home. What my mother had done was unheard of – five children and she'd upped and left her husband, Cora's own son. Worse still, she hadn't gone off quietly to her family but had thrown herself and her brood on the mercy of the Church in this poor house in Midleton. The story of how Cora Coleman's daughter-in-law had run away was all over the town. She was a laughing stock and it was mortifying because people who weren't fit to lick her boots were laughing at her behind her back. Worst of all, the priests knew and she was ever a devout, respectable woman.

She'd come prepared to coax and cajole. She *had* to get this stupid tart back to Cobh by hook or by crook and she'd have to do it herself. Maude was useless, standing there gawping at the silly bitch and her bruises. Cora assured Kathleen that, on pain of death, John would never touch her again and eventually my mother gave in and agreed to go back. She didn't have much choice. Everything conspired to drive her back to my father. Her family wouldn't help her and there was no assistance from the state in those days. Our stay at the convent was only a stop-gap and where was a woman with five children going to go then?

When we arrived home after our adventure in Midleton, life was good for a while. My father smiled more than usual and my grandmother helped when the next baby, Sarah, was born about nine months later, but as time passed and the memory of Midleton faded, his smile wore thin and his violent anger engulfed us all once again.

It's funny what you take to be normal when you're a child. I thought nothing of the fact that there were so many of us, nine at the final count (seven children and two adults), crammed into a small two-up two-down terraced house. We didn't have a bathroom and our toilet was outdoors. We didn't go outside for nocturnal pees, as in Midleton, but kept a plastic bucket on the landing, with a newspaper over the top as a lid. In the morning, it was always full to the brim, mostly with my father's strong brown piss and his cigarette butts. We took it in turns to empty the bucket, which meant carrying it slowly and gingerly down the stairs, along the hall, through the kitchen and out the back door to the lavatory.

One Sunday morning it was my turn. I hated this chore but I didn't grumble. How could I? I was happy with the sunlight flooding in and the house so clean and tidy. Everything sparkled and smelled divinely of furniture polish. I'd just complete this one onerous task and then I'd go out to play. So I bent down to pick up the bucket and, as it had no handles, I hooked my fingers under the rim to lift it. It was full and the sheer volume of urine made it wobble. Nevertheless, I started on the first step of the stairs. The wobbling increased. I took another step and then disaster struck. I slipped on the polished linoleum and lost my grip.

Numbly, I watched as the bucket got away from me and four litres of piss, stools and tobacco shreds arced out and crashed onto the stairs below me. There was no carpet to soak it up and I watched, transfixed with horror, as it cascaded downwards and splashed onto the hallway and up the walls onto the new wallpaper that my mother was so proud of. The stools came to rest all over the place and the smell made me gag but I couldn't move and I couldn't believe what had happened. It was my mother's screams that made it real for me. She came running from the kitchen, shrieking at the sight before her. I didn't want to step in the piss but she yanked me down the stairs and clipped me hard across the head. Then she made me clean it up. Now it was my turn to cry. Under my mother's blunt supervision, I started on the upstairs landing, picked up the turds and cigarette butts, mopped the piss off each step into a basin and went over everything with hot soapy water.

Our sleeping arrangements were thus: we children shared the front bedroom and our parents had the back one. In the bad times, my mother slept with us and my father was apt to burst in, in the middle of the night, and thump her where she lay in the dark, calling her a "fucking cunt" or suchlike, before retreating angrily to his empty marital bed. We'd wail in terror at the malevolent silhouette weaving between the beds but my mother would soothe us, cooing softly: "It's all right. It's all right. Go back to sleep." And when I was very young, I believed her and I did go back to sleep.

When my parents stopped sleeping together for good, we were thus: my father, Joseph and Peter in the back room; my mother, Grace, Hannah, Rose, Sarah and me in the front. We were desperately overcrowded and watched with shame and envy as our neighbours upped their standards and added bathrooms and extra bedrooms to their homes. It's not that we couldn't afford any improvements; my father was a qualified tradesman and his income was above average. It wasn't that he *couldn't* give us more space; he *wouldn't*. He hated us. And above all, he hated going out to work to provide for us so he was damned if he was going to do anything to make us more comfortable.

We did our ablutions on Saturday evenings in a tin bath in the kitchen and when we were older we snatched what privacy we could, with a basin of hot water and a sponge, in the front bedroom. I often stood in our back yard looking up at our neighbours' new bathrooms, wondering what it was like to sink into the luxury of a hot bath. When I entered my teens in the early 1970s and started having periods, it felt shameful to be still using an outdoor toilet and washing in a basin the way we did, and I felt dirty and greasy all the time.

Once, in an effort to demonstrate that nothing needed to change, my father improvised a shower in the back yard, using the kitchen tap and a length of garden hose. He explained nothing to us so we watched in puzzlement as he busied himself with the hose, connecting it to the kitchen tap and rigging up the nozzle end just outside the back room window. This spot gave him maximum privacy from the neighbours and when he was satisfied that he couldn't be seen by them, he began to undress. We watched in astonishment as he proceeded to strip naked and soap himself vigorously under the cold water, his big, pale torso filling the window frame. I'd just caught a glimpse of his wet buttocks when my mother pulled us away and closed the curtains. He only did it the once because winter was coming on and the hose kept slipping off the tap.

Our cramped conditions could have been improved in one fell swoop by moving to a bigger house, which was also something we could have afforded to do. At one point, there was a suitable property for sale just up the road. It had four bedrooms and that most coveted of things – a bathroom. There was a big garden all around it and an orchard. It was called The Ranch, a curious name for a pretty old cottage, and we fell in love with it. My mother enquired about the price. It was reasonable, well within our reach. I got excited, imagining myself, bathed and fragrant, inviting friends around for picnics under the apple trees. My father, who at first dismissed the idea of moving, wavered and seemed to be agreeable, and my excitement grew. Thinking of the four bedrooms and the bathroom, I could feel our overcrowding untangle like a greased knot and our standing in the community increase exponentially. Maybe, just maybe, he'd say yes and we could move up in the world too.

But after discussions with his mother, he said no. Our house belonged to her and she was damned if she was going to let Kathleen Leahy, that bitch from Donegal, benefit from it. Not after Midleton. So the answer was no. We wouldn't be moving.

Instead we got a bed settee, a forerunner of the sofa bed, and it was installed in the front room alongside my mother's prized possessions – a flimsy display cabinet filled with china, which we called the Glass Case, some books and a sheepskin she got from the butcher, which she'd salted and cleaned herself. Grace and I slept in the bed settee first. Then Grace, the first-born, went back upstairs to her mother and Hannah came down to take her place. It was thrilling being downstairs in the pitch dark and a bit scary, but all the more exciting for that. Some nights,

Hannah and I would snuggle under the blankets and whisper until we fell asleep. Other nights, we fought like wild animals and had to be separated. Other times, we opened the curtains and watched clouds scudding across the moon.

We took my mother's china out of the Glass Case, just to have a closer look at it. There was a tea-pot, a coffee pot, a set of cups, saucers and plates and a velvety box of silver-plated cutlery. The crockery was fine bone china and it came from the better life she'd known before she got married. Its translucence was magical. We only ever used dense, practical crockery and I loved the fact that I could hold these cups and saucers up to the light and see my fingers through them. Sometimes, when she was out, we cooked eggs and fried bread and ate off the delicate little plates and drank tea out of the paper-thin cups, making sure to wash up and put everything back before she came home. The Glass Case itself made me nervous. Touching it was playing with fire because its three glass shelves teetered dangerously on the edge of tiny pegs. Anything other than the most delicate handling would bring the whole lot crashing down and if that happened there'd be hell to pay.

I worried about the Glass Case on the night that my parents were in the room. It was late when my mother slipped in and went to sit on a chair in the corner. She was hiding from my father, hoping and praying that he wouldn't find her; hoping that he'd forego the encounter he wanted and just go to bed. The light from the hall and her presence in the room woke me up.

"What's up, Mam?" I called out sleepily.

"Nothing. It's all right. Go back to sleep," she whispered, but I couldn't go back to sleep. What was going on? Why was my mother cowering in the corner of the room, in the dark? I waited. Then I heard my father's stomping footfalls approaching and my heart accelerated until it was beating like the wings of a trapped bird. He thumped the door open and smashed the light on. Now Hannah was awake too. I could feel her close beside me, shrinking down in the bed. My mother sprang to her feet and tried to leave the room but he blocked her path and was foul from the moment he opened his mouth.

"LOOK AT YA! HIDIN' IN HERE LIKE A FUCKIN' RAT!" he shouted, fists clenched. Oh God. I dreaded what was coming. My heart was galloping and my breathing was fast and shallow as I too shrank down under the covers.

My mother said nothing but stood before him with her arms folded, trapped and resigned to the imminent beating, while he continued, in a mock curious tone that was grotesque and frightening: "What did ya do when I was at work?"

No answer.

"I said: WHAT DID YA DO WHEN I WAS AT WORK?"

No answer.

"WHO DID YA TALK TO WHEN YE WERE DOIN' YER SHOPPIN'?"

No answer.

I was willing her to speak, to placate and appease him and thereby avoid the terrible beating but she knew there was no hope of that. The interrogation continued:

"WHICH SHOPS DID YA GO INTA?"

"The Spar," she conceded in a small, tight voice.

"WHAT?" he bellowed.

"The Spar," she said more loudly.

"SO YOU GOT THAT ROTTEN FUCKIN' STEAK YOU GAVE ME FOR ME DINNER IN THE SPAR, DID YA?"

No answer.

"DID YA?"

"Yes."

"IS CASEY'S NOT GOOD ENOUGH FOR YA?" Casey's was the local butchers.

No answer.

"NOW YOU LISTEN TO ME, YOU CUNT! IF CASEY'S IS GOOD ENOUGH FOR ME MOTHER, IT'S GOOD ENOUGH FOR YOU, YA DIRTY DONEGAL CUNT! GET YER MEAT IN CASEY'S IN FUTURE, D'YA HEAR ME?" There was a brief silence during which he pumped his fists – open . . . closed . . . open . . . closed – and stomped from foot to foot before he moved closer to his true purpose which was to draw relief from giving his wife an unholy beating: "I SUPPOSE THERE'S SOMEONE IN THE SPAR YE'D LIKE TE GET OFF WHORIN' WITH, ISN'T THERE? YA UGLY FUCKIN' CUNT!"

His obscenity knew no bounds and we heard *cunt* over and over, on and on and on. I was numb from hearing it. Hannah and I hid in the bed, not moving a muscle or making a sound so as not to draw attention to ourselves. Petrified and helpless, we had to leave our mother to the beating she was surely going to get. His shouting had woken the whole house and probably the neighbours as well. Peter, Sarah and Rose were crying upstairs, but my mother couldn't get past him. Grace would have to see to them. The tension was unbearable so I focused my mind on the number of times I heard "cunt". Thirty-one. I was worried about my mother's proximity to the Glass Case. They were standing so close to it that if he hit her, she might lose her balance and fall against it. If that happened, the shelves would collapse and my mother would fall onto deadly shark's fins of broken glass.

The inquisition went on regardless:

"YE'D LOVE TO BE OUT WHORIN', WOULDN'T YA, YA UGLY FUCKIN' CUNT. BUT WHO'D HAVE YA, YA UGLY BITCH? LOOK AT YA! LEGS LIKE A FUCKIN' PLOUGHMAN!" He was referring to my mother's lumpy varicose veins, made worse by child-bearing. Still she said nothing and her passive silence infuriated him. He wanted her to say something, anything, to bring the moment on and to make him feel righteous when at last he lashed out with his fists.

"I SUPPOSE YER FUCKIN' THAT DANNY O'BRIEN" – the butcher at the Spar – "TE PAY FOR YER MEAT, AREN'T YA?"

Silence.

"AREN'T YA?"

More silence.

"THAT'S WHERE ALL YER SWILL COMES FROM, I SUPPOSE."

By "swill", he meant us, his children. He was in a frenzy now, clenching and unclenching his fists, folding his tongue over and clamping down on it with his bared teeth so that it bulged out grotesquely between them. A tongue sandwich, with yellow teeth for bread. The tongue sandwich signalled the end of dialogue, such as it was, and the start of violence.

My mother mumbled something about the children crying upstairs and tried to get past him but the next second he was on her. She shrieked in agony and in an instant we were up and out of bed, the pretense of being asleep abandoned. We flew to her, where she was crouched by the Glass Case, holding her head. He'd pulled out a clump of her hair. That's what had made her scream. I heard it ripping. Then he lunged again. Knock, knock, knock with his knuckles on her arms, shoulders and head. I could hear his fists clouting against the bones of her face. Hannah and I were shaking and screaming. We had to stop him. If we didn't, he was going to kill or maim her, he was thumping her head so much. Hearts racing with adrenalin, we put ourselves in the path of the blows and begged him to stop. "Daddy" – invoking that word that was so strange to us – "Daddy" we repeated over and over. "Please stop, Daddy. Pleeeeze, pleeeeze stop, Daddy. Pleeeeze stop. Pleeeeze stop, Daddy."

Our intervention worked. His arms fell to his sides, although his fists were still clenched. He backed away slightly and unrolled the tongue but then my mother's dam burst: "GOD DAMN YOU, YOU MADMAN!!" she shrieked through bitter desolate tears. Oh Jesus, this was awful. She was going to start him off again, so now we turned to her and implored: "Pleeeeze be quiet, Mammy, pleeeeze be quiet." I even put my hand over her mouth to hush her but she flicked me off and continued: "GOD CURSE YOU! MAY YOU BURN IN HELL!" His tongue was between his teeth again and we closed in around her, our faces and hands upturned to him, beseeching him to stop but he lunged at her once more, calling her a fucking cunt, and landed a sickening blow on her head.

And then he was done. His fury spent, he stomped off upstairs to bed, signalling an end to the night with a deafening slam of his bedroom door. We were shaking and our hair was standing on end. I was crying and biting down hard on the length of my index finger as I watched my mother pull herself up off the ground and tell us, in a dead voice, to go back to bed. With that, she staggered away to the kitchen to get it ready for the morning.

We got back into bed and I was relieved to see her moving, still alive, still my mother but it was a long time before I fell asleep. I was electrified and trembling and the echo of his hateful words bounced off the walls. The horror of what had just happened played over and over in my mind.

*Cunt* reverberated through my whole being. Thirty-one times he'd said it. And *swill*. We were swill. We weren't even piglets. We were the foul slop that farmers feed to pigs, animals that will eat absolutely anything. Did he hate us so much that only the foulest image would do? It wasn't the first time I'd heard it. He was fond of saying that my mother was a sow and we were her swill. My mother was a sow and a whore and a cunt and we were swill. It was official. My father said so. But surely he'd got mixed up. I desperately hoped that was so. That he was just so angry he got mixed up and what he really meant to say was *piglets*.

Thanks to his influence, we swore like soldiers. I thought nothing of saying *fuck* – fuck this, fuck that, fuck you, fuck off – and regularly called my sisters *cunt* and *whore*. One day in Junior Infants, sitting among the frilly dolls and playthings of that babies' room, I called my neighbour a cunt. It didn't upset her because she didn't know what it meant. Neither did I really – I was only four – but I knew it was bad because my father said it when he beat my mother. The teacher, an elderly nun, heard me and, to her credit, she ignored it. As I got older and realised how my father's foul language raped our minds and shamed us, I hardly swore at all.

I could hear her in the kitchen, silent, way beyond tears now, preparing things for the morning. Then she climbed the stairs and fell into a sore and exhausted sleep. Hannah and I were left to square away this trauma as best we could. We denounced him and said things we'd said before in similar circumstances: "Madman!"; "I wish he was dead!"; "Please kill him, Jesus!" and "Please God, make him go away!" Then we turned away from each other and were silent except for our sobbing.

When I woke the next morning, my body ached and I was afraid because I could hear my father slamming and banging in the kitchen. I hoped my mother was upstairs. On his way out of the house he slammed the front door so hard that it hopped open and a cold wind blew into the front room and over the bed settee. We got up but I didn't want to. Even the very air frightened me that morning. No one referred to the previous night and I ate my mother's lumpy porridge without complaining. We went to school silently and with lowered heads. At lunchtime we hurried home. Our dinner was ready when we got there: lamb's liver cut into cubes, mashed potatoes, cabbage and gravy. My mother dished it out and finally sat down to have her own meal. When I was getting up from the table, I noticed a dull, red patch, the size of a five-penny piece on the side of her head. It was the spot where he'd pulled her hair our. I stared at it and it made me feel sick.

On days like these, we tracked our father's movements to the minute. If it was Days, he finished work at four o'clock in the afternoon. The Steel Mills where he worked as a fitter was on an island in the harbour and Cobh was on another and the ferry back took fifteen minutes. He usually called in at his mother's on the way home and he'd be arriving there about twenty-five past four. He'd definitely do that today; he'd be needing his ma. The neighbours must have heard the rumpus last night and now they'd be pointing the finger and laughing at him. Ma would give him a bottle of stout and tell him it was all right, the cunt deserved it. She hated the ugly fucking sow, after all, with her Donegal airs and graces. He'd be there until about twenty past five. The timing was good because old Bob, my grandfather, would still be napping and he and Ma could talk. It was only a short walk from my grandparents' house to ours so we could expect him a little before half past five. It was vital to sense his mood as soon as he walked in.

When he did arrive, we recoiled but were ever watchful. Silently and making no eye-contact, he washed his diesel-covered hands and arms in the deserted kitchen. Then he made a cup of tea, took his cigarettes and newspaper and went up to his room. With a bit of luck, he'd stay there all night. His dinner would have to be taken up to him but we could pull straws for it. That evening, it fell to Hannah, who was so afraid of him that she refused to do it on her own. I offered to go with her and while my mother cooked, we readied the tray. He was having one of his favourites – three lamb chops, boiled potatoes, cabbage and onion gravy, followed by three custard slices and a pot of tea. It was the best of food, cooked to perfection, on a spotlessly clean tray. Everything was done to mollify him and avoid a repeat of the previous night.

When it was ready, we took the meal up and followed a set procedure. First, knock on the door (we were not to open it) and wait for a response. This would take the form of a hostile: "WHAT?" Then, call out politely: "Your dinner's here, Daddy." Daddy. He'd robbed us of that term of endearment. I was so uncomfortable with the word that I clenched my buttocks whenever I uttered it. As soon as he grunted acknowledgement, we put the tray down and took the stairs two at a time, desperate to be gone before he opened the door. Next, we had to wait in the back room for the knock on the ceiling that told us he'd finished eating and the tray was on the landing, ready for collection. Then we took up his dessert, the custard slices – delicious ovals of puff pastry, filled with vanilla cream and topped with lemon icing – which were his favourite cakes.

After our own dinner, eaten hastily and with an ear to the ceiling, we ranged ourselves along the leatherette couch in the back room, in front of the TV. My mother sat at one end, knitting, and everyone wanted to sit right beside her. No one would sit in *his* chair, in spite of its prime position by the fire. We were constantly vigilant for any movement overhead, especially if it sounded like he was coming down. If so, we decamped first to the front room downstairs and, when he was installed in front of the television, up to the front bedroom for the rest of the evening, with only the occasional foray to the kitchen for nappies or babies' bottles. Later, Hannah and I would tiptoe downstairs to sleep in the bed settee and, as we crept along the hall, the back room would seem to throb malevolently with his presence. The door was shut tight against us but electric light and cigarette stink oozed out through the cracks. We'd scuttle past and get into bed as quickly as we could. Then we listened out for any untoward sounds – the back room door opening violently perhaps and heavy footfalls rushing upstairs – until we fell asleep.

Nothing bad happened for weeks at a time but fear lurked constantly in my heart. One night at bedtime, my father came home from work early. I was so surprised to hear the slam of the garden gate and his stomping footsteps approaching the front door that I jumped into bed fully clothed, my shoes and socks still on, and pulled the blankets up to my ears. I stayed like that for a good hour, convinced that this change in routine heralded trouble. I expected my mother to appear in the room looking for a place to hide and him following her with his fists clenched, but nothing happened. He banged around in the kitchen making himself a cup of tea and then he went up to his room. When I was sure it was safe, I got out of bed, got undressed properly and got back in.

My grandmother, Cora, was a small woman who cast a long shadow over our lives. We were wary of her because we knew that she'd killed a baby when she was a child. Her sister Maude, who couldn't keep a secret, told Kathleen, our mother. The incident was shrouded in mystery. The only details we knew were that she'd dropped her baby brother and he'd hit his head on a stone and died. A committer of infanticide, Cora was a notorious outcast in her home town and when she was fourteen, she came south to work as a chambermaid in a hotel called The RobRoy, a prominent feature in old photographs of Cobh. When she first arrived, she felt like she was in a foreign country. Breezy, elegant and full of Georgian houses and Victorian villas, her new home in Cobh was completely different from the place she'd left behind. She'd never seen the sea before and now here she was right beside it. In fact you couldn't get away from it, the town was so hilly, you saw it from every vantage point. Ships of all shapes and sizes came and went, day and night, and the broad sea front was constantly filled with people, horses, carriages, carts, bicycles and occasionally, an automobile.

She didn't tell anyone about what had happened, but prayed and prayed for forgiveness. It was her terrible secret and as she grew older she learned to hide it behind a mask of dour Catholic piety. She was joyless and to hear her tell it, there wasn't a trace of affection in the functional, symbiotic way she married my sea-faring grandfather, the well-respected old Bob Coleman. "He wanted a house-keeper and I wanted a husband," she'd recount with bitter satisfaction. They had three children: John, Cora – my other namesake – and Thomas.

Having children stirred up ugly feelings in her and when she looked at John, her first-born, Cora saw the baby who had died and the likeness awoke in her an inferno of anger and pain. Why did he have to die?! Why did he have to slip from her grip that day?! Overnight she'd lost everything she held dear. They made her go away and now she was stuck with this bloody baby, in a smelly, damp harbour, married to a whiskery old sailor. She was consumed by unhappiness – and John bore the brunt of her pain. She beat him frequently and the neighbours could hear the little boy crying through the walls. She forbade him to go out on the street and what the world saw was a solemn child playing in the garden on his own or scuttling along the road to school. She also slaked her anger on Cora junior, but Thomas, as the youngest, escaped the blows and had a sunnier disposition than his brother and sister. He was John's only friend; they were altar boys together, they fished and swam in the sea, they built dens, and when the coast was clear, they made fun of their mother's nasty temper.

When Thomas was thirteen, he got sick. He complained of stomach pains and they got worse and worse. There were two doctors in Cobh, one cheap and the other more expensive. My grandmother, always penny-pinching, sent for the cheap one. When he prodded Thomas's abdomen, the child screamed and the doctor, who was inept, took a wild guess and said he had worms.

"Worms?" echoed Cora, perplexed. She'd never known worms to cause such pain.

"Yes, that's right," continued the doctor, proffering a sachet of white powder. "Give him this three times a day for a couple of days and that should shift them. Good bye."

Cora Coleman

With that he took his fee and was gone. Cora mixed the powder with water and gave it to Thomas, hoping against hope that it would cure him. The delirious child drank the potion and for a short while the pain stopped but then it came back, worse than ever. Thomas was screaming in agony and fear shot up Cora's spine.

The other doctor was sent for and Cora wrung her hands as she told him about the worm powder. He examined Thomas gently and said, "We have to get him to hospital as quickly as possible." Seeing the anxious faces around the bed, he explained further: "He's got appendicitis. The problem is the worm powder and what that's done to his condition. If the appendicitis isn't too advanced, he'll be all right, but you say he's been poorly for some time?"

"Yes."

"Mmm," and the doctor was silent.

An ambulance pulled up outside. The doctor gave Thomas a tincture of morphine but every bump in the pre-tarmac roads made him scream, and he was sick too. By the time they reached the hospital, his appendix had burst and now he had peritonitis. Poisonous fluid from his tattered appendix was spreading through his bloodstream and he had a raging fever. Some days later, with yellow pus oozing from his eyes and nose, he died.

The town was stunned. People couldn't believe that old Bob Coleman's strapping young son was dead. Peritonitis. Few had heard of it. A huge crowd attended the funeral. My grandfather said that Tommy appeared at the end of his bed that night and told his father not to worry, that he was all right.

22

The image of my tragic uncle as a child-ghost haunted me throughout my childhood. As I grew up, I realised sadly the depth of my grandfather's grief. My grandparents' marriage ended in all but name when Tommy died. Bob blamed Cora for his son's death and he hated the sight of her. He stayed out as much as possible, as did Cora junior, so my grandmother turned to John. His mother was nice to him now, but John just wanted her to leave him alone because she made him cry when she talked about Tommy. "Was it my fault?" she asked, knowing that, from her hungry son, there'd only be one answer. "No," he assured her, his throat closing and tears welling up in his eyes. They'd cry together and when the tears subsided, they'd have cups of tea and she taught him that life was hard and people were bad and thus he never left her.

When my father was in a good mood, he washed, shaved, dressed well and talked to us like any other father. Once, bizarrely, he took me to a rugby match. He loved rugby and the All Blacks were playing at the Mardyke in Cork. But what was I doing there? Where was Joseph? I can't have been more than six or seven. I distinctly remember the wall of legs as I stood on the ground, frightened by the tremendous roaring of the crowd.

He had nicknames for Grace and me: Mina Tonk and Mala Pol respectively, culled from some Hollywood film about Red Indians. So they wouldn't feel left out, my mother christened Hannah Frieda Fieldmouse and Rose was Rocky Graziano because of her hard little fists. My father John would sit amiably, waiting for his dinner and while he did so, he watched rugby on the TV or listened to Glenn Miller or Frank Sinatra on our little portable record player.

Although it was the sixties and seventies, our house reverberated to the sounds of the thirties and forties, the music of my father's youth, and I knew every note and every lyric of Glenn Miller's "Pennsylvania 6-5000" and Frank Sinatra's "Close To You", to name but two. His smile lit up his face and we forgave him the fact that he called us "swill". We buried it deep with all his other slights and threw ourselves into the celebratory spirit of the moment – Daddy-in-a-good-mood. However, we never quite forgot what he was capable of and when he wanted little favours done, we knew better than to refuse.

One such task was to give him a sort of head massage, in which we had to trace the tip of a knitting needle all over his head, neck and shoulders. This had a soporific effect on him and that was good because anything that relaxed him benefitted us. I hated this chore. It was intimate and laborious and he never wanted it to stop. On and on you had to go with the knitting needle while hopping from foot to foot to ease the aches in your legs, which you couldn't mention because that would spoil his fun. When it was my turn, I'd go off with a heavy heart, in search of a knitting needle and when I found one, I'd mimic stabbing him with it, good mood or no good mood. On my return, he'd be waiting, head bent in anticipation, shirt collar tucked in, a sebaceous smell rising from his white, hairy skin.

When my mother left school, she worked in a hairdressing salon in Athlone, a busy market town, many miles from her home in County Donegal. Every Saturday night there was a dance and the girls at the salon and their customers talked excitedly about the band that was playing, who might be there and the prospects of meeting someone special. CIÉ, the national railway company, was upgrading tracks locally and there'd be eligible young men around. Over the stench of burnt hair and perming lotion, they planned their make-up and clothes and, sure enough, one Saturday night, my mother and her friend were approached by a tall, handsome stranger. He'd watched them come in, get their drinks and sit down. One of them, a blonde, was quite pretty. He'd shag her given the chance but the other one, a brunette, wasn't his type. He thought he might try his luck with the blonde before someone else did so he went over. They saw him coming. He addressed the blonde but the band was loud and the brunette misunderstood. She got up and he didn't have the gumption to turn her down. He swallowed hard as they moved onto the dance floor. The blonde disappeared. Six months later he and the brunette got married.

My parents, John Coleman and Kathleen Leahy, look very happy in their wedding portrait. The sun is shining and they're grinning from ear to ear; even the church wall behind them seems happy, with the quartz in it glinting brightly. It's strange to see my father smiling so broadly. It was such a rare event. Was he drunk? He is tanned and wearing an expensive suit and my mother is a picture in an A-line organza wedding dress with white peep-toe high heels. She has her arm in his and seems delighted to have found her prince and married him. Gazing at this photograph, I wonder if he beat her before they got married. Did he never hit her before they tied the knot? I find it hard to imagine. Did she have no inkling of what he was like? Was there nothing and no one who could have forewarned her? I imagined him keeping up a big act during the months of their courtship and the strain behind the broad wedding-day grin.

In any case, after the wedding, her dancing days were well and truly over. The beatings began as soon as the first baby came along, screaming its bloody head off and her always going to it and neglecting him. How dare she put that shitty, noisy thing before him? The first blow taught her a lesson and it made the next one easier and the one after that was easier still. She could get rid of all her fancy outfits as well because she wouldn't be going anywhere in them. Henceforth, her life revolved around him and my father wore away her self-esteem to the point where she neglected her appearance. Thus her hair was often greasy and she'd usually be found in smelly old tops covered in baby-sick and an apron to which nappy pins were always attached.

But one day something new came along – the Avon Lady. She was a woman from Cork who went from door to door selling the latest thing – Avon Cosmetics, newly arrived from England. Like a visiting dignitary in her smart suit and make-up, the Avon Lady took cups of tea with the mothers of the neighbourhood and we all watched, engrossed, as she laid out her lipsticks and nail polishes in shades of red, orange and pink; foundation, powders, rouge and face creams in a variety of pretty little pots. All our neighbours bought something so my mother had a pearly pink nail varnish and lipstick to match.

We were delighted with her purchases and wanted to make her up as soon as the Avon Lady was gone. Obligingly, she sat on a kitchen chair and we set to work. First, we combed her soft chestnut hair and pulled it back into a ponytail. Next, we opened the slick, shiny tube and twisted up the pristine stick of pink lipstick. She showed us how you stretched your lips out when you applied lipstick so that it got into every little crevice, and then, slowly and carefully, we painted it on, being fair-minded, taking turns. She blotted her lips on a piece of paper and smiled at us. What a transformation! She was beautiful! And we hadn't even finished. There was still the nail varnish. She showed us how to shake the bottle, unscrew it and remove excess polish before applying it to the nails. The little brush glided over my mother's ten fingernails, painting them opalescent pink, hiding the dirt that always seemed to be under them and redeeming them, if only for a while, from the drudgery of housework.

We were having so much fun with the make-over that we hadn't noticed the time. It was a quarter to five and my father would be home at half past. It was time to return my mother to her usual Cinderella state. The lipstick was easy to get off but the nail varnish had dried rock hard. It wouldn't just wipe off. We had never had nail varnish in the house before, let alone nail varnish remover. She was frantic to get it off before he got home so I volunteered to sprint at full speed to Lenihan's chemist at the far end of the town, get a bottle and sprint home. *Please God, let them have a bottle*, I prayed as I ran along. They did; I ran home with it and she wiped the nail varnish off and hid the cosmetics in her handbag.

Then we all hurried upstairs to await his arrival. He had slammed out of the house that morning and his mood was unlikely to have improved at work. He'd be stopping in at his mother's, which was a worry because we knew she fanned the flames of his violent anger.

We were in the front bedroom waiting when we heard the gate bang and his pounding footsteps on the path. Then he was inside, the house filling up with the smell of cigarettes and diesel oil, stomping his way down to the kitchen. He was having his dinner downstairs because he wanted to watch a rugby match on TV. His place was set at the table and his meal was ready. Good. While he was washing his hands and arms, he noticed my mother's handbag on top of a pile of washing. He had to keep track of what the sow was up to, so when he'd dried off he owed it to himself to have a look inside. What was this? Nail varnish! Lipstick! What the fuck was she doing with nail varnish and lipstick? Was she out whoring while he was sweating bricks in the Steel Mills? Enjoying herself while he was flogging himself to death in that fucking place? What the fuck was going on? The fucking bitch! Only whores wore paint like this. Agitated, he made a note to get to the bottom of it. But not now. First he'd have his dinner and watch the rugby. What grub was it anyway? He lifted the lid on the frying pan. Steak and gravy. Okay. And for his afters? Custard slices. Okay.

My mother went downstairs to serve his dinner and then retreated to the kitchen while he ate. There was no conversation. The only sound was the *pap pap pap* of his thick forefinger on the salt and pepper, the stabbing of his knife and fork in the food and the chomping of his mouthfuls. When the chomping stopped and the cutlery clanged with finality onto the plate, she went in and cleared the table. She returned with the custard slices and the tea and then rejoined us upstairs. The TV went on. A sports commentary could be heard. Please God, let his team win. Time passed. We could hear his cup going down heavily on the saucer and smell his after-dinner cigarettes. He whooped and yelped as his team won points but when the match ended, he was straight on the stairs and as he neared the top step, I fervently hoped that he was going into his room but I was wrong.

With a suddenness that made me jump, he burst in. Instinctively we closed ranks around our mother, whimpering and biting our fingers and nails. He lunged at her, brandishing the cosmetics and bellowing:

"WHAT THE FUCK ARE YA DOIN' WITH THESE?"

His face distorted with anger as he continued:

"YER OUT WHORIN' WHEN I'M AT WORK, AREN'T YA, YA FUCKIN' CUNT?"

My mother was deeply reluctant to answer his demented accusations but he bellowed louder and we pressed in closer, so she had to say something.

"I got them from the Avon Lady."

"THE WHO?"

"A woman who sells cosmetics door to door. I didn't want her to go away empty-handed."

That was all right, surely. It was a good answer. She was just being kind. He couldn't argue with that, could he? Please God, let him realise her kindness and just go away.

There was a short vacuum and then he mocked her in a high, mewling voice: "I didn't want her to go away empty-handed." With the mocking, we knew something bad was coming and the air was filled with our petrified beseechings: "No Daddy, pleeeeze don't do anything!" My eyes blazed into his. I held his gaze, begging him not to hit her and if she'd remained silent I don't think he would have but she *did* speak and in spite of our distress, what she said was not placating but inflammatory.

"Your sister wears make-up so I don't see why I can't."

Recognising that she'd just made matters far worse, we turned to our father and begged him:

"Pleeeze Daddy. Don't do anything! Pleeeze! Pleeeze!"

But it was too late. Ignoring us, he roared:

"DON'T YOU DARE MENTION MY SISTER, YOU DIRTY FUCKING CUNT! DON'T YOU FUCKING DARE!"

He made a tongue sandwich and then two loud knuckle blows connected with her head. THUNK, THUNK. Our screams erupted and our mother lost her balance on the bed. His arms were big, hairy pistons, delivering blows like a jack-hammer to her prone frame. "Pleeeeze stop, Daddy. Pleeeeeze, pleeeeze stop, Daddy. Pleeeeze stop." I was crying wildly but he neither saw nor heard me. There was another resounding blow to her head and then a warning:

"IF YOU EVER MENTION MY SISTER AGAIN, I'll FUCKIN' KILL YA! D'YA HEAR ME, I'LL KILL YA! YA FUCKIN CUNT!"

With that he spat at her, the gob landing on her cheek, hurled the lipstick and nail varnish at the wall and stormed out. For a moment we were all stunned. I felt her humiliation at having his spit on her face but I didn't go near her. I knew from experience not to. These moments were the nadir of her life and she'd just push me away. Bloody kids! She'd never escape from him because of us. It was our fault she was trapped and we knew it, because she told us so, thus:

"If it wasn't for you lot, I wouldn't be here."

She always regretted her words when she saw our wounded little faces but she couldn't help herself. It was all too much to bear without occasionally speaking the truth. I hated myself deeply because I knew I was the cause of those dreadful assaults. I was a ball and chain for both of them and I despised and regretted my very existence.

Frank Sinatra was starting up in the bedroom next door. Macho lyrics filled the air. "The Tender Trap". It seemed anything but tender to me. He'd treat us with contempt for the rest of the evening but that was all right. Contempt didn't break any bones. Presently my mother went down to the kitchen and I crawled under one of the beds, curled up and stayed there until she called me for my tea.

My father had a horrible job. He was a fitter-turner at Irish Steel Mills on a never-ending cycle of shifts. I never knew what a fitter-turner was, but he spent a lot of time on cranes – not driving them but doing some kind of maintenance. Apart from two false starts – one in merchant shipping and the other on the railways when he met my mother – he spent all of his working life there. He didn't need to. Old Bob was a harbour pilot and he'd have set his son up in a good job with the Harbour Commissioners but their relationship was frosty and John's closeness to his mother didn't help.

His shifts were from eight in the morning to four in the

afternoon, which we called "days"; four in the afternoon to midnight was "four-to-twelve"; and midnight to eight in the morning was "nights". We lived our lives around those shifts. During the school holidays, days was good because he was gone all day and bad because he was home all evening. Four-to-twelve was good because he was gone all afternoon and evening, bad because he came home in the dead of night. Nights was all bad because there was frequent ugliness before he left, he was back before we woke and he slept all day, so that my mother was constantly on edge in case we disturbed him.

It was worst in summer. He picked fights with her and reduced everyone to tears right up to the moment of leaving the house. Sometimes he feigned illness and didn't go to work. Once, he removed the plugs from the TV, the radio and the kettle and took them with him. At least he'd have the solace of knowing that we had no pleasure while he had none. When he was at home, he insisted that we stay in the house or garden for no other reason than to deprive us of the freedom that he no longer had. If children ventured in to play with us, he'd tell them to go home, which was mortifying, so we didn't encourage our friends, like the Mac Neices, to come round.

During four-to-twelve, we kept our swimming things rolled up and hidden all day and counted down the minutes to his departure, at which point we would explode out of the house, run down the hill to the sea and dive headlong into the water. Our mother's only proviso was to be back before dark. If we could, we went swimming two or three times a day.

All states of the tide were good. High tide meant the

water would be deep and green from the seaweed underneath, and lapping right up in the throat of the old slipway where we parked our towels. The seabed sloped away sharply from the slipway wall and it was like a natural swimming pool. There was always a streak of danger in the deep undulating water, which seemed alive and sentient to me and I marvelled at the recklessness of the boys, Joseph among them, running along the wall, hurling themselves into mid-air and belly-flopping into the water with a great splash.

Low tide exposed a stretch of sand and we played there as well as swam: chasing each other, shouting and laughing, paddling in the shallows, kicking up spume and lying down in the path of the soft, frilly waves, letting the cool water trickle over us. Later, I'd wade out hand-in-hand with a sister until we were up to our waists and there was nothing for it but to plunge into the cold water, my heart knocking with the shock. Then I'd do a sort of gangly doggy paddle but give up quickly in favour of floating and gazing up at the blue sky, the tops of familiar trees just in my field of vision.

Although my father got an annual three-week break in August, we never went on holiday. He sometimes hired a car and took us on day-trips. We were proud of the fact that he could drive, because in the 1960s a driving licence wasn't very common, even among men. We'd all squeeze into the rented Cortina or Anglia and it was fun to pretend we were a happy family, basking in our father's loving care. Look! There goes John Coleman with the driving licence! He loves his family so much, he's bought them a car! On the contrary, it was indicative of my father's miserable nature that we didn't own a vehicle. He himself only ever went to work or mass and he could do both on foot, he reasoned. True, he went to Cork occasionally, but there was the train for that. As for buying a car to make my mother's life easier (what with seven children and so much shopping to do), he'd rather have died. If *his* daily life was a grind, he was going to make sure *hers* was as well. Thus it was that my mother pushed a pram and humped carrier bags up the steep hills of Cobh, year after year, and we walked the long road to school in the pouring rain when all the while my father had a driving licence and the means of buying a car.

Still, we had the rented holiday car and it took us to places we wouldn't otherwise have seen, like Garryvoe, a sandy beach outside and to the west of our stony harbour. We went there once or twice, loaded down with sandwiches, biscuits and red lemonade and when we arrived, part of me was afraid to get out of the car, so dazzling was the broad plain of white sand that stretched in every direction as far as the eye could see. The windy, sunny air took my breath away and it felt like I was stepping onto the moon. And the ocean! It glistened and shimmered in the distance and its big, sunlit rollers pounded and splurged onto the shore. While we paddled in the foamy shallows and played with the sand, our parents would sit on a blanket, my mother tending Sarah and my father smoking and reading the paper; clothes, sandals, towels, biscuit packets and lemonade bottles strewn all around them.

The end of his holidays was always terrible. Back to the Steel Mills. No more smiles or clean-shaven jaws. No more Mina Tonk and Mala Pol. The scowl returned and eye contact disappeared. We were swill again and we knew that, inexorably, something bad would happen.

It would come about like this. One evening he'd allow us to watch the television with him; the next evening, we could watch television but he'd have his hand up to his face, like a blinker, to block us out. The evening after that, he'd use the clothes horse to make a screen around his chair so that he could still see the TV but not us. The evening after that he'd tell us to get out and then we'd spend the rest of the night upstairs in a state of mounting trepidation. We didn't care about the TV. He could have the stupid television and the back room all to himself forever more if it would prevent the bad things happening.

At times like this, I worried constantly about my mother's safety. I longed for a good man to come along and stand guard over her and beat the shit out of my father – knuckle *him* in the head and rip *his* hair out, so that he knew how it felt. The neighbours were useless. Our walls were thin and they heard everything but they chose to ignore our plight and did nothing to help us. Their excuse was that marriage was sacred. Only the Church could intervene and if the priests weren't bothered about what happened to our mother, neither were they. The priests had known for years that my father viciously abused my mother but they did nothing to stop him. On the contrary, they were ready with bucket loads of platitudes for women like her and fielded pleas for help with old staples like: "These things are sent to try us" or "You'll get your reward in Heaven".

Ironically, we were surrounded by relatively happy

couples, with marriages so different from my parents' that they seemed exotic to me. I was fascinated that our neighbours not only *didn't* beat their wives but actually took them out on Saturday nights, to dinner-dances or the cinema where they met and chatted with other couples. I couldn't understand their civility. Why did they do it? Were they just pretending to be nice? Weren't their children ashamed of themselves as we were? I wanted them to be ashamed of themselves. I wanted the men to abuse their women and children and call them "sow" and "swill", if only so that we weren't the only ones. But they didn't. They lived together respectfully and peacefully and we were alone with our shame.

We were similar in many ways to the Mac Neices who lived two doors away. We had seven children and they had six. Both fathers were local men who worked at the Steel Mills. Both mothers were farmers' daughters from far-flung parts of Ireland. My father had known Paddy Mac Neice all his life but he never spoke to him. He ignored him in the street and at work, sure in the knowledge, handed down by his mother, that the Mac Neices were beneath the Colemans. I'd heard how stupid and low Mr Mac Neice was all my life but I couldn't equate that with the friendly man, beloved of his wife and children, who went off to work every day whistling a tune, with a kind word for everyone.

In the summer, Mrs Mac Neice wore sleeveless dresses and she never had bruises on her arms. Quite the contrary, her husband bought a car and taught her to drive. He put in a bathroom and we heard that Mrs Mac Neice even had an electric blanket for the cold, winter nights. I envied her and her children deeply. And if I couldn't have what they had, the next best thing was to keep our dysfunction secret.

But it was useless. We had visits from the police when my mother, under a hail of blows, would scream for one of us to go and get them. I was deeply ashamed to see the patrol car outside our house and my father shouting insults at the policemen, calling them "chicken feed" and telling them to fuck off. It didn't seem to happen to any other family in the town. I was sure my father was notorious and that people were talking about us behind our backs. I felt like an outcast and never mentioned my father to other people, in the vain hope that they didn't know about him.

It happened at school sometimes that Lillian Mac Neice would tell my classmates little snippets that she gleaned from eavesdropping on her parents' conversations. I froze and bit my cheeks until the spotlight passed over the subject of my awful father. She sensed my shame and threatened to tell everyone what was heard through the walls unless I gave her sweets and did her bidding. She was a little bully and she was blackmailing me.

One awful day I was walking home with her when I saw Joseph approaching in the distance. His face looked strange but I couldn't make out why. Lillian was speaking but I didn't hear her. I was staring hard at Joseph's contorted face and as he got closer I realised, with horror, that he was crying. Oh dear, sweet Jesus, here comes my older brother and he's crying on the street.

And we weren't alone. At my side was a malicious little gossip and her eyes were on stalks. Two emotions assailed me: panic at what had reduced Joseph, a tough little boy, to this; and shame that our dirty secret had spilled out in public. When he drew level with me, he didn't stop but said as he passed:

"Don't go home, Cora. You know why."

"Why? Why?" shot in Lillian but I ignored her. Don't go home? Of course I was going home! In fact, I quickened my pace. My companion had fallen silent and soon I was able to leave her at her gate. I ran the rest of the way and was horrified to find my mother standing outside the house trying to stem her tears on her apron. Her face was red and swollen and her hair was standing up in clumps as if someone had been pulling it. She was afraid to go in and she couldn't stop crying. Tears flowed noiselessly down her face from her blood-shot, red-rimmed eyes. She didn't speak, just cried and stared into space and as I watched, her traumatised emotions invaded me. I felt an urgency to get her inside but I didn't know how. Anxiously, I tried to hug her but she pushed me away. It was a bright sunny day and the house was in shadow. I couldn't see *him* but I could hear him crashing and banging in the kitchen and shouting out "WHORE!" and "CUNT!" Eventually he went upstairs and we ventured in.

The kitchen was a dreadful mess and a fugue of smoke from burnt chops hung in the air. The chops were for his dinner, not ours, and he was doing them himself. He must have been bellowing at her not to touch his food, that he'd cook his own dinner; keep her dirty fucking hands off it – imperatives I'd heard before in similar circumstances. The frying pan was black and the sink was full of broken crockery, food scraps and tea leaves. My mother had recovered slightly in that she'd stopped crying and combed her hair. We set about tidying up and getting the dinner. We were having one of our staples, "egg dinners" – mashed potatoes with a fried egg on top, covered in white sauce with tinned peas. I put my all into cleaning up and then I set about peeling potatoes and chopping onions.

Meanwhile the others arrived. We ate silently, all the while aware of him overhead and the possibility that he might come down. He often did that. If he hadn't quite exhausted his rage, he'd descend from the bed where he lurked, fists clenched and bare feet scuttling on the lino of the stairs. Once, he came down wearing only a shirt and we watched in disbelief as he went through the stages of his assault with his big purple penis dancing and jiggling for everyone to see.

He was on night shift that night and I passionately hoped he'd be killed at work. Gruesome accidents sometimes happened at the Steel Mills. Men were cut in two by falling girders or burnt alive in the furnace. I implored Jesus to let it happen to him.

But there was the consolation of the bed settee, its warmth and security and the giggling, whispering and snuggling up with Hannah. Until one night, when she was nine, she fell silent with a headache. The next morning, the headache was worse and she was vomiting as well. I lay beside her, distressed, as she moaned and cried in pain. My mother wanted to ignore Hannah's illness because she was afraid to call a doctor. My father had hated doctors since Thomas's death and he wouldn't allow one in the house. He shouted insults at *them* too and if he knew a doctor had called, he'd beat her. Hannah was getting worse, however, so one morning, when *he* was on days, Dr Keane arrived. He was slightly nervous, knowing he was calling at the home of mad John Coleman, who blamed all doctors for his brother's death, but to his great relief, the door was opened by the wife, a polite little thing from County Donegal. She had a dirty old bandage around one of her shins, which was seeping pus; but that wasn't why she'd called him. It was one of the children she wanted him to see.

"What happened to your leg, Mrs Coleman?" he asked.

"Oh . . . I bumped it on a chair," she answered lamely. He looked at her varicose veins and caught a whiff of the wound. It was putrid.

"I'll take a look at that when I've seen to the child. Which one is it and how old?"

"Hannah. She's nine."

My mother took the doctor to where Hannah lay in the bed settee, a bucket beside her and a reek of vomit in the air. He examined her and emerged briskly from the room.

"Your daughter has meningitis, Mrs Coleman; she'll have to go to hospital immediately," he explained tensely, enquiring which neighbour had a phone and went to call the ambulance.

When he returned he asked: "Has she been sleeping with any of the other children?"

"Yes. Cora." As she said my name, she nudged me in front of the doctor to be examined. He peered at my face, eyes and tongue and pronounced me unaffected.

While they waited for the ambulance, he turned his attention to my mother's leg. The bandage was a strip of bed sheet, underneath which there was a huge, weeping ulcer. She'd had it for some time and I'd got used to the flesh-red disk, the size of a fifty-pence coin, and its horrendous stink. She'd started covering it up lately to soak up the pus that was oozing from it. When the doctor saw it, he started tutting. The disc was now elongated and well on its way to forming an anklet around her shin.

"You're a lucky woman, Mrs Coleman. That's gangrene you've got there. If you'd left it much longer, you might have lost your foot."

Looking her straight in the eye, he asked: "Did you really get this from a bang on a chair?" Sensing the doctor's sympathy, she shook her head.

This is how my mother really got her ulcer:

It was a wet night and the rain was lashing the window in the back room. My father had my mother backed into a corner and it was serious because my grandmother was in the room and the TV was off. Pinned behind the door, Kathleen couldn't stand but had to sit on an old armchair which lived there. Peter, the baby, was in her arms and frightened children were closed in around her. My father's fists were clenched and his every demented accusation was followed by:

"DIDN'T CHA?"

"WOULDN'T CHA?"

"AREN'T CHA?"

Unusually, there were no expletives. This was out of respect for his mother. I was standing at some distance, next to the sideboard, and I regarded my grandmother nervously as the assault unfolded. She was in her coat and head scarf and wearing her good leather bootees because of the rain. Watching the action keenly, she knew that at some point my father was going to strike my mother and she was waiting for it. I knew this was the case and that depressing knowledge made me cry. My crying rang out like a bell in the charged atmosphere and it startled her. She came up to me, slapped me hard across the face and spat: "What are *you* crying for?" I couldn't answer.

Frustrated by my mother's silence and unable to pound her head and shoulders because of the baby, my father kicked her shin; taking aim and burying his heavy, oily work boot in her varicose veins. She shrieked in pain and then everyone was crying. The startled baby was crying so my mother gave him to Grace, who was crying. She took the baby, disappeared into the front room and locked the door. Cora, who was not usually present during my father's assaults, found all the crying unnerving. What was the matter with these stupid children? Copying their bloody mother, I suppose. She decided to go home. Anyway, she'd got what she came for – to see my mother bear the brunt of life's unfairness. She deserved it, the stuck-up tart with all her bloody kids. Where were they all coming from, for God's sake? They couldn't all be her John's. The bloody bitch must be mad for it. Before she left, she screamed at my mother to forget her airs and graces and be a good wife to her son. When she left, my father's work was done and he too scuttled away.

I was stunned by the state of my mother's leg. I'd never seen anything swell up so quickly. Within minutes, the swelling was the size of a tennis ball and we were all trembling and sobbing and staring at the super-fast swelling lump. The skin over it looked like it was going to crack. She told us it was all right, not to cry, soon she'd get the tea. What about one of our favourites – fishfingers, chips and beans? Oh, yes please! The thought of chips sent a frisson of excitement through me in spite of the circumstances. We hardly ever had them because it took so long to make enough for everyone. But now, as my mother hobbled around on one foot, I set about peeling and cutting up a huge pile of potatoes. Meanwhile, Grace emerged from the front room, puffy-eyed, needing a clean nappy and a bottle for Peter. We had to do four batches of chips, three packets of fish fingers and three tins of beans to feed everyone. And that was before we started on *his* dinner: boiled potatoes, lamb chops, onion gravy and cabbage, followed by queen of puddings. Someone would have to take it up to him. It fell to me and when the meal was ready, I took the tray and slowly ascended the stairs. On the way up, I could hear Frank on the record player. How could he play music after what he'd just done? I hated Frank Sinatra. His music was the soundtrack to our misery. I wanted to pick up the record player and smash it over my father's head.

It took a long time for the swelling to go down but gradually the tennis ball was replaced by a golf ball and then a black-and-purple bruise. As the bruise faded, a little ulcer developed in the middle of it, which got bigger and bigger. My mother groaned with the smarting pain and when it started to weep pus, she bandaged it with the bed sheet.

Dr Keane had just enough time to treat it before the ambulance arrived. He told her to bite on something because it would hurt, so she picked up a tea towel and folded it, ready for use. He took a blunt-edged surgical knife and scraped out the pus and rotten flesh. Next, he took some white powder and shook a generous amount into the gaping raw hole. My mother bit on the tea towel and whinnied as the powder burnt down to the healthy living muscle. Finally, he packed the wound with sterile gauze, covered it in a snow-white bandage and the stinking, yellowed strip of bed linen went on the fire.

When the ambulance arrived, Hannah went to hospital. We couldn't believe how seriously ill she was – so ill that she could have died. And now she was in hospital in Cork. My mother went in the ambulance, and Grace was holding the fort. Meningitis was such a serious illness that Dr Keane went too and he gave my mother a lift back home afterwards. Hannah would be in hospital for three weeks, having lumbar punctures to take antibiotics straight up her spinal column into her brain. Lumbar punctures sounded very strange. I hoped they wouldn't hurt her. When she came home, she was like a little doll who didn't belong among us. She was pale and thin and her gleaming, blonde hair had been meticulously combed and plaited and dressed with two little red bows.

During my childhood, Ireland was a theocracy. Cobh was typical – stuffed to the gills with Church establishments. Religious fascism ruled our lives. We went to confession every Saturday, mass every Sunday and our schools were owned and run by the Catholic Church. There was religious iconography everywhere. Every home had a crucifix and a picture of the Sacred Heart – that iconic picture of Jesus, the one where he looks serene (in spite of the stigmata) as he gives a blessing, his sunburst heart hovering in the middle of his chest. Ours was in the front bedroom and I sometimes drifted off to sleep soothed by the gentle face of the Christ and the knowledge that he loved children. Jesus would never call a child "swill". If Jesus didn't think I was swill, then how could I be? Surely my father had got it wrong.

At school, we sat under a big plaster crucifix of the agonised, dying Jesus – monstrous nails driven into his hands and feet; a terrifying crown of thorns embedded in his skull; blood on his face, chest, arms and legs. I was taught by nuns, most of them harmless, if a bit eccentric. However, there was one, Sr Jocelyn, who enjoyed her power and the freedom it gave her to bully vulnerable children, the ones whose family problems were common knowledge, whose parents were unlikely to complain about ill-treatment. There was Noreen Hegarty, who came to school in rags; Maria Duffy, whose face and hands were covered in warts; and me, with the violent father.

Jocelyn sat on a padded chair on a rostrum at the front of the class. She had a big, man's body, a deep voice and large white hands which bore the silver ring that meant she was married to Jesus. I tried to picture Jesus and Jocelyn together but, try as I might, I couldn't imagine the olive-skinned wraith on the crucifix with the big man-woman at the front of the class. He was handsome, albeit in a feminine way with his long wavy hair and delicate face, while she was so ugly it frightened me. As well as small, lashless eyes and a big, bumpy nose, she had a mouthful of yellow, vulpine teeth, which she clenched and bared at regular intervals. She was my teacher for three years and during that time I hated going to school . . . and never more so than the one day I lied about my homework.

"Cora Coleman, where's your homework?" she demanded, the long yellow teeth bared in an ugly grimace.

"I lost it, Sister."

"How?"

"I put it down and it got lost," I reiterated, hoping the chaos of our house would provide a good cover. She was silent but stared hard at me:

"CORA COLEMAN, DID YOU DO YOUR HOME-WORK?" she boomed.

"Yes," I insisted.

"WHERE IS IT?"

"I don't know."

"DID YOU DO IT?"

"Yes."

Suddenly she lost control in a way that reminded me of my father. A switch flipped in her and dynamite exploded. She lunged at me, pulled me out of my seat by the back of my uniform and dragged me to the front of the class. She ordered me to stand on an empty desk. She pushed me forward so that I stumbled onto the seat and then, prodded from behind, I stepped up onto the desk top.

The class was deathly quiet and I was trembling. I was on a level with the crucifix and I begged the bloody, impaled Jesus to help me.

"Now, Miss Coleman . . . I'll ask you once more: DID YOU DO YOUR HOMEWORK?" My knees were knocking and I felt faint with the weirdness of being up on the desk, sensing rather than seeing the stunned faces of my peers far below. I was much too afraid to continue the deception.

"No," I whispered, shoulders sinking, head drooping, trying desperately not to cry.

"NO? NO? SO YOU'RE A LIAR, ARE YOU?" she bellowed triumphantly.

"Yes, Sister," I whispered inaudibly.

"ARE YOU A LIAR, CORA COLEMAN?"

"Yes, Sister," I repeated more loudly.

"Did you hear that everyone? CORA COLEMAN IS A LIAR!" she announced to the hushed ranks of little school girls.

"Well, you'll have to be punished," she pronounced, judiciously jabbing a big doughy finger in under her veil and scratching her head. "Pull your socks down!"

Knee-high white socks were part of our school uniform and now I bent over and pushed one and then the other down to my ankles. I straightened up and waited while she went to get the slapper. This was a thick, heavy paddle of wood like a small cricket bat. Gripping it tightly and angling it for maximum impact, she whacked me on the calves. The pain was intense like a burn and it rippled out to every inch of my being. I wanted to cry out but was afraid to. The first blow was followed by another and another and another and for each one she bellowed out a word, slowly and deliberately: "DON'T – YOU – EVER – TELL – LIES – IN – MY – CLASSROOM – AGAIN!!!"

At last she finished.

"Get down! Get down!" she snapped impatiently. As soon as I was on the ground, she pushed me to the foot of the crucifix.

"NOW SAY AN ACT OF CONTRITION TO THE LORD JESUS CHRIST, WHO DIED TO SAVE US FROM OUR SINS . . . GO ON!!" she bellowed, pressing me downwards so that I crumpled under the force of her big hands and knelt in front of the cross. The thing that I dreaded most, the laughter, began behind me but she quelled the mirth with a finger to her lips because she wanted to hear my act of contrition. I closed my eyes, held my hands in the prayer position and began:

"O my God, I am heartily sorry for having offended Thee, and I detest all my sins, because of Thy just punishments, but most of all because they offend Thee, my God, who are all-good and deserving of all my love. I firmly resolve, with the help of Thy grace, to sin no more."

As I recited the prayer, she fetched the bottle of holy water (like the slapper and the crucifix, every classroom had one of these) and showered me liberally with the sacred liquid. I finished and waited for permission to get up. The sight of me kneeling on the ground, dripping holy water, was just too much and in spite of her embargo, my classmates exploded with wild, disbelieving laughter. I waited for permission to move and when it came, I went back to my desk and pulled my socks up over my sore red legs.

For the rest of the morning, I was in a state of shock. I sat at my desk in a sort of paralysis and let the blessed numbness protect me. At eleven o' clock the bell rang for morning break and we all filed out to the playground. Nobody spoke to me. I was the one they'd been laughing at and now no one knew what to say. I desperately wanted to hide so I made for a bench in the far corner, half-hidden by a hedge, and scanned the crowd. I saw my classmates with their friends, who were looking over at me and giggling. I was even funnier now that I was hiding behind the hedge. Suddenly, I saw Hannah playing hopscotch and a huge sob welled up in my chest. I wanted the two of us to go home, get into the bed settee and never get out again. I was going to start crying and I had to stop myself so I bit my cheeks until they bled and the pain focused my mind and calmed me down. I spat out bloody saliva and probed the teeth marks with my tongue. Then the bell rang for the end of break-time and I went back to the classroom.

Jocelyn assaulted me many times and although my mother knew, she never protested. In private we had come adrift from norms like Catholicism and mocked the clergy, calling the nuns "penguins" and the priests "sky pilots", but, in public, she was as obsequious as the next parishioner. She wasn't going to rock the boat. Not for my sake. If I'd gone home that day, she'd have sent me straight back. When Jocelyn beat me and I was laughed at by my classmates, the only defence I had was to withdraw deep inside myself. If classmates passed our house in the wake of these mortifying episodes, my solution was to hide. I'd run indoors until they were gone.

As I got older, I shrank away from people more and more. I loved the darkness of winter and the cupboard under the stairs at the home of Cora and Old Bob, where I retreated with a candle whenever I could.

I trusted nature, not people, and knew every flower in every hedgerow and every bend in every country lane. I especially loved the trees; being among trees was the best thing I knew. Near our house was a windbreak of majestic old cedars and we little girls gave them fancy names like Penelope, Samantha and Isabella. Samantha was the biggest and the place where her trunk met her branches was like the palm of a huge hand. Sometimes I went to her on my own, climbed up and listened to her soughing – the merest whisper, like the brush of a feather on summer days or a great creaking and roaring when the autumn winds blew in. She was old and strong and her bark was gnarled and twisted like an elephant's hide. Curled up in Samantha's big, generous hand, I sucked comfort out of her as out of a mother.

In summer, when it was really hot, a haze rose from the waters of the harbour enveloping our island, until it became Avalon for us. I spent my summers swimming in an inlet called White Bay, just down the hill from our house. There was a white-washed cottage on the hill with orange nasturtiums crowding around it and tall trees soaring up behind. To me it was like a picture from a fairytale. There was a well, and a spring that issued from a dry-stone wall.

When we were very young and he was in a good mood, my father took us for walks down to the bay and on the way we'd stop at the spring for a drink. He'd cup his huge hands and we'd incline our little heads forward and lap up the pure hill water from the bowl that they made.

My mother knew the woman who lived in the cottage and, contrary to my idyllic imaginings, she said it was a damp, gloomy hole of a place. She'd lived there all her married life and she longed for a modern home in the town, away from dripping trees and underground streams.

The spring flowed down White Bay Hill in a little channel that was cobbled with purple stones. We'd follow it down, keeping our eyes peeled for frogs and other such creatures until, at the bottom, the change in the air told us that the sea was nearby. Like the other children charging past us, we were ozone-crazed and made a mad dash for the beach. From White Bay, you could see the great expanse of the harbour and I gazed in wonder at the huge oil tankers and cargo ships anchored there, my chest filling with that rarest of feelings – family pride, knowing that my grandfather, Old Bob Coleman, had taken the helm of those huge ships and steered them up to the docks in Cork, back down again and out to the far horizon from where they'd come.

The front bedroom was our territory. It was where the Sacred Heart was; where we all slept together; where I could always find my mother if it was four to twelve and a bad day and *he* was getting ready for work. She'd get his packed food ready – beef or ham sandwiches (cut thin, the way he liked them), four scoops of loose leaf tea, four scoops of sugar, and milk in a miniature whiskey bottle – leave it ready and withdraw upstairs. While she waited for him to go, she'd sit by the window and gaze out at the children playing in the road. If I saw her there, I waved.

She'd study the front garden and make a note of what needed doing. The grass might need cutting or she'd need to get some manure for the roses. Like the other women in our street, she grew flowers out the front but she didn't touch the back garden. That was my father's preserve. He grew vegetables there and lavished great care and attention on them, sending off for seeds, not trusting in those that could be bought locally. When he was in a good mood, he spent his weekends digging, sowing and harvesting but when he was in a bad mood he lost interest and cats peed on his prize marrows while slugs ate the cabbage and all the lettuce went to seed.

At about half past three, he'd emerge, sandwich box tucked under his arm, and I'd hold my breath as he stomped past and left me unacknowledged, as usual. It was awful when he ignored us like that. It was damning. We meant nothing to him and he was letting everyone know it. The worst occasion was in the town one afternoon when I was about eight or nine. I was with Grace and we were horror-struck to spot him in the distance, barrelling down the hill, going in on four to twelve. I could see he was glowering even though he was a small figure far away. We watched him reach the bottom of the hill with mounting anxiety and instinctively held hands. He got bigger and bigger, nearer and nearer, and Grace's grasp on my fingers got tighter until she was crushing them. He'd seen us. That was for sure. The long straight street was nearly empty. I hoped he'd speak to us. I willed him to say something, just to acknowledge our presence. But he drew level and then, with his big sulking nose in the air, he passed us by.

When my mother saw him going, she'd spit one word after him – "Madman!" – and go downstairs where there'd be an unholy mess to clear up, our tea to get and babies to put to bed. Soon she'd be back upstairs in the front bedroom, reading stories for drowsy children as the twilight fell across the gardens, the road and the fields beyond.

We were in the front bedroom the day I was staring at her bandage. I was probably about five or six and I remember my gaze being fixed on the brilliantly white gauze that was wrapped around her right hand. I was feeling the badness of it, knowing it wasn't an innocent wound that was underneath. We were all there and I remember our reflections in the dressing table mirror – mouths open, bewildered. *He* was downstairs getting ready for four-to-twelve. There was a tingling on the side of my body nearest the door, as if it was covered in little feelers that were listening out for any movement on the stairs that might signal his approach.

The day before my parents had been upstairs alone. We children were playing downstairs. He was shouting. The usual elements were present:

Foul language: "FUCKIN' WHORIN' CUNT!"

The coarsest of insults: "UGLY CUNT! LOOK AT YA! NOSE LIKE A FUCKIN' SHARK! LEGS LIKE A FUCKIN' PLOUGHMAN!"

Paranoid accusations: "I SUPPOSE YA THINK YER GOIN' OUT WHORIN' IN THEM SHOES!"

He punched her viciously but this time it wasn't enough. He saw a lump of metal and picked it up. It was a toy gun of Joseph's, but big and heavy. He lifted it over his head, tongue-sandwiched with the satisfaction he anticipated. My mother screamed, put her hand up to protect herself and a jagged edge of metal ripped her palm open, such was the force with which he brought it down on her.

The scream made us rigid with tension and we waited, hyper-vigilant, for more. Then we were at the foot of the stairs and our mother came down, in a blue coat and white high heels, very pale in the face as if she was going to faint. She was holding onto the wall with one hand to steady herself while the other one was pouring blood. Drops were plopping rapidly onto the red lino. My father had disappeared into his room. She told Grace to fetch a tea towel from the kitchen. I couldn't move and could hardly breathe at the sight of my mother's blood. Once she had staunched the flow with the tea towel she wrapped a clean pillow case neatly around it and went to the little clinic in the town, where it was stitched and dressed properly.

In spite of her injury, I wanted my mother to tell me everything was all right, take me in her arms and lift me up out of the chaos and pain that formed the broader context of that bandaged hand. But there were too many of us and I made do with pressing in as close to her as possible. Seeing us staring at the dressing, she made light of it, telling us jokingly that we'd have to have sliced pans for a while. (Sliced pans – pre-sliced loaves of bread, in their shiny, waxy wrappings – were a novelty in the 1960s. You could fold a slice of the light, plasticky bread and almost fit it in a matchbox and I loved it so much that one day after school, I ate a whole loaf with butter and marmalade.) We stayed huddled in our tight knot until we heard him leaving and then we loosened off a little bit, so she could get up, and trailed closely behind her when she went back downstairs.

It was nature that helped us most to survive our father – by giving us walls. But walls keep everything out, good as well as bad, and every time he traumatised us, the wall got a bit higher and our lonely anxiety manifested itself in a variety of nervous symptoms: Grace shaved her fingertips with a razor blade; Joseph and Sarah sucked their thumbs into their teenage years; I bit my nails to the quick; Hannah had an eating disorder and Rose's hair fell out. I don't remember Peter having nervous problems. Grace protected him and thus I think he escaped the worst excesses of my father's violence.

When my grandfather died in 1972, my grandmother Cora was distraught – not at his passing but at the vacuum he left behind. What would become of her? Cooking and cleaning was her life but who would she cook and clean for now? It was decided that one of us, her despised non-grandchildren, should move in with her and keep her company. My mother asked for a "volunteer", but my siblings would sooner have plucked their eyes out than live with their grandmother. She had no love for them and they knew it. She didn't believe my sisters and brothers were her grandchildren because she couldn't see herself in their faces. They were simply the issue of the tart from Donegal. They, in turn, only ever referred to her as "the Nannygoat" or "the Old Bag".

It was my misfortune to be named after her. Cora. I felt branded, not named. Cora by name, Cora by nature. It set me apart from my siblings, none of whom had been burdened with Coleman names. Moreover, I had the Coleman genes, bore a strong resemblance to her daughter and spent more time with my grandmother than all my sisters and brothers put together. When I fell out with my siblings, I was the enemy, a spy in their midst. A Coleman among the Leahys. I was called Thick Lips and Big Head because of my Coleman features, name-calling that my mother made no effort to stop, and told to get back to the Nannygoat's, where I belonged.

I went on a school trip to Shannon Airport once. Cora might have paid for it. I know I went from her house and took food that she'd prepared for me. There was far too much: a whole packet of Goldgrain biscuits, three rounds of luncheon meat sandwiches, a banana, an apple, three fairy cakes and a bar of chocolate. I realised that I'd be eating all day to get through it. It was packed into a small battered case that I think had been Thomas's school satchel. I lugged it along with me and sat on my own because no one wanted to sit with Cora Coleman and her suitcase of food. In Limerick I started on the sandwiches and after Shannon I had some more. I felt I had to eat everything. It never occurred to me to throw some away. I was so afraid of my grandmother that I was sure she'd find out that I'd dumped her food and I knew the trouble her displeasure could cause at home. Furthermore, I sensed the pathos that had gone into its preparation, quantity and packing into Thomas's old school case. I felt obliged to eat it all for the sake of my tragic family.

It was dark on the journey back to Cork. Outside, there was still a glimmer of the setting sun on the horizon. You could just make out fields, mountains and the odd cottage with its lights on. I imagined wolves on the prowl, will-o-the-wisps and mist-shrouded bogs. I was on my own again, at the front of the coach with the satchel open on the seat beside me. I only had the Goldgrain to go. I opened the packet and began chomping. A girl opposite watched me in disbelief as I worked my way through the whole packet. Singing started up at the back. It was "Nobody's Child", a lament of embarrassing sentimentality that we all knew and loved. I was eating so I had to sing along in my head. I often sang this old song to myself. It comforted me when the Coleman looks got me down. It touched me so deeply. It was how I felt – nobody's child – and I put an ocean of feeling into each mawkish word.

We all knew that I was going to be the volunteer. It was only a matter of when I'd say yes. During the weekend that I went to live with my grandmother, I had my first period. It was the early 1970s and menstruation was still a shameful bodily function in our community. Sanitary protection changed hands swiftly over shop counters and sanitary towels were only ever referred to as "STs". No one ever admitted that they were having a period. Menstruation was never discussed and I was startled when a school friend told me she'd started her periods and described what it was like. I felt sorry for her but in my ignorance I didn't think it would happen to me.

I was shocked when I dried myself after swimming on the Friday of that weekend and found a streak of blood on my towel. I kept it secret and plugged up the flow with toilet paper but by Sunday evening, it was heavy and the wads of toilet paper weren't working anymore. I had to be at Cora's by six o'clock for my tea. Pushed by necessity and cringing with embarrassment, I approached my mother and uttered just one sound – "p" – willing her to understand and not to get it confused with urine or little green vegetables. She did understand, gave me half a packet of sanitary towels (tampons were unheard of) but no explanations or advice. Stealthily, I washed and changed my knickers and then I went off to live with my grandmother.

And I liked it. Although she was a bitter, spiteful woman, her house was clean and quiet. Furthermore, she was a good cook and I was always hungry. There were three bedrooms and only the two of us, so there'd be no overcrowding, and best of all I wouldn't have to be around my father. If I organised my timetable carefully I might never have to see him again.

There was a price for all this luxury, however – we'd be saying the rosary every night and, horror of horrors, I'd have to sleep with her! *What!* I thought when she told me, *I'm not sleeping with you!!* I reeled from the idea. As a teenager, I didn't want to sleep with an old woman. Especially *that* old woman! The thought of it disgusted me but she insisted. She was frightened in her own room. She said she heard noises during the night and I thought of Thomas at the end of my grandfather's bed. Spring was just around the corner, she argued, and she'd move back into her own room then. So I had to agree. Anyway, the gap I'd left at home was quickly filled and I couldn't go back.

That first evening our routine began. Without preamble, she switched off the television and got out her prayer beads. We knelt and recited the rosary, an interminable list of prayers and beseechings, involving the invocation of the Father, the Son, the Holy Spirit, the Blessed Virgin and various other saints, depending on the time of year. There was a lot of repetition of the "Hail Mary", of which she'd recite the first section: "Hail Mary, full of grace, the Lord is with thee, blessed art thou among women and blessed is the fruit of thy womb, Jesus." At the mention of Jesus we bowed our heads, then I'd continue: "Holy Mary, mother of God, pray for us sinners, now and at the hour of our death. Amen."

While she was deep in prayer, I looked around. I'd known this house all my life but I'd only slept in it once before, when it amused my visiting cousins to have me there. I loved this little room, with its green leather suite, terracotta fireplace and gleaming brass fender. There was the little cupboard under the stairs where I'd often secreted myself with the door locked, while my grandfather banged and shouted for me to come out. The old wind-up clock ticked loudly on the mantelpiece. My grandfather's things – his rack of pipes, his books and his radio – were still where he'd left them. I used to watch him prepare the tobacco for those pipes. It came in a compressed block and he'd get out his little penknife with the mother-of-pearl handle and cut thin shavings from it, slowly and pensively.

When he had enough, he'd roll the tobacco in his palms until it was finely shredded. Then he'd fill his pipe. When he lit it, the smell was wonderful, rich and aromatic, quite unlike my father's stinking Majors. I liked to play with the pipes when he was out, inhaling the smell deeply, imitating the way he sucked on the mouthpiece and the way he curled his long thin fingers around the bowl. Next to the pipes was his wireless and at the table was the place where he'd always eaten alone, his meals served by a dutiful wife who also ate alone, in the kitchen. Being an old sailor, he was resourceful; using snippets of his own hair, he'd made paint brushes with which he painted pictures of the ships he'd sailed on during his long life. And there they hung, on the walls of the living room.

After the rosary, Cora gave me hot milk and biscuits and then I went to bed. I dressed in one of her flannelette nighties, freshly laundered and smelling of lavender, and got into the double bed between cool, clean sheets. For company I had a statue of Jesus, a statue of the Virgin that glowed in the dark, a crucifix and the ubiquitous Sacred Heart. I had cramps but I didn't ask her for aspirin because I didn't want her to know I was bleeding. In spite of her own pregnancies, she believed that menstruation was the badness in a woman being flushed out of her body every month. I knew she'd only add to my shame so my packet of sanitary towels was hidden under the bed. I was afraid I'd stain her pristine sheets so I pulled my knickers up as tight as they'd go and lay in the dark, listening to every sound.

All too soon, I heard her bare feet slapping heavily on the lino of the stairs. She'd taken her teeth out and was gummily muttering prayers as she climbed. At intervals, she stopped to groan as if every step was agony. I had to suppress an instinct to run away, so I did the next best thing – I scuttled to the edge of the bed and pretended to be asleep. Soon, she was in the room and then beside the bed. She had a hot water bottle which she positioned where her feet would be and got in, all the while muttering prayers. The mattress depressed and I clung to the edge to prevent myself rolling towards her. I felt sick when I thought of our bodies touching during the night, her gummy spittle in my hair maybe, us spooning each other in our sleep.

The next morning, she was up before I woke. I could hear the wireless from downstairs and the clatter of breakfast crockery. I lay there for a few minutes, startled by the strange surroundings, and then I remembered where I was and that I lived here now. The curtains were still drawn but the morning light caught the crucifix on the wall above the dressing table. Suddenly I felt the sanitary towel between my legs. Oh Jesus. I leapt out of bed to check the sheets. They were okay. And so was the nightdress. But the towel was sodden. It wasn't going to hold any more blood so I took it off and looked for somewhere to hide it. The wardrobe. With a bit of luck she'd never find it in there. I dropped the sanitary towel onto the dark floor of the wardrobe, making a mental note to bag it up later and take it away. Then I put my school uniform on and waited to be called for my breakfast. Downstairs, I sat in my grandfather's chair and she served me just as she'd served him. First, an orange cut into segments, then a large bowl of cornflakes with hot milk, followed by thick slices of toast dripping with butter and dark chunky marmalade, with a cup of strong brown tea to wash it all down.

On my way to school I called in at home. It was a typical Monday morning. Everything was missing: school ties, socks, shoes, school bags and the comb. We only ever had one comb and it was always lost on Monday mornings. There was a system to the search for it. First down the sides of the bed settee; then under the sideboard; next down the back of the couch; and if that didn't turn it up, we were dispatched all over the house to look for it. My mother would be tense, with my father on nights maybe, and so many tousled heads to tidy. "Where is it?" she'd snap, "It can't have disappeared into thin air!" That was her standard response to the missing comb. It had disappeared into thin air. Stung by her bad mood, we'd mimic her as we walked to school, laughing at the expression "thin air" and wondering what *thin* air looked like. I stood there watching the chaotic scene with a sense that everything was the same but different. I'd slept with the enemy and I'd be sleeping with her again tonight. I'd eaten a large, leisurely breakfast while my siblings had had a rushed, lumpy bowl of porridge.

I was clammy and smelly and in the warm classroom I whiffed slightly of blood. After school, I had a wash and then I went back to my grandmother's and my strange new routine started all over again – me in my grandfather's chair; a large meal; on my knees for the rosary; and finally, in bed with my grandmother.

As time went on, I got better at coping with my periods but the problem always remained of how to dispose of used sanitary towels and bloody knickers. I only ever came up with one solution – hide them and forget about them. Spring came and went and when the days were long and the nights were short, Cora finally went back to her own room. At long last, I had my own space. I was thrilled and set about removing all the statues and holy pictures from the walls. I put up posters from *Jackie* magazine, mainly of Paul McCartney and Donny Osmond. I covered the walls with them and went off to school delighted with my handiwork. However, when I came home, I found that they'd all been taken down and the statues and pictures were back in situ. I switched them again. Out with religion and in with sex. When I found the key to the bedroom door, I locked it and took the key to school with me. That evening, my grandmother was incandescent with rage and came at me in a fury:

"HOW DARE YOU LOCK ME OUT OF MY OWN PROPERTY, YOU DIRTY LITTLE BITCH!" she screeched. "GIVE ME THE KEY TO THE BEDROOM! *GIVE IT TO ME!*"

I fetched the key from my school bag and handed it over. Snatching it from me viciously, she snapped:

"DON'T YOU DARE TOUCH MY THINGS AGAIN, YOU DIRTY LITTLE BITCH! THE NERVE OF IT! HAVE YOU NO SHAME, INTERFERING WITH THE HOLY FAMILY!"

*Dirty little bitch*. The words rang in my ears. I was hurt by them. I thought I was her favourite grandchild, at least when my cousins weren't around. So did my brothers and sisters, and they punished me for it. I wished they could hear her now. *Dirty little bitch*. I needed to know what she meant.

"I'm *not* dirty," I countered, to provoke elaboration.

"YOU ARE! YOU DIRTY BITCH! WITH YOUR MEN ALL OVER MY WALLS AND YOUR KNICKERS COVERED IN BLOOD ALL OVER MY HOUSE!"

So she'd found them. She shouted at me to get out:

"GO ON! GET OUT OF MY HOUSE! GET BACK WHERE YOU BELONG, YOU DIRTY LITTLE BITCH!"

Her words were music to my ears. Clearly she hated me just as much as she hated my siblings. How wonderful! It was evidence that I was one of them, after all. I went home feeling like a true Leahy. Rose was persuaded to replace me. Before long there were fights and I heard those hateful words again – Big Head and Thick Lips and "Get back to the Old Bag's where you belong". Everyone seemed to think I belonged somewhere else. I refused to go but Rose came home in tears one day and after all the fighting and name calling, I went back. My grandmother and I compromised on the pictures so that I ended up with mostly religion and a smattering of sex. I never saw the key again and I knew that she went through my things when I was out, but we rubbed along together for another year or so until, finally, we got our extra bedroom and then I went home for good.

Amazingly, when I was fifteen, my father agreed to the building of an extension. It would consist of a kitchen and a small bathroom and bedroom. A man called Mr Brennan was employed to build it and an important prerequisite of the project was that *he* was not to be inconvenienced. This was difficult because our old kitchen would be out of action and our meals had to be cooked on an open fire in the back room. He was still to get his nice dinners even if my mother was burnt and blackened in the process. Another prerequisite was that she was not to talk to the builder. *He*'d certainly not be talking to him and she was to do the same.

"How is he supposed to get his instructions?" she asked evenly.

"One of *them* can tell him," he suggested – meaning us. Upstairs in the front bedroom, my mother fumed at the madness of it.

"Just imagine," she cried, to no one in particular, "a builder coming into a house and he can only talk to the children. Have you ever heard anything so crazy?" She laughed bitterly and added: "What about when they're at school?"

Sanity reigned because she decided to ignore my father's orders. Assuming that, during the construction, she'd probably get beaten anyway, she told Mr Brennan whatever he needed to know and made him cups of tea as well, while my father skulked in his room and watched the extension take shape through a chink in his curtains.

It was strange having another man in the house and one so different from *him*. Mr Brennan had a sweet nature. He smiled at us, asked us about ourselves and whistled snippets of songs all day long. My mother could be heard chatting with him and because of that I waited with bated breath to see what my father would do. I fully expected him to attack her and call her a whore and a cunt. I waited day after day for the onslaught, cringing deeply at the thought of his obscene imaginings and their imminent expression but the ambush never came. The reason was his fear of the other man. My father hesitated because Mr Brennan was bigger and stronger than he was. If he hit her, he wagered, she'd be showing off her bruises again and it was none of that builder cunt's business.

When the extension was finished, we didn't know ourselves. The new kitchen was huge. You could fit four of the old one into it. It had a range for the winter and an electric cooker for the summer, a dresser, a refectory table, a big pine sideboard and a big picture window that framed our back garden and the fields beyond. At long last, after many years of longing, we had a bathroom with a sparkling white bath, toilet and wash basin! It was like *Dr Who*'s Tardis, with Mr Brennan as the magician who had conjured it into our midst. The day that it was ready for use was like Christmas morning to me. I couldn't believe that now I'd be able to bathe like everyone else, to sink into hot water and foaming bubble bath for the very first time. To top it all, there was a lock on the door so that every sensation of this long-awaited and utterly delightful experience could be savoured at leisure and in private.

The walls were a dull grey from the plaster. Mr Brennan said it would have to sweat before we could decorate. The walls were sweating. It was curious language. I imagined the walls straining and perspiring in some great, mysterious effort. While we waited for the walls to sweat, the kitchen floor had to be tiled. Always keen to please, I volunteered to do it. I was nervous because I was only fifteen, it was such a big room – the biggest kitchen in the street now –

and I'd never tiled anything before. If I did it well, my
mother would lavish praise on me and I'd be in heaven,
but if I messed it up, I'd feel her angry frustration, hot
and heavy. In order to avoid that, I read and reread the
instructions slowly and carefully. The tiles were white
with a blue fleck and as they went down, they transformed
the concrete shell into a room. My mother was delighted.
She praised my efforts lavishly and I was her best girl for
the day. The furniture followed and when we'd added a
venetian blind to the window, we were so proud we could
have invited the Lord Mayor of Cork in for tea.

Two of my father's pleasures were newspapers and
pornography. He bought a daily newspaper but also had
seven on Sundays. They were the *Sunday Press*, the
*Sunday Independent*, the *Sunday Times*, the *Observer*,
the *Sunday Mirror*, the *Sunday Express* and the *People*. I
knew this litany by heart because Joseph and I collected
them every Sunday morning after nine o'clock mass. The
pile weighed as much as a breeze block. It was crazy. He
was the only man in Cobh who bought seven Sunday
newspapers. How could he read them all? The newsagent
certainly must have wondered that as she handed them
over to his puny little children. Once we got them home,
we left them on the kitchen table, if the mood was good,
or outside his bedroom door if it was bad. He didn't
throw them out either but piled them up on top of his
wardrobe and under his bed, so there was always an
overpowering smell of damp newsprint in his room.

He hid his pornography well, but on black, unshaven
days, he pulled out all his dirty pictures and spread them

around the room. He had a variety of material, some of it home-made. There were cut-and-paste montages – bits of images from magazines and newspapers tweaked and scratched at; pictures of near-naked women made fully naked by careful scratching at their briefs and the addition of tiny tufts of his own hair as pubes. A page-three model, holding two coconuts, was scratched at until her breasts and the coconuts merged and two lurid red nipples were added to give her enormous boobs. There were little booklets of pictures which, when flicked through, showed women doing striptease and a myriad other shocking images.

I knew all of this because one day I discovered it for myself. It happened like this. It was my turn to take his dinner up and I found his bedroom door ajar. I didn't know what to do because this had never happened to me before. It was usually shut tight. Where was he? What should I do? If I left his dinner on the floor it might get cold. I decided to go in and leave the tray on the cabinet beside his bed. I swallowed hard and entered. It was dark and smelly and in the gloom I whispered the strange word: "Daddy". There was no answer so I turned the light on.

At first my brain refused to acknowledge what I saw – every possible surface was covered in lurid images. There were naked women, vaginas, breasts, spread legs and couples having sex everywhere I looked. Under a lingerie model whose corset had been scratched off, there was this hand-written annotation: "My sister Cora finally agreed to let me see her in the nude. Of course, I shagged the arse off her." His sister. My name.

I blushed. I put the tray down on top of a naked

woman and turned to go but suddenly he was there in the doorway, doing up his flies. I was shaking and breathing fast. It was just him, me and his dirty pictures. It seemed a long way down to the safety of my mother in the kitchen. His door was open because he'd been to the toilet. It was a rare slip-up. Gruffly, he told me to get out and never to go into his room again, even if the door was open. Speechless with fright, I darted past him and took the stairs two at a time. I felt hot and sweaty and sick with shame. In my mind's eye, I saw the horny faces and purple-red genitals that had shot out at me from the walls and the bed and the floor. I didn't know people did things like that.

Sex was taboo in our semi-rural, Catholic world. It was rarely mentioned and the only way it reached us was through TV and then in the most oblique and censored fashion. Pornography was doubly taboo. If sex had different shades, pornography was deepest black. It was from the far side, completely alien to family life, sick and depraved, a most terrible form of sin – and yet my father's room was full of it. The pictures I saw there had a profound effect on me. I saw couples having coarse, visceral sex and there was one particular image that I couldn't erase. It was of a man dragging a woman onto a bed by her hair. He had an angry, red erection and she was naked from the waist down. She wore a pained expression and he looked furious. Is that what sex was like, I wondered? Is that what my father did to my mother when we were conceived? I imagined it must be, given the violent context of their marriage. Was I the product of rape? Is that why no-one ever talked about sex, because of its inherent violence?

I plucked up the courage to tell my mother what I'd

seen in my father's room but she already knew. I wanted to know where he got his magazines. You couldn't buy magazines like that in the local shops and he didn't have any friends to get them from.

"In Cork, I suppose," she answered tightly, wanting me to stop annoying her with my questions, not wanting this dirty business coming to the surface. Cork. That made sense. In our small world, Cork was a distant place where anything was possible. It had extensive quays and that meant loads of foreigners and prostitutes. It also explained his mysterious Saturday excursions when, dressed to the nines, he'd take himself off and return hours later with packages that he spirited straight up to his room. When I was older, I surmised that he visited prostitutes in Cork and I imagined him in cheap rooms by the river, asking girls if they minded him calling them Cora.

Our sleeping arrangements were now thus: my mother and Grace in the new bedroom; my father, Joseph and Peter in the back bedroom; Hannah, Rose, Sarah and me in the front. The bed settee, now old and tattered, was taken to the dump and the front room, after many years of doubling up as a bedroom, became a study for Grace, who was preparing to go to university. Ear-piercing screams would emanate from there as she struggled with her studies and I swallowed hard because I knew that in two years' time I'd have to do the same.

Educating her children was my mother's escape route and as many of us as possible would go to university. We were all in awe of Grace's bravery, the first in the family to go to college. I admired her greatly, but from a distance. Up close, I could hardly remember a smile or a kind word from her in my whole life, but I didn't blame her. I put it down to my Coleman genes. My grandmother resented her simply because she was my mother's first-born and bore no resemblance to her. *He* hated her from the moment she was born because his mother did, and because now that he had a child, he felt trapped. I have an early memory of him hiding behind the front door and Grace coming home from a birthday party. She was about eight or nine. Him pouncing out, startling her and making her jump, hissing: "Where have *you* bin?" About to strike her, I think. My mother getting between them, cursing him for ruining her child's life. The naked hatred between them. Grace caught in the middle. I knew that Grace feared and loathed her father and grandmother with good reason and because of that my mother loved her all the more dearly.

Although I was jealous of Grace, I accepted that she had a special relationship with our mother. It had always been thus. Our inequality was the very essence of normality. It was like knowing the sky was blue and the grass was green. I'd breathed it in all my life and never questioned it. But now, in my teenage years, I became jealously attuned to their intimacy. In the atmosphere of fear and loathing that ruled our home, they whispered a lot behind closed doors. I'd hear them and, instead of walking away, I tortured myself by eavesdropping. The walls of the extension were thin and if you stood in the bathroom, you could hear their conversations next door, in the new bedroom. If one was uncertain, the other was reassuring. If one was confused, the other was enlightening. There was sometimes soft laughter and their voices were very low

71

when important information was being exchanged. Plans for the future perhaps – and I felt sure those plans didn't include me. I knew that if they struck out for a new life, I'd be left behind in the bombed-out ruins of my childhood. That was where I belonged; a Coleman left behind with *him*.

We younger girls were constantly rearranging the furniture in the front bedroom, sometimes having the beds parallel and sometimes at right angles. We left the sheets on until they were grey and the pillow cases stank of mouth dribble and hair grease. We thought everyone's bed linen was like that and that crisp, clean sheets and pillow cases only existed in hospitals or hotels. Sometimes there were fleas on the sheets and our mother was adept at catching them and cracking them on her long fingernails. Deftly and with focus, she'd position them on one thumbnail and crack them with the other before they could hop away. I imagined every flea was my father, tiny and crushed and dead.

In the back room, Joseph and Peter slept on narrow metal bunk beds, doing their best to ignore the stink of old newspapers and my father's presence. Joseph started staying out late and always came home drunk. If my father was out on nights, he played records, which woke us all up. It was torture to be woken night after night by the morose sound of Neil Young's *After the Goldrush* or Bob Dylan's *Desire*, the two albums he played over and over. Although miserable from disrupted sleep, I didn't protest because I was afraid of Joseph. I knew he'd thump me if I did. He was solitary and truculent and dropped out of school early. We made allowances for him because he had no one to look up to. At least we, being girls, could model ourselves on our mother, after a fashion. Drunk, he sometimes burst into the kitchen where we were usually gathered and shouted this at us:

"RATS!"

Rats. It was horrible. Almost as bad as "swill". And, just like "swill", it cowed us. But one day I couldn't go cow down and marched up to him, spat in his face and shouted:

"WE . . . ARE . . . NOT . . . RATS!"

With that he grabbed me by the hair and pulled me around the kitchen. Such was my father's influence on his first-born son.

Joseph never seemed to sleep peacefully. His metal bunk bed rattled as he twisted and turned and shouted in his sleep. In a sleepy grumble my father could be heard telling him to settle down and if that didn't work, he'd wake up properly and roar across the few feet that separated their beds:

"HEY YOU! . . . HEY YOU! SSSHUTT UPP AND GO TO SLEEP!"

One day they locked horns and careened around the new kitchen, smashing into the dresser and breaking my mother's ornaments. Joseph swore at *him* and staggered drunkenly out of the room. My mother, her face buried in a tea towel, wept inconsolably. She could have nothing. Everything nice was swept away. I stared at the ugly black wound on the new pine table where a drunken Joseph had stabbed it with a fork and imagined another era of violence just beginning, with Joseph as heir to his father's crown. I desperately hoped not. I put my arm around my mother to console her as I'd seen Grace do, but she shook me off roughly.

"Get off me!" she snapped. Clearly, I wouldn't do as a substitute. Smarting from the rejection, I sought the solace of the front bedroom and collapsed on the bed I shared with Hannah, too low to cry, wishing I was dead or, better still, that I'd never been born. What was the point of my life? Nobody wanted me. I stayed on the bed for a long time, beyond tears, wrapped in numbness, my survival suit, staring at a cardboard box on top of the wardrobe. It had a bunch of bananas printed on it in red. Eventually I started to have thoughts that brought me back to the world. Boys. Clothes. Paul McCartney, who'd replaced Jesus in my heart as the man least likely to do me wrong.

I looked around the room. We'd made our own of it, my younger sisters and I. We all had our little flourishes with posters and pictures on the walls. Hannah and I sketched and painted in our corner. We did art at school and tried out our own little flourishes at home. Hannah liked portraits while I preferred landscapes. It was the safest place I knew but even the front bedroom couldn't keep *him* out entirely. Hateful reminders, like his cigarette smell and Frank Sinatra, seeped in, as they did now, from the next door bedroom.

One morning around that time, I was woken by that voice shouting below in the kitchen. He was just back from the night-shift. As so many times before, I listened to the formulaic build-up to his assault – the menacing, sexualised accusations, dredged up out of nothing, and my mother's silences or short, reluctant replies. The silences were unbearable because I knew they made him worse. Oh please Mammy, I begged now, pleeeeze, pleeeeze say something. Something nice. Something to calm him down. Something to make him go away. All she had to do was say the right thing and it would stop. Or so I thought. Of course, I didn't understand, as she did, that there was no "right thing". There was no way out; his lust for violent release was inexorable and insatiable. My mother didn't waste her breath but tried to conserve her energy to deal with the coming pain. She gave reluctant monosyllabic answers infuriating him. The name-calling ensued and then there was the vacuum in their exchange when I knew he was punching her.

I didn't have to be down there to know it was happening, my body told me. My temperature rose, my heart beat faster and anxious sounds escaped from my throat. My younger sisters were asleep, and I was glad. At least they'd been spared this one episode. Presently, he stomped upstairs to his room and slammed the door with a ferocity that shook the whole house. John Coleman, champion door slammer! That was his talent in life; he could slam a door louder than anyone else. Mr Mac Neice told us that, at work, the men called him "Slam-Bang-Alakazang". Everyone woke up. Rose and Sarah, frightened by the sudden loud noise, shot out of bed and bumped into each other like headless chickens. Hannah remained curled up with her eyes closed although she was awake. I didn't move either because moving meant leaving the security of the bed with its warm embrace and going out into the world, raw and hurt.

Within minutes, my mother was in the room rousing

us for school. She had that roughed-up look that I recognised so well. I could see that she'd been punched and her hair had been pulled. My heart cried out to her: *I'm sorry. I'm so sorry.* I dearly wished to stay at home, not to have to face the day with my heavy heart but her voice was hard and I knew I'd have to go to school, like it or not. She wanted some peace. She didn't want kids in the house as well as *him*.

On my way to the bathroom, I noticed that my father's door was open. It must have rebounded on its hinges with the slam. He was standing at the window, wearing a blue blazer that his mother had given him. The collar was turned up as if against the wind and his hands were clasped behind his back, in the manner of a ship's captain. And what was that rich, sensuous smell? A cigar! Yes, he had a small slim cigar, of all things, between his fingers! I couldn't believe it! That symbol of wealth and celebration, here in the home that he'd made so poor and unhappy. I detested the very sight of him in his blue blazer smoking his cigar. He looked bizarre, as if in the grip of some vain fantasy: the eligible young man desired by the finest girls in the town and he was thinking now that he could've had his pick. Why, oh why did he have to go to Athlone and get snared by that ugly cunt with her varicose veins? I wondered if Joseph and Peter were still asleep in their bunk beds. Hardly. They had probably escaped from the room with their school clothes and were getting dressed downstairs.

My father's room was a foul hole that no child should have to sleep in and with that in mind my mother set about improving it for the sake of her sons. When I was sixteen, she persuaded him to agree to a fitted wardrobe. It would have twice the space of the old one and the boys' clothes could go in there too, instead of on the floor. As usual, it wasn't easy to talk him round. He was afraid because something would change. The stacks of ancient newspapers would have to go, along with the dour old wardrobe that was their home. But it happened, and the new closet was beautiful. It had louvred panels for doors and it was a treat, when he was out, to go in there and just gaze at it.

Things were looking up. Now that we had a bathroom, we no longer needed the nocturnal bucket. Furthermore, we now had three bedrooms instead of two, the biggest kitchen in the street and the air was sweeter since the piss and the newspapers had gone.

Change kept happening and he couldn't stop it. We weren't small children any more. Grace, Joseph and I were as tall as him now and although he still attacked my mother, it wasn't as easy as it used to be. Frustrated, he turned his attention to the furniture. One Saturday afternoon, I heard strange creaking sounds coming from his room, followed by banging and the sound of splintering wood. Then I heard his window open and, seconds later, something crash to the ground outside. His door was closed but muffled obscenities were clearly audible: "Fucking cunt and her fucking built-in wardrobe!"

I hurried downstairs to see what had landed in the yard. Hannah and my mother were at the back door, looking out in disbelief at the new wardrobe, in bits on the wet, mossy ground. The frames were all twisted and splintered and the delicate slats of wood that made up the louvres were everywhere. There'd be no mending them. Next came a flurry of clothing: the underpants, vests, socks and shirts that my mother had just bought him. It all lay in a pathetic pile outside the back door. We waited tensely for more but there was nothing, only silence.

He had his dinner in his room that evening and at eight o'clock he came stomping down the stairs. We held our breath and huddled together in the living room but he didn't come near us. Instead, he went out leaving a trail of aftershave in his wake. It was strange. He never went out at night and he rarely wore scent. He was acting out of character and we fretted all evening as to what it meant.

At half past eleven, when the pubs shut, he came home. My mother, Hannah and I were sitting by the embers of the fire when the front door opened and someone staggered in. My breathing quickened and I hoped it was only Joseph, who'd go straight to bed. Suddenly, the door burst open and my father stood there, swaying in front of us like a stunned rhinoceros. He was managing to stay upright by hanging onto the door handle but his mouth wouldn't form the words he wanted to say and all he could get out was "Ya fuchin cunsshh!" With that, he wheeled around and headed for the kitchen from where we could smell cooking and burnt food. After the sound of retching and groaning, he went upstairs and fell into bed. We waited until we heard snoring, then my mother put down her knitting and stood up wearily. I followed her out to the kitchen, steeling myself for whatever we'd find. Sure enough, there on my lovely white and blue tiles was a huge pool of vomit. Lying abandoned in the middle of it were his false teeth and good tweed jacket.

For one sweet moment we weren't afraid of him. "God damn you to hell!" my mother snarled, as she lifted her foot and stamped down hard on the dentures, snapping them in two. I picked up the puke-covered jacket and, holding it at arm's length, checked the pockets for cash before throwing it back into the foul-smelling mess. I used it as a mop, which wasn't very effective; but that wasn't the point. It was poetic justice. He'd spewed his vomit all over our lovely new kitchen and I, in turn, was using his finest jacket, an expensive tweed from the best men's outfitters in Cork, to clean it up. I felt triumphant and had a fit of the giggles. My mother joined in. I laughed at what she'd done to the teeth and she laughed at what I'd done to the jacket. We called Hannah in and she laughed too. We laughed at our own brazenness after a lifetime of fear and in a final act of defiance we threw the jacket and the teeth out into the yard where they landed on top of the broken louvred panels.

Once we'd cleaned up properly, it was time for bed. In bed, I could hear his drunken snores through the wall and I worried about what he'd do when he saw the jacket and the teeth. Luckily, the next day he was so hung-over he couldn't remember a thing. He never mentioned the dentures and must've had a second pair. He stayed in his room all day except for visits to the bathroom and we knew if he was abroad when we got short bursts of the Majors. He went out again the following Saturday night, his after-shave lingering for ages in the hallway. When his smell and bad energy had dissipated, the house was quiet and peaceful. I never tired of marvelling at the new kitchen. Proudly, I feasted my eyes on the lovely things we now had: the venetian blind at the big window, the stove, the long pine table and of course my tiled floor, recently mopped and gleaming. My mother was laughing at Rose, who was a great mimic and I was looking forward to the *Late Late Show* at ten o'clock, when we'd have our traditional Saturday night supper of chicken noodle soup and buttered sliced pan. I was happy.

But it was too good to last. At half past nine, much earlier than expected, we heard the dreaded stomp, stomp, stomp up the garden path. He punched the front door open and pounded purposefully along the hall to the kitchen. Adrenaline flooded my veins and my heart raced, knowing this Saturday would be different from last. The kitchen door burst open. With his fists clenched, he went straight up to my mother where she stood at the cooker, stirring the soup. He wasn't drunk tonight so all his words were in sharp definition.

"LOOK AT YA, YA UGLY CUNT! WHORIN' AROUND THE COUNTY DONEGAL SINCE YOU WERE FIFTEEN!"

I blushed to my roots – not because he called her a whore; I was used to that. It was the fact that he was suggesting she'd been a whore when she was a child. Younger than me. A child whore. The idea shuddered through my being. Awful questions went through my head in spite of myself. Fifteen. County Donegal. Was it true? What did he know that I didn't? And then I was disgusted with myself for having such thoughts. He'd put them there, the dirty mind-raping bastard!

And then in my head I was shouting: *STOP IT! STOP*

*IT! STOP IT!* Hardly knowing what I was doing, I came up behind him with my fist clenched and pounded his hateful back for all I was worth. I thumped him over and over, shrieking:

"SHUT UP! SHUT UP! SHUT UP! SHUT UP! MY! MOTHER! IS! *NOT*! A! WHORE!"

He turned around and looked at me with his small grey-green eyes but he didn't see me. There was no acknowledgement of my being, let alone my distress. My hysterics had interrupted his overture, that was all, and he stood there nonplussed, clenching and unclenching his fists and shifting his weight from foot to foot.

Young, tall and strong, we, his children, regarded him with the hatred he'd instilled in us; so he turned on his heel and retreated up the stairs to his room, slamming the door with the usual outrageous force. I crumpled onto a chair and wept desolate tears. Hannah and Rose comforted me but it was an awful moment for all of us. He'd raped our minds with the image of our mother as a child, having sex for money.

Strangely, my mother ignored me and carried on stirring the soup. I didn't understand. Surely she was glad that I'd thumped him for her and defended her honour? But she wasn't. She didn't want me interfering, making a scene like that, making it obvious that her marriage was driving her children out of their minds.

I felt foolish sitting there being ignored by her. It felt like I was the mad one, not him. So I fled the kitchen and found the privacy of the bathroom, anger and jealousy pulsating through me. I felt murderous and I wanted to kill them all: my father for hating me, my mother for not loving me enough and Grace for being the one she *did* love. I cried copious tears but eventually they subsided and I felt better. I was seventeen and I lived on hope, dreaming that one day I'd leave them all behind. I'd meet a prince who would love me and never beat me or call me foul names and we'd live in a big house and not have children. I'd be someone important like a heart surgeon and look beautiful in my white coat with a stethoscope hanging around my neck.

I had a further reason to be cheerful because Grace was going away for the summer. She was starting her final year at university in October so she was going to be an *au pair* in France for the summer to improve her French. She and my mother were planning her trip meticulously. They went to the Green Shield Stamp shop in Cork, came back with a set of suitcases and one beautiful morning in early July, we accompanied Grace to the airport. She was pale and silent and my mother was tearful at the thought of their separation. I was angry at the sight of her tears and jealousy burned inside me like an inferno.

We were all silent on the way back from the airport, our minds filled with the memory of the airplane taking off and bearing Grace away to a foreign land. But my jealousy raged on. As I walked along behind her, I sensed my mother's whole being bereft of the beloved child who'd gone away. Her grief made me mad. I wanted to scream: NEVER MIND HER! SHE'S GONE! BUT I'M HERE! WHY ARE YOU SUFFERING WHEN I'M HERE? CAN'T YOU LOVE ME INSTEAD?

But Grace was everything to her mother: friend, sister,

confidante and spouse, and compared to that I was nothing. I made a fist and wanted to thump her hard for the pathetic figure she cut, shuffling along in her tight court shoes, missing her first-born child.

I managed to contain my anger. As soon as we got back home, I disappeared for the rest of the day. I went to Delph Head, a pine wood on a cliff top, far from the town. Deep among the trees, on the cliff edge, you could sit and watch the water ebbing and surging far below. It was cool and silent except for the soughing of the trees as the sea breezes blew through them. I listened and slowly I calmed down but I was shocked at the intensity of my anger. Maybe I was a Coleman in more ways than one. Was violence a trait I'd inherited from my father? I squirmed at the thought of being like him. It was bad enough to look like his sister and bear his mother's name but any resemblance to *him* would be like a disease. Gradually the beauty and solitude of Delph soothed me and by the time I got home my demons were still.

My mother was in the kitchen making sandwiches for the tea and I helped by buttering bread and chopping tomatoes and onions. She'd arranged to ring Grace at eight o'clock but we didn't have a phone so, at the appointed time, she went to the phone box on North Hill and came home beaming. Yes, she'd arrived safely and the family seemed very nice. The *Monsieur* was about to take her on a tour of Paris. No need to worry. Everything was fine. She'd write soon. We made a pot of tea, opened a packet of biscuits to celebrate and spent the rest of the evening picking over the details of the phone call. Going on a tour of Paris. Wasn't that great!? They were nice people. What a relief! She'd write soon. How long did it take letters to come from France?

Not long, as it turned out. Within days, a letter with French markings and airmail stickers plopped onto the doormat. Now we got more information: the family were wealthy and had a large apartment near the Champs Elysées as well as a *chateau* in Provence. The money was *Madame's* and had come from sugar and slaves. She had no qualms about her slaving ancestors and there were portraits of them all over the apartment. The tour of Paris had been wonderful, with an open air concert in the Tuileries, conducted by Daniel Barenboim. I wondered if *Monsieur* was handsome and imagined Grace with him in an open-topped sports car and wished it was me instead. The children were well travelled, musical and conversant in English. The youngest, a little girl, could stone, section and devour a peach with adult precision. They'd be in Paris for the rest of July and then at the chateau for the month of August.

In the letters from Provence, Grace was miserable. It was too hot and there were enormous spiders in her room. It wasn't near the coast and there was nothing to do. *Madame's* mother was there and she treated Grace like a maid. She could hardly wait until she came home and neither could my mother, who was counting the days and kept the letters from France safe in a drawer in her room.

Unexpectedly, while Grace was away, my mother and I did get close. We were unified by an event that came like a bolt out of the blue. My father tried to kill himself.

It happened like this. In that glorious summer of 1976, my father hated his life. He'd already spent fifteen years in the Steel Mills and he was looking at fifteen more. He had to go in there tonight, which meant sleeping all afternoon while the sun was splitting the stones and we, the swill, were lazing around, with our young tanned bodies, doing nothing. We always hid our beach things until he was gone and we thought he didn't notice, but he noticed all right. He knew everything in this, his mother's house. He imagined us skipping down White Bay Hill, mocking him and laughing at him, while he sweated to put food on the table and keep a roof over our heads.

He stood in the middle of this expensive new kitchen that the sow had wanted – not for him of course, for her swill. He saw the dresser that he didn't like, the stove that never warmed him, the table that he never ate at. There wasn't a vestige of him in any of it, and yet he had to pay for it all. He felt trapped. It was like being in prison. No, worse: prison had a limit. This would go on till he dropped dead. It was hell! He thought of escape, as he'd done for years. Why didn't he just pack a bag and go? He wanted to so much. But where would he go and what would he do? There was no answer. He feared the world and his mind was blank. In the meantime, there was always one more rugby match to watch, one more tasty meal, one more plate of cakes. And now time was running out. His hair was thinning and greying. He didn't look so great anymore. It'd been a long time since a pretty young girl had looked at him. They were all tarts now anyway, with their skirts up to their behinds, not knowing their place.

He saw his dinner keeping warm on the stove. How long had it been there, he wondered? He hated reheated food, with the veg all soft and wilting. He liked his veg crunchy, she knew that. The least he deserved was his grub freshly cooked and straight from the pot. She'd be here in a minute to serve it to him, in icy silence. Or maybe not. Maybe she was out whoring. Ma had always said to watch her because she was a tart. And he had. He'd beaten the shit out of her over the years for her whoring. She'd been roundly punished for that, don't you worry Ma! But, notwithstanding his mother's conviction and in spite of himself, a doubt squirmed around in his brain. Had she ever really done any of that? Ma had always been so sure but all he'd ever seen her doing was knitting. Knitting and bringing her fucking swill up. Ah, fuck it! He didn't know what was true and he didn't care. He lifted the saucepan lid covering his dinner to see what there was. Lamb chops, spuds, carrots, cabbage and gravy. The cabbage was limp. Jesus Christ! He hated overcooked cabbage and she knew it. The fucking whore knew it! He didn't grow it just for her to ruin it.

"FUCK IT!" he howled. Biting his tongue, he picked up the plate and hurled it against the wall, where the thick, brown gravy made a big splat. The chops and potatoes fell to the ground and spun off under the table. The carrots and cabbage, stuck in the gravy, slowly oozed down the wall. The next wave of anger hit him and he picked up the heavy steamer that had cooked his vegetables and hurled it at the window. There was a tremendous crash as the pots hit the big pane of glass and flew through it. Glass went everywhere. There was a gaping hole in the window and the venetian blind was bent and buckled. Next came the frying pan used to cook his chops. It glanced off the hole and made it bigger. More glass flew through the air. Stillness descended and he felt better. That is to say, he felt empty rather than despairing. With that, he went up to his bedroom.

My mother, who was making the beds when she heard the sound of exploding glass, crept downstairs with her heart in her mouth, took one look at the mess and fled. The scene was unchanged when Rose, Hannah and I arrived home from school. The first thing I saw was the hole in the window but the devastation was too much to take in and I started trembling. Rose was crying and Hannah stood looking around in stunned silence. My mother arrived and told us what had happened but I was in shock and it didn't sink in. He'd turned his rage on the furniture before but it was nothing like this. I could feel his intense, black anger and the madness of it still in the room. I stepped gingerly over the debris and looked through the jagged hole to where the pots and pans were lying in the back garden. It was surreal. There was the frying pan and the saucepans lying in the soil among my father's precious brassicas.

We started cleaning up. I picked up the broken glass, potatoes and chops while Hannah scraped the carrots, cabbage and gravy off the wall. My mother found a piece of cardboard and taped it over the hole in the window. A gloom descended on the room and we turned on the light. I was still trembling and my teeth were clenched. I couldn't relax at all. We had a quick, simple tea of boiled eggs and toast and then the evening was arranged so that we'd all be in bed with the lights out before he got up for work at half past ten. When the time came, I was in bed but I certainly wasn't asleep. I waited and waited and finally there was the familiar, angry grab at the door knob as he came out, trailing a heavy Major smell, and went downstairs. I was tuned into his every movement in case he headed up to my mother's bedroom. Thankfully, that night, he slammed out of the house without incident. A few days later, a new pane of glass was fitted and the venetian blind was bent back into shape.

But that wasn't the end of it. One night, not long after, we couldn't wake him for work. We weren't unduly worried because he often took sleeping tablets and could be difficult to wake. Half past ten came and went and at a quarter to eleven my mother asked for volunteers to go up and wake him. Rose went first. I could hear her knocking on his bedroom door. She knocked and knocked and even called out the strange word, but to no avail. He was sound asleep. Hannah tried next. She took a wooden spoon and banged on the bedroom door with it. No good. My mother was knitting very fast, the needles clicking furiously. It was puzzling. How could he still be asleep? Clearly, someone was going to have to go into his room and shake him awake. It was my turn and I recoiled from the thought of approaching him in his bed and touching him. But I knew I had to.

Reluctantly, I went upstairs. Taking a deep breath, I turned the door handle and went in. The light from the landing was enough for me to see his bulk in the bed. He was lying on his back, with his mouth open, snoring loudly. I edged closer. There was a magazine on the chest of drawers so I rolled it up and poked him with it. I jabbed him hard several times but to no avail. He was dead meat.

I went downstairs and my mother looked at me hopefully but I shook my head and her face tightened. She stared at her knitting, flipping the needles over for another row and knitting it. Suddenly she slammed the whole lot down and went up to have a look for herself. I went with her. Neither Joseph nor Peter was there so she turned on the light. I gave her the rolled-up magazine and she poked him as I'd done. Nothing.

Then we noticed two empty pill bottles. My mother picked one up. Sleeping tablets. Had he taken these and if so how many? We had no idea so we put the bottles back where we'd found them and left the room. Meanwhile, my father snored on. We decided to leave him. It wasn't the end of the world if he missed one night's work and hopefully he'd right himself during the night. Although we suspected that he'd taken an overdose, we couldn't admit it to ourselves and we felt no driving need to save him. He hated us and therefore we hated him. Instead of frantically searching for help it was natural for us to say things like: "He's probably just taken a few more than usual", "There probably weren't many left anyway", and "He'll be all right in the morning."

But he wasn't all right the next morning. In fact, he was much worse. He was lying exactly as we'd left him but his breathing had changed. The snoring had turned into an ominous growling and there was nothing for it now but to ring for an ambulance. When it came, the paramedics went up the stairs; footsteps moved around and came down slowly, bearing him along on a stretcher.

He had a tube up his nose and a bottle of saline solution was lying beside his head. They confirmed that he was in a coma but they wouldn't know how bad it was until they got him to the hospital. When had we discovered him? This morning. A white lie. Did my mother want to accompany him in the ambulance? No.

We were all bewildered at what had happened and when the ambulance left, we sat, stunned, at the kitchen table trying to take it in, aware that something had fundamentally changed. My father, my awful father, wasn't there anymore. He'd been taken away and before us stretched an indefinite period when he wouldn't be coming back. We drank cups of tea and went over everything that had happened: trying to wake him, the snoring, the pill bottles and the ambulance.

Then my mother and I went up to his room and searched it. We shook everything out and found his savings book, gathered up all his dirty pictures and burnt them in the back garden. Then we stripped the bed, boiled the sheets and pillow cases and washed the blankets. I was overjoyed. My father had disappeared, might even die for all we knew, and I found myself where I wanted to be: in Grace's shoes at my mother's side.

It was late afternoon when my mother and I went to the phone box to ring the hospital. He was in a critical condition. His heart had stopped and he'd been resuscitated but they couldn't tell us any more. We should ring back in the morning. We were quiet on the way home. I thought about his heart attack. After years of violent strength, he was as weak as a kitten and no more than a hair's breadth from dying. I wanted his heart to stop again, for good. I begged God to give him another, more powerful heart attack to finish him off. I prayed for it before I fell asleep and I woke up the next morning relishing my father's absence and hoping he was dead. I couldn't wait to get to the phone box to hear the good news, but alas, the news was bad. He'd improved during the night and was on the mend.

I was crushed by disappointment. He'd grown smaller and smaller until he was just a dot on the horizon, so distant that we'd been able to boil and wash and burn his befoulment out of our lives. I'd been confident that he was gone for good but, sadly, he'd clung to life and now the dot was getting bigger and bigger and coming back.

The doctors wanted to see my mother to discuss his treatment so, in a spirit of bitter disappointment, she and I went to St Finbarr's Hospital that afternoon. It was a busy place, where people came and went quickly and purposefully. We were just about to ask for directions when a voice rang out behind us:

"MISSIZ COLEMAN!"

It was a local woman called Marion O'Sullivan, another one who'd scandalised Cobh by leaving her husband. She and her children were renting a flat in Cork and she was cleaning in the hospital to get by. For some reason, she felt she had to explain her actions to my mother. Candidly, on the forecourt of the A&E, she described her husband, a naval officer, as a brute and a sex fiend. She said she couldn't even get down on her knees to polish the floor without him jumping on her. My father's pornography flashed through my mind and I imagined Mr O'Sullivan grabbing his wife by the hair and raping her. I blushed and shuffled my feet uncomfortably. She assured us that she didn't miss the old town one bit. She was alone now but she had peace and quiet. An ambulance drew up amid a screech of sirens and we watched as people with bloody, bandaged heads were rushed inside on stretchers. I felt sick, and I hadn't even seen my father yet. My mother and Mrs O'Sullivan parted warmly and we made our way to Intensive Care.

A well-meaning nurse tried to nudge us into my father's room but we stood stock still in the corridor like a pair of donkeys. I saw him through an open door, connected to tubes and monitors and that was enough for me. I sat on a chair near the exit while my mother talked to a doctor and signed some forms. He explained that my father was alive because he had an exceptionally strong heart. "A heart like a bull," the doctor said. Yes, I thought bitterly, he was like a bull all right – big, stupid and dangerous.

The news wasn't all bad, however. He wouldn't be coming directly home. In a few days' time, they were transferring him to a mental hospital and he'd be there for a couple of weeks. My spirits rose as we digested this news and recognised it for the gift that it was. He wasn't gone for good but he'd be gone for a bit longer. The weather was glorious and for the first time in our lives, apart from our stay with the nuns in Midleton, he'd be somewhere else. Those blissful weeks, which came near the end of my childhood, were the happiest days of my life, thanks to the simple fact of my father's absence. I played pop music in the house and danced and sang and laughed with my mother and siblings. Friends visited and

Mrs Mac Neice and Mrs Allen from the end of the terrace came in for cups of tea. I was so thrilled with our new fatherless status that every moment was absolutely wondrous and unforgettable.

A second hospital visit was required – this time to the mental hospital, St John's. We laughed at the irony of the names. John Coleman in St John's mental hospital – how appropriate! We had to go to Glanmire, a rural area north-east of the city and we caught a bus outside the railway station. Shamefacedly, I asked the driver to let us off at St John's, hoping he'd know it and I wouldn't have to explain that it was the mental hospital. He did and when we got off the bus, there was a long trek along a country road which skirted a wooded valley. We walked on and on in the shade of oaks, chestnuts and silver birches, the sun occasionally glinting at us through breaks in the foliage. It was a lush, verdant place and two of my favourite smells abounded – wild flowers and farmyards. I breathed deeply as we walked along, thrilled by the perfume and having my mother's undivided attention. When the hospital finally came into view, my expectations of a Victorian madhouse with gothic windows and turrets were completely dashed. St John's was a complex of modern, low-rise units set in landscaped parkland. It was like a golf course with buildings on it.

We rounded a bend and suddenly, something awful happened. I saw my father. He was sitting on some steps outside a building marked "B", far away across a rolling lawn. "Look!" I blurted out and then my mother saw him too. It was a jolt. It was as if he'd come back from the dead. We hid behind a tree and studied him. I noticed how happy he seemed. He was sunning himself and smiling and he'd never looked better – shirt unbuttoned, sleeves rolled up, tanned a deep brown. A man came out and sat down beside him and they chatted like old friends. How weird! I'd never known him talk so openly to anyone. He didn't seem like the same person. We carried on up to reception and a nurse told us to go to Block B.

"No," my mother said flatly.

"But you have to," said the nurse. "That's where your husband's consultant is."

"NO!" my mother repeated more loudly. "I'm not going down there while *he's* there!"

With that, she sat down and stared straight ahead and I sat down beside her. The nurse consulted her matron, who glanced over at us. She could see from her crossed arms and general demeanour that my mother was not going to budge. A phone call was made and presently a psychiatrist appeared. He beckoned us into a consulting room. He was young and handsome and in a cheerful tone he invited us to sit down. He explained that he wasn't in charge of my father's case; that doctor was in Block B and, at some point before we left, we'd have to speak to him –

"I'M NOT GOING DOWN THERE WITH THAT BASTARD SITTING ON THE STEPS SUNNING HIMSELF!"

My mother interrupted with such emotion that I lifted my gaze from the ground and looked at her. Her face and neck were flushed and her eyes were moist. She couldn't bear to see him so carefree, even if it was in a mental hospital, after all the misery he'd caused. In her nervous system, there was a record of all the pain she'd suffered at his hands and she hoped that the overdose had drawn a line under it. Like me, she was choked with disappointment at his survival and she never wanted to see or speak to him again.

"Your husband has been very ill, Mrs Coleman," the doctor said reproachfully.

"I don't care. It's no more than he deserves," she countered coldly.

"I'm sure you don't mean that," the doctor opined patronisingly.

My mother got upset again: "YES! I *DO* MEAN IT! HE DESERVES TO BE DEAD, NOT ILL! ASK MY DOCTOR AND THE POLICE! ASK THE NUNS IN MIDLETON. ASK MY CHILDREN. THEY'RE TERRIFIED OF HIM!!"

"I don't think you should bring your children into this," he admonished, glancing at me.

"WHY NOT?" she demanded. "HE'S WRECKING THEIR LIVES!"

"Anyway," he interjected, in an effort to regain control of their exchange, "in discussions with the doctors here at St John's, your husband feels it might be best if he goes to stay with his mother for a while."

"How long is 'a while'?" my mother asked in a calmer, more even tone.

"Well . . . that could be negotiated at a later stage," he answered, running his hand through his glossy, well-cut hair. "There *is* one condition though. We feel it would be good for the family if he visited for Sunday lunch."

Sunday lunch. The term was foreign to us. It conjured up images of bone china, napkins and other civilised things and we were to partake of this delightful meal with a man who loathed us, a man who called us "swill" and "sow". There was black humour in the sheer implausibility of it and my mother and I looked at each other and laughed uproariously. It was partly nerves. The young doctor was nonplussed. The last thing he expected us to do was laugh. He shifted nervously in his seat.

When our laughter died down my mother asked, "What else do you want from me today? I have a houseful of children to get back to."

"You'll have to see Dr Clark down in B –" he snapped in spite of himself.

"I told you I'm not going down there if *he's* sitting on the steps."

"Yes, yes," spat the doctor, rattled that his suggestion about Sunday lunch had been met with derisory laughter.

"Your feelings will be conveyed to Mr Coleman and we'll see if he won't stay in his room for the next half an hour or so." With that he left the room, grateful to be escaping from us. We waited for the all-clear and then made our way across the sweeping lawn to Block B. Climbing the steps, the spot at the top where *he'*d been sitting seemed to be scorched with his presence and we steered well clear of it. Once inside, my mother was whisked away to an office and I waited for her in the foyer, where a woman, followed closely by a nurse, wandered up and down beating herself with her fists and crying hysterically. She frightened me so I went outside.

The sun was hot but I felt cold. I looked at the distant

trees through the shimmering heat haze and normally the beauty of the scene would have gladdened my heart but at that moment I felt very bad. Disturbing questions went through my mind: if my father had wrecked my life, how was I going to carry on? Why had my mother stayed when other women, like Marion O'Sullivan, had left? Couldn't she have saved my life from being wrecked if she'd left? My father had looked so happy without us. Were we, in fact, the cause of his unhappiness? The crying woman came out so I went back inside, where an elderly man engaged me in conversation. He was tweedy and bespectacled and asked me what I was doing there. I said I was waiting for my mother. "Is she a patient?" he asked. "No!" I said shortly and then added, "But my father is."

"Oh. What's his name?"

"John Coleman."

He thought for a minute, muttering:

"Coleman . . . Coleman? Ah yes, Coleman in B6. He's had a lot to say for himself, that one. You know, when he first came in, he thought your mother was giving birth to twins. He went on about that at length."

The tweed suit studied my disquieted face with relish as the image of my mother, in the throes of begetting twins, formed in my mind, closely followed by the image of my father raving about it in a mental hospital. He was about to relate to me other imaginings of my father's when Dr Clark's door opened and my mother emerged smiling. This psychiatrist had informed himself of my father's background and it felt like, at last, someone was on our side.

The tweed suit slipped away as my mother approached and we started the long trek back to the bus stop. I hoped we'd be well away before my father returned to his sunbathing. I didn't want him to see us. I felt that if he saw us we'd become real for him again, as he had for us, and that would form a connection that might hasten his return. I hoped that if we faded from his mind, he'd never come back.

On the way back to the city, we went over every aspect of the visit, my mother commenting indignantly on everything. About seeing my father on the steps, she said, "Did you see the set of him, sunning himself without a care in the world?" As for the young doctor, "He's got a lot to learn, with his Sunday lunches!" The memory of how we'd laughed at his suggestions and his disconcerted face made us laugh again. Dr Clark was, she said, "A lovely man! He said *he* had problems. Bloody madman, he means!" She didn't recognise the old tweed suit and I didn't tell her what he'd said. We revelled in the delightful news that my father would be going to stay at his mother's. It was an extension to our freedom – maybe a permanent one, if he decided to stay there.

We rejoiced as we retraced our steps back along the road to the bus stop, drunk on the possibility that he'd gone for good. The thought of our home and how much things had changed there made me giddy with happiness. By the time we got to the station, the train had gone   but we didn't care. In festive mood, I suggested hitch-hiking and, equally gay, my mother agreed. No one offered us a lift but we only laughed. We were clowning around and having fun – giggling and doing silly things like thumbing lifts from bicycles and milk floats. I took pride in the fact that we were having so much fun together. I was definitely her suicide buddy. Eventually we gave up and went back to the station, tired and happy, to wait for the next train.

The heatwave continued and nothing seemed to move on our little island. The fields were full of golden crops of wheat and barley. The trees were bone dry and the tarmac on the roads was soft and stuck to my feet. Grace came home from France at the end of August and when my mother went to the airport to meet her, she was lit up with happiness. Grace looked wonderful with her tan and her sun-bleached hair. She was Cinderella after the ball as she stood in the kitchen and the reality of being back among us hit home. Touched by another world, she had magazines that we couldn't read and cosmetics that we couldn't use because they were in French; cheese that smelled like sweaty feet; and a recipe for stuffed marrow, which she tried on us and we refused to eat.

My mother told her about the overdose and the fact that *he* was staying with the Nannygoat. The private conversations resumed. Tea was made and knitting needles clicked. I wanted so much to be included in those conversations and I felt it was my right. I'd been at my mother's side throughout. I was the suicide buddy, after all. But that was now over. I was no longer needed and two pairs of brown eyes kept me at a distance. There was a lot for them to discuss. My father's attempted suicide changed everything because my mother could now apply for a legal separation (divorce was impossible), citing unreasonable behaviour, and Grace would be finishing university soon. They really had to plan.

My father didn't stay at his mother's very long because she wouldn't let him. He was back at work now and she wanted him back in her property as well, to reclaim it from us – his wife and children – who she considered not much more than squatters. As the only "real" grandchild, I was the go-between.

"Tell your mother not to bolt the front door tonight. Your father will be coming home."

With these words, my grandmother ended the long, hot summer and I walked the short distance between her house and ours in a state of disbelief. He was coming back. Tonight. Oh God, no. I walked up the garden path and into the house, feeling cold and numb. I knew that as soon as I said the words "He's coming back tonight" everyone else would feel cold and numb too. I entered the kitchen but it was hard to get anyone's attention, there was so much noise.

"He's coming back tonight," I said, my voice faint with shock. No one heard me. "I SAID *HE*'S COMING BACK TONIGHT!"

"What?" asked Hannah, turning down the radio.

"He's coming back tonight. *She* said not to bolt the door because he'll be coming here after four-to-twelve."

Joy drained out of the house and silence descended as we struggled to take in the bad news. He'd be back in a few hours' time, in the dead of night when we'd be in our beds and at our most vulnerable, and we couldn't keep him out. I was deeply frightened because he'd had a lot of time to think and he must have analysed the night of the overdose from every possible angle. We'd left him until morning, which had nearly killed him. He must know that by now. He'd be wanting revenge and I was terrified of what he might do. My mother was ashen-faced. She turned to Grace and they closed ranks. Taking their knitting and two mugs of tea, they went up to their bedroom and closed the door. I wanted to follow, to feel included and protected, now more than ever, because the bad thing was coming back, but I knew my place.

My friend Anne called and we went for a walk. We chose one of my favourite routes – along the quay to a corner of the island called East Point, where you could sit on a jetty and gaze out at the water and the whole southern sweep of the island. To Anne and the people we passed, it was a hot, sunny day but I was cold and numb and none of the beauty touched me. I could see nothing but my father, stomping home from work with his lunch box under his arm.

Night time arrived and we were in bed, all except Joseph, who was out getting drunk as usual. The front door was left unlocked, as instructed. I lay awake with my ears pricked and, sure enough, just after midnight, a familiar pounding could be heard, getting louder and louder as he came along the hushed, darkened road. The old reactions returned: adrenaline pumped, muscles tensed up and my heart pounded. I expected to hear the gate slam. Strangely, it didn't. He closed it gently as if he didn't want to wake us up. Ah! So that was his plan! He was going to sneak in and slaughter us all in our beds. He opened the front door even more quietly, tip-toed along the hall to the kitchen, made a cup of tea and smoked a cigarette. He seemed to be down there for a long time. Then he tip-toed upstairs and went to bed. I waited and waited to hear something ugly, some signal to tell me it was time to get up and fight, but there was nothing. Still I kept my vigil until I heard him snoring. Then I gave in to sleep.

My father never touched my mother again or said any of the vile things he used to say. In fact he only ever mumbled now and sometimes said "please" and "thank you". We put it down to the tablets he'd started taking at the hospital. Also, the world had acknowledged his unhappiness and that made him less angry. From then on, my perception of him changed. He was still frightening but in a different way. He was like a zombie. The living dead. He'd been to the edge of the void and come back. He spent most of his time at his mother's and only came "home" to sleep. Although the violence had stopped, it was still an unhappy home. The bombs had stopped falling but our lives were in ruins. Everything seemed to fall apart. My father was back but my mother was waiting for a chance to escape. These days she carried important documents, like her marriage certificate and savings book, in an over-stuffed handbag which she never let out of her sight. She got a job in the canteen at a shipyard, saved every penny she could and we lived on the leftovers she brought home.

Joseph moved to Cork and started a life of binge-drinking in mouldy rented rooms. There seemed to be a family within a family, which comprised Grace, Peter, who was Grace's pet, and my mother. This centre was strong and self-sufficient. Those inside would survive. At that time, we others orbited at varying distances: Rose and Hannah close in because they were Leahys; Joseph and Sarah farther out because he was a troubled youth and she was a wilful girl; and me farthest out of all because I was a Coleman. I shouted at my mother one day that I was "a second class citizen" compared to Grace; a mild rebuke, I thought, a mere statement of the obvious – but she reacted with boiling rage. Picking up the sweeping brush, she came at me and whipped me ferociously with the handle. I put my hands up to protect my face, and the thick, wooden pole smacked down painfully across my fingers. I put my hands in my armpits and it came down hard on my unguarded head and shoulders. The blows were driven by a fierce energy and her face was contorted with it. In her opinion, she'd done her best for me, yet here I was with my loathsome Coleman features telling her it wasn't good enough.

Just before the drama of my father's overdose, I did my final exams at school and qualified to go to university. I didn't want to. I wanted to go to art school but my mother wouldn't hear of it. She dismissed art as nonsense that was only for the idle rich. It was university or nothing, her way or the highway, and I felt lost enough already, so I went.

The exams were the culmination of years of febrile study, sandwiched between two obsessive students, Grace and Hannah, who studied every evening and all day Saturday and Sunday. It was crazy, but I felt obliged to follow suit because it soothed my mother to see us studying hard. She made Grace stop at midnight but Hannah and

I carried on until we dropped, usually about two or three o'clock in the morning. Hannah rocked back and forth as she studied, as if the fate of the world depended on how well she did at school. Sometimes I couldn't go on and I stopped "early" at one in the morning, cold and exhausted. I went on and on like that for months, enjoying my mother's tacit approval, until the chronic lack of sleep showed in my long, pale face; so much so that my teachers thought I was ill and would miss the exams. But I was there and I passed with flying colours. Of course I did. Failure was untenable.

# Part Two

## Not on her face

After the intensity of my childhood, my early adult years seemed flat and empty, like a lunar terrain, devoid of the faces and voices that had previously crowded my life. Grace and I rented a bedsit in Cork, directly opposite the university campus. Our room was long with two windows, a double bed, a cooker, sink and some cupboards. Between the windows there was a table and two chairs and when Grace wasn't at lectures or at home with my mother, she was there, bent over her books for hours on end. Clearly, the obsessive studying that had got me to university was meant to continue here.

We shared the bed but, disliking each other, cringed at doing so. I slept on the inside, turned to the wall, and every morning I woke at the crack of dawn, my whole body aching and churning with anxiety and homesickness. Whenever I thought about my mother and younger siblings at home I cried and wanted to go back to them. I stared at the wallpaper that was inches from my face and picked at it until the alarm went off. Then I got up, went across the road to the college and attended lectures.

My subject was Applied Psychology. I'd chosen it at random and for no other reason than the fact that it was well clear of Grace's patch, English and French. I just knew she wouldn't want me around. My first textbook was as big as a telephone directory, with a lot of glossy pictures of the brain. When I first opened it, terms like *corpus callosum* and *hippocampus* jumped out at me and I snapped it shut.

At weekends, I did go home and both Grace and I cried as we left on Monday mornings. Seeing our tears, our mother also cried as she pushed us out the door. I was lonely and frightened and at night I smelt turf fires. It felt so strange not to be at home with my family, squashed along the couch in front of a roaring fire, my mother knitting and all of us engrossed in something on the television.

I couldn't stay in the bedsit because Grace was studying so I went to the university library because it was warm and bright. One such evening, I was sitting in front of my unopened textbooks when I heard a voice at my side.

"Hello, Cora."

I looked up at a pair of familiar blue eyes smiling down at me. It was Eamon Harris, who'd taught me English and Irish in second and third year at school. I blushed, remembering the crush I'd had on him. I could still see him as he strode into our classroom on his first day, a copy of *Romeo and Juliet* under his arm. All eyes were on him and you could hear a pin drop as he introduced himself, just the slightest quiver of nervousness in his voice. We all liked him. One of the other teachers even set her cap at him. He was young, about twenty-four, and passionate about teaching but my mind strayed from his lessons and my eyes scanned his rugby player's physique, always wondering what he was like without his clothes on. I loved his English lessons and under his instruction I excelled. He praised my homework assignments formally in front of the class. I was a star, an A-plus student. The teacher said so and it wasn't just any old teacher. It was hunky Mr Harris, who everyone fancied. I wrote poetry and he liked it enough to stay after school and help me with it. He'd squeeze himself into one of our little desks. I'd be weak at his presence and would gulp down his undivided attention like an alcoholic. I loved TS Eliot and he tried to interest me in Irish poets. He loaned me volumes of poetry, which touched me deeply although I didn't read them. Inspired by his praise I sent some poems to the *Cork Examiner* and they were published. He was proud of me and said so. I was in heaven. I was unused to compliments and his praise was giving me heart attacks of pleasure.

I stared up at him now, blushing at the memory of his attention and my lascivious undressings. I smiled back and held his eyes but didn't know what to say. Should I call him Sir, Mr Harris, or Eamon? No, not Eamon. That was too familiar. I was flustered and in the end I just said:

"Hello."

I was so glad to see him with his familiar friendly face that I felt like a lost child whose parent had come to claim her. Things raced to get out of my mouth but I was too shy to say them, although I almost blurted out: *My father tried to kill himself, you know.*

We stayed like that for a while – him looking down at me and me looking up at him while he enquired about my welfare. Was I enjoying uni? Was it a big change from school? There was a funny little room just off the main library full of antiquarian textbooks and he'd been in there researching something. Nervously, he invited me to the cafeteria for a coffee. In spite of my blushes, I went. We crossed the Quad and the night air was so sweet – cool and autumnal but perfumed with wood and turf smoke. He got me a drink and asked if I was hungry. I said no but he shared a snack with me anyway. We caught up on the missing time. He asked about various classmates of mine, and what the "applied" meant in Applied Psychology.

"I haven't a clue," I answered with a miserable laugh.

There was a short silence and then: "I'm surprised you didn't do English."

I shrugged and stared at my coffee. Yes, if art school was out, I should have studied English; but I couldn't tell him the truth – that my older, mother-hogging sister hated me and my genes and wouldn't want me in the English Department.

"How are you finding it?" he asked.

I sighed and, almost crying, answered: "It's like Irish all over again."

He laughed out loud at this, remembering the difficulty I'd had with our ancestral language. He loved it and was a fluent Gaelic speaker but try as he might he couldn't teach it to me. He was bemused that I did so well at English but failed miserably at Irish. He couldn't understand the discrepancy. If I had the ability in one language why didn't I have it in the other? Again, I hid the truth and shrugged. I couldn't betray my mother by admitting that she'd poisoned me against it. And I couldn't hurt his feelings by describing it in her terms – uncouth, risible, a waste of school time and a joke compared to English. Under my mother's influence, I did my Irish homework in a cursory and furtive way, if at all, and I was used to being beaten by the nuns for failing to produce it.

We were amazed to discover that we lived just two doors apart in College Road. A short silence and then, a little nervously, he asked me out that Saturday night. There was a popular folk singer at the Opera House and the support was a young band from Dublin. Really blushing now, I accepted. Great! He'd call for me about half past seven. Great! We parted with broad grins and I arrived back at the bedsit floating on air. Grace was bent over her studies. Normally, I slunk in, tip-toed past her and went straight to bed but tonight I couldn't contain my excitement.

"You'll never guess who I've just met?" I trilled, dancing around the room.

"Who?"

"EAMON HARRIS! Do you remember him? He was my teacher at school."

There was a pause and then:

"So?"

"He's asked me out! I'm going out with him on Saturday night!"

I sat down, got up, sat down again. What would I

wear? And my hair! What would I do with my long curtains of black hair?

"You can't! We'll be at home," Grace announced with finality.

"I'll stay here."

"You can't! There won't be anything to eat."

"I don't care. I won't be hungry."

"There won't be any heating." We had a little paraffin heater that we took home to be filled at the weekend.

"I don't *care*, Grace, I won't be cold." How could I think of the cold – I was red hot with excitement.

I went to bed and curled up around my treasure – my date with Eamon Harris. I couldn't sleep it was so wickedly delicious. Jesus Christ! He'd asked me out! The number of times I'd dreamt about that and now, by some amazing quirk of fate, it was actually happening. I went over and over every frame of our encounter: the library, the coffee, the chocolate biscuit snapped in two, the looks, the smiles, the date, the parting.

The next morning dawned grey and overcast but it was bright and sunny in my mind. For the first time since I'd started university, I woke up free of anxiety. I thought about Eamon, just two doors away, and I could hardly believe he was so near. I bounced out of bed and went about my business without a care in the world.

Finally Saturday came around but the weather inside me had changed. I was self-conscious and nervous. This was my very first date and I was in the realms of the unknown. Moreover he'd been my teacher and I didn't want to look stupid. But what would we talk about? We'd exhausted all the familiar topics in the cafeteria. I knew nothing that would interest him. I thought about sex. I'd pictured him naked from the safety of my classroom desk – and now it might happen for real. Oh Jesus! I blushed to my roots. My teacher naked. Christ Almighty! I couldn't believe this was really happening.

At half past seven the doorbell rang. I looked in the mirror and didn't like what I saw. I was wearing glasses now because my sight had weakened and they were horrible plastic things. My hair was up in a sort of bun and with my blue corduroys and old clumpy brown shoes I hardly looked seductive.

My landlady answered the door. There were greetings. I realised that they must know each other, being neighbours. I stood above in the room, paralysed with shyness. As I heard him coming up the stairs my heart started pounding. Part of me looked for a way to escape. Then he was at the door and I let him in.

It was surreal to have my former teacher standing in his overcoat a few feet from my bed and we both felt it. He smiled to break the tension and indicated one of my little paintings that was propped up on a shelf. He liked it and I nodded my thanks, too nervous to speak. He filled the room with his size and vitality, his smell, his soap-washed face, the spots of rain on his shoulders. I got my jacket and we left.

The gig was a sit-down affair. No dancing in the aisles. Afterwards, we had a drink and I relaxed a little. We talked about the show – that young band, they weren't his cup of tea. We laughed at their antics and at the front man in his red jumpsuit. The folk singer was better.

Eamon took me home and as we approached my gate I wondered what would happen next. Ironically, for a girl who knew all about whores and cunts, I knew nothing about the protocol at the end of a first date. I assumed he did, being in his twenties, so I followed his lead. We lingered at the gate and then he asked me out again, this time to a pub by the sea.

"Yes, I'd love to."

"Next Saturday?"

"Yes, great!"

"Do you mind if I kiss you goodnight?"

"No."

He came closer and first he hugged me to him so that my head rested on his shoulder. Ah, the soap still lingering, the utter wholesomeness of it, and a note of something else . . . masculinity. Good and sweet. Not like my father's, which was bad and sour. Our lips met and his tongue explored my mouth so I explored his and soon we were having a dance of teeth and tongues. Finally we parted.

With Grace at home, I spread out and luxuriated in the bed for once. All I could think about was Eamon. As with the library encounter, I went over and over every detail of the evening, especially the kiss at the end, and I came to the same delightful conclusion each time. He *wanted me! He* wanted *me! He kissed me!* My God, Eamon Harris had *kissed me.* My whole being was in a state of blissful shock.

Bonnie Kinellan's was a pub perched on a rocky bit of coastline miles from the city. It was set in rambling gardens that sloped right down to the crashing waves.

The countryside we drove through to get there were as black as ink. Tree trunks stood out ghostly in the headlights. I loved their bosky spookiness, with me and Eamon so cosy in his warm little car. We talked about poetry, a safe subject, and there was a dreamlike quality to it all: the trees, the pitch dark, the poetry, us going off together into the depths of the countryside.

The pub was busy but we got a table by the door and Eamon went for drinks. There was a crush at the bar and he was gone a long time. So long that people were looking at me. Not looking. Staring. And then looking away and talking and laughing. Laughing at me. The stupid cunt sitting by the door on her own. What the hell did *she* want? Sitting there as bold as brass, the dirty fucking cunt. Oh God Eamon, hurry up! My face reddened. Any minute now someone would come over and tell me to get out. I'd put my hair up for this date as well and now I fidgeted with the clips and it all fell down. I hid behind it.

Finally Eamon came back and I wanted to scream at him for leaving me alone for so long that people were looking quizzically at me. I took a long swallow of the lager he'd got me and felt a bit better. With no idea of the self-destructive filth that had just gone through my mind, he was asking me about my painting. Why hadn't I gone to art school?

"Because my mother wants me to get a degree," I answered stiffly, with a huge lump in my throat as I thought of my mother at home, never quite out of danger as long as *he* was in the house. I hoped that the absence of us bigger, more adult children hadn't given my father the confidence to attack her again. My heart tightened as I realised that it was gone – that tight knot of children around their mother, the unity and focus of it, the fierce struggle for survival.

"But it's your life, not your mother's," Eamon was saying.

"Yes, I know," I acknowledged lamely, finishing my drink way before him. I drew his attention to the pub – how busy it was, the smoke, the wall of legs right behind our chairs – and away from the painful thing that was throbbing inside me.

Back in Cork he parked just off College Road, laid his arm gently along the back of my seat and played with my long hair, winding it in his fingers and tugging delicately at the tips. It was divine. He ran a finger down my neck and shoulder and over the outline of my right breast. All my nerves responded to his touch.

"Would you like to go out again?" he whispered.

"Yes, please," I answered, weak with pleasure, relieved that he still wanted to see me in spite of my obvious lack of direction. He drew me to him and again I breathed in the strength and the goodness.

Our next date was at the Irish Society, Conradh na Gaeilge, where he was a member. I was nervous. Enemy territory. Everyone would be speaking Irish.

"Will I have to speak Irish too?" I asked tentatively.

"No. Not if you don't want to," he reassured me, twisting my hair into ropes with his fingers.

"Will anyone speak to me in English?"

"Yes, of course people will speak to you in English!"

He laughed at my Nazi vision of Gaelic revivalism and

the mistrust that had been handed down to me by my mother. I practised a few phrases that I thought would be useful: *Dia duit* (Hello), *níl a fhios agam* (I don't know) and *slán* (Goodbye).

We arrived hand-in-hand, on our third date. Almost a couple now. People nodded to him from all directions as we headed upstairs and into the bar. It was hot and crowded. People were quaffing deeply from pints of Guinness and glasses of red wine, laughing uproariously and speaking fluent Gaelic. I was amazed. I felt as if I was in a parallel universe. It certainly wasn't what I'd expected, which was something furtive, a few old men mumbling in Irish and nursing glasses of stout. But these people weren't furtive. Quite the contrary; they were having a great time. They were actually enjoying themselves in Gaelic! This language, my ancient tongue, was being spoken fluently and happily by the throngs of people around me. My mother was wrong and I'd been beaten time and time again by the nuns for my poor school work because I was loyal to her and believed she was right.

Before long, Grace confronted me about Eamon. She relayed a message to me from my mother. It went like this: I seemed to be doing nothing but enjoying myself. What was happening to my studies? Was Eamon Harris going to pass my exams for me? It was all right for him, he didn't have to scrape the money together for university fees. Had I forgotten what Mammy had to put up with? I didn't realise how lucky I was, that was my trouble. We were there to study and nothing else . . .

I sat on the edge of the bed, deflated, and watched

Grace as she criticised my nugget of happiness. She was a paragon of virtue – studying hard for her degree, determined to bring the family the honour and dignity it so sorely lacked. I, by comparison, was a much lesser being – a wastrel, bent on selfish pleasure. All was not lost, however. A compromise was offered: if I'd knuckle down, I could see Eamon once a fortnight. Take it or leave it.

It was an Indian summer and he wanted to take me on a picnic before the winter set in.

"I can't," I said in a guilt-induced trance.

He looked at me. "Why not?"

"I have to study."

"What?" Nobody but the Colemans studied hard in first year.

"My mother doesn't want me to go out with you . . . so much. She says I have to study."

He was silent for a moment; then he asked, "How much is *so much*?"

"I can only see you once a fortnight." I was gormless and spineless with guilt. The warmth went out of his eyes and he regarded me crossly. We both fell silent. There were no more caresses.

The silence was finally broken.

"Well, I'm sorry, Cora, but I don't want to be pigeon-holed."

*I don't want to be pigeon-holed.*

I've never forgotten the words with which he let me go. If he couldn't see me whenever he liked, he didn't want to see me at all. He wouldn't fight for me or wait for me and I for my part didn't fight for him. I could have

116

left home. I was eighteen and I could do what I wanted. But I didn't. We let go of each other that easily.

We spent another few minutes watching the frost form on the bonnet of his car, then we got out and made for our respective front doors. And that was that. My relationship with Eamon Harris was over. I saw him a few times after that, when he brushed past me, offended, not making eye contact, despising me for my lack of gumption. And once at a pub I was working in when he came in smiling with a group of teachers. I think he married one of them.

It is difficult to describe much of my life after Eamon Harris, my mentor and would-be lover, walked out of it, because it was so meaningless. The lack of direction that he'd noticed came from the very essence of my being. Awareness of violence, not ambition, was at the heart of my existence. I was punch-drunk and numb to the normalcy of life. Frozen up. The survival mechanism that had helped me as a child – the *don't feel it* reflex – wouldn't go away. I couldn't just switch it off. I'd been exposed to violence from the cradle and numbness was hard-wired into me. It'd grown on me like a flesh-and-blood shell. I interpreted intimacy as a threat – idiots trying to yank my shell off – and I distrusted everyone I met. I knew of an alcoholic who'd set her bed alight because she couldn't feel her cigarette burning her fingers and her sheets had caught fire. That was me as a result of my childhood – always walking into danger and not knowing it, or knowing it but not caring. Although I'd been traumatised by so much violence, I'd no consciousness of having been wounded and needing help. And neither did anyone else. I was like someone who'd been hit very hard and couldn't feel the pain. I blamed myself for my unhappiness: it was my personality; I was a bad person. Bad Cora – that was me.

I called myself a cunt on a regular basis, like that time in Bonnie Kinellan's with Eamon, because I'd internalised that awful word, among others. It came up out of my subconscious of its own accord and one part of me used it to rip shreds out of another. I feared men because I thought they were all violent like my father. I thought violence lurked in men and only needed the right stimulus to bring it out. I was even afraid to contradict a man's opinion in conversation and flinched inwardly when I did so. I also hated women. The friendships I had were always strained. Secretly I thought women were whores and cunts like myself. If they had other friendships I was full of jealousy. I had visions of their relationships with men in terms of the pictures I'd seen on my father's bed. Lurid carnal enjoyment and rape. Black and red vaginas. Erections. And I drank excessively to shut it all out. I lost my virginity to one of my tutors, a lean country boy with a long stabbing penis. In the morning his landlord looked in and he shoved me forcefully under the covers. Another woman might have been indignant at being hidden away like something dirty and shameful, but to me it was acceptable, the norm.

I struggled on dutifully with psychology, my heart always thumping in my chest with the fear of failure. I felt like an imposter, intimidated by and alienated from the work we had to do. I was doing the honours degree and we had to gather statistics, use computers (huge machines, almost unheard of in 1976) and read books with names like *Memory: Broadbent's Filter Theory and Other Models*. I was bewildered by it all and had no intrinsic interest in the subject to help me. In the library, I envied students browsing in the English section. I wished now that I had done English and to hell with Grace. I'd have cruised it. My classmates were going into research or personnel, applying for jobs in England and America, but I'd no idea what I was going to do once I finished university. All I knew was that I had to get this degree.

When I thought about the future my mind was utterly blank. It was like a TV screen with static but no sound and no picture. Pleasing my mother and assuaging guilt, that's all there was to life. I was a mother-pleasing zombie and would do anything to get her approval. Confusion wore me down and I became depressed.

One day, there was excitement in the Psychology Department. The night before, a classmate of mine, a popular good-looking boy from the country, had broken away from his friends and jumped into a deep, fast-flowing section of the River Lee. He'd refused all attempts at rescue and drowned. Everyone was shocked. I couldn't get this boy out of my mind. I had a constant image of him bobbing on the churning water, surrounded by the clamour of panic-stricken voices, rejecting the ropes and outstretched arms that could easily have saved him. I was drawn to the spot on the river where he died and stared down into the water. Although I knew nothing about his background, I projected my plight onto him. I imagined that he too was pushed beyond endurance and in a cowardly sense he was my suicide by proxy.

I scraped through the end-of-year exams and went back home. I got a summer job at a factory where they made TV dinners. You could smell the kitchens from two hundred yards away – a sewage-like but not unpleasant aroma. Smells abounded. The packaging department, for example, reeked of glue and when I was on duty in there I ended up high on the fumes. The work was monotonous but I loved it. I forgot all about university, had money in my pocket and I made a friend, Ali, a cheerful intelligent woman who was a few years older than me and took me under her wing. The women I worked with were jolly and we were always laughing at something, especially if it was at the expense of management.

I was in a little gang. There were six of us in all, including Ali and me: two spinster sisters Doreen and Joan, putting foil trays full of food on the conveyor belt; Ada, the fading beauty with the beehive, half-way along, stepping on a pedal that released a sauce; Jean, who wanted an office job, stamping foil tops on; and Ali and I loading up pallets with the finished item.

That summer the company was beset by problems, no more so than when a mountain of chicken drumsticks arrived that were too big for the aluminium trays they were to go in. There was much scratching of heads and it was decided that the only thing for it was to bash the chicken flat enough to fit in the trays. It was a huge order and all hands were needed. Even the managing director was there, in a white coat and hairnet, setting the pace, showing us how it was done. We laughed and skidded around in the chicken fat, brandishing our mallets and smashing the drumsticks to smithereens. No one seemed to worry about consumers choking on splintered bones. We stuffed chicken into our pockets, up our sleeves and down our knickers. There was chicken everywhere – sticking out of handbags, in cloakroom lockers and on the dashboards of cars. The practical joke of the day was to sneak up behind someone and smear their faces with chicken fat.

As the summer came to a close I absolutely dreaded going back to university.

"I can't do it! I can't do it! Oh, Jesus Christ, I can't do it!" I began wailing one night. Although my mother wasn't in the room I addressed her:

"PLEASE DON'T MAKE ME GO BACK, MAMMY! PLEEEZE, PLEEEZE! I CAN'T DO IT! I CAN'T DO IT!"

Concerned siblings enquired: "What? What can't you do?"

"PSYCHOLOGY! I CAAAN'T DO IT!! I DON'T UNDERSTAND IT! I . . . I HAAATE IT!"

I cried a marathon of tears. Even my father, the suicidal wraith, put a brief comforting hand on my shoulder, but I couldn't stop. No one could console me and eventually they all recoiled from my elemental howling. I sought out the privacy of the bathroom, went in and locked the door. I vomited up my dinner and released a whole year's worth of stress in loud, inarticulate lamentations and sobs. I couldn't stop and during a lull I said to the walls:

"I just want to be a painter."

The simple truth of this soothed me but I didn't stop crying. It wasn't until hours later, in bed, when Hannah begged me to be quiet that I managed to quieten down.

My mother, who'd been in the new bedroom and could hear me clearly through the wall, was worried enough to let me go to the art school for an interview. I didn't have a portfolio, just a few drawings stuck in a piece of cardboard and, like a pilgrim in the new world, I was astounded by what I saw: studios bursting with light, huge spaces painted white, easels, canvases splashed with colour, brushes and pots of paint, enormous skylights and oily smells that made my heart race. I watched a long-haired boy stretching a canvas. I'd no idea how to do it; I still don't. He smiled at me and I blushed.

The interview went well and I got a place but I didn't take it. I told myself it was because I knew nothing. All I had were a few drawings and I couldn't turn up there in October with my pathetic little pencil and copy book. But that wasn't true. The truth was that mother-guilt was an all-consuming beast which bit and mauled me. Testing it, attempting to do something for myself as opposed to my mother, felt terrible. God love her, she'd suffered so much for us. My memories of the savage beatings she'd received were very vivid. So I put my art away and, in the guilt-trance, started my second year of Double Honours Applied Psychology.

I discovered drugs and binge-drinking and had my only happy times when I was drunk or stoned. I suppressed my artistic nature, forgot about it and anchored myself to the pernicious beliefs that my mother's hard life was my fault and that adversity was the norm.

I got pregnant for the first time when I was twenty-one, at the end of my third and final year at college. The father's name was Gerry and he was my first real boyfriend. He was a candidate for head of the Students' Union when we met and that made him glamorous in my eyes. I say "my first real boyfriend" because we lived together, in a succession of rooms around the city. It wasn't hard to move. We'd put our few belongings in bin bags and off we'd go, sometimes owing rent, sometimes not, living on peanut butter sandwiches and spending most of our money in the pubs.

One night Gerry and I were so drunk that we had sex without precaution. I waited and waited for my period to come but it didn't. Reluctantly, I went to a doctor who confirmed that I was pregnant. Dumbly, as if I had no knowledge of how conception happened, I couldn't believe it. He asked me if I wanted to have a baby and my answer was a resounding no. I was too young and I was unmarried. Being unmarried and pregnant in Ireland, even as late as the 1970s, was a frightening prospect. Women became social outcasts overnight. I thought of a flame-haired farm girl near home who'd kept her baby. She only ever came into Cobh to go to mass. I think my father beat my mother once just for talking to her.

Gerry certainly didn't want to be a father. He was bewildered by the tyranny of sex. One minute we were gay and free-wheeling; the next we were both running scared from the seed he'd planted in me. Surprisingly for the time and place, the doctor suggested a termination. In fact, he was insistent that I should not have a baby if I didn't feel ready for it, vaguely citing the biblical spilling of the seed as proof that God didn't always want us to have babies. Needing little encouragement, I found a number for the BPAS (British Pregnancy Advisory Service) in the back of *Cosmopolitan* and decided to ring them the next day.

I was nervous and my heart tightened as the door of the phone booth swished closed behind me. The smell of damp newsprint filled my nostrils and reminded me of my father's bedroom. I nearly ran away but forced myself to stay put and ring the number I was clutching in my trembling hand. A calm voice on the other end of the line gave me a date – the fourth of January – and an address in Liverpool, which I wrote down. Leaving the phone booth, I realised that I'd have to go abroad to get this thing done and I'd never been abroad before. I spent Christmas at home, holed up in the bedroom going over and over the stages of the journey: 1. Cork to Dublin; 2. Dublin to Liverpool; 3. The ferry to the clinic; 4. Liverpool to Dublin; and 5. Dublin to Cork. With these five steps it'd all be over. I tried to tell my mother I was pregnant. I said:

"I've missed two periods."

"You must be pregnant, so," she replied in a hard flat tone, turning her back and walking out of the room.

Gerry was no help either. He'd gone slack-jawed and dead-eyed. On the morning of my journey, I met him at the railway station in Cork. I was terrified and desperately wanted him to come with me, at least part of the way. I had enough money for him to come as far as Dublin but he refused. He told me so as we stood there on the street, me with my travel bag by my side, him with his shoulders hunched, hands deep in his pockets.

"Why not?" I asked.

He had to go home to Wexford for a family dinner.

"You . . . have . . . to . . . go . . . home . . . for . . . your . . . dinner. Can't you get out of it?"

"No."

"Why not?"

His mother was expecting him. She was keeping some Christmas cake for him. I paused to take this in.

"What?" I asked incredulously, my voice rising.

I lost control and screamed, "WHAT THE FUCK ARE YOU TALKING ABOUT?"

I mocked him, mewling: "I have to go home for my dinner." And then I was shouting again: "WHAT THE FUCK ARE YOU TALKING ABOUT?"

Christmas cake! A dam burst and I screamed and cried and thumped him. He put his arms up to shield himself from the blows and then he started crying as well. Our current bedsit was nearby so we hurried along there and got indoors. After splashing his face, Gerry went to the shop for milk and cigarettes. While he was gone I resigned myself to going it alone. That's just the way it is, I thought. When he came back I was more amenable. The tea was comforting but the cigarette I smoked made me nauseous. Soon it was time for the train so we locked the door and went back to the station.

Night was falling and it was raining as the train neared Dublin. The crossing was rough and I threw up twice. A steward advised me to lie on the floor, which I did and I felt much better. At six in the morning the ferry docked in Liverpool and I got up and followed the crowd. There was a bus to Lime Street railway station and I arrived there at half past six. Most of the station was still closed but the Ladies toilets were open so I went in there. My appointment wasn't until nine o'clock. Two and a half hours to go. I fell asleep on a long narrow bench but was rudely woken by a cleaner who shook me and told me I couldn't sleep there. At half past eight I left the station and hailed a taxi, which whisked me into the centre of Liverpool. The driver was silent until I tried to pay him with Irish money.

"Jesus Christ," he wailed, "I can't take da! Haven't got any sterling, love?"

"What? . . . No."

I hadn't even thought about currency. He turned around and looked at me for the first time.

"Haven't ya got any English money? I can't take da!"

"I'm sorry! I haven't got any . . . sterling!" It was my turn to wail. "Please take it. Please!" and I proffered the Irish pounds.

"But I can't, I'm telling ya! It's not legal tender here, is it?"

"Please take it!" I begged. "I'll pay you double if you take it."

As if by magic he agreed, so I handed over £10 instead of £5 and got out of his cab. The last word I heard him say was "Paddy" and then he tore off in a cloud of exhaust fumes.

The BPAS office could have been a solicitor's reception

room or an employment agency. There was a smiling receptionist, a sofa, spider plants and magazines. I was examined by a doctor and then I had an interview with a counsellor who asked me these questions:

"Why do you want a termination?"

"I'm not ready to have a baby."

"Are you sure you want to go ahead with it?"

I'd travelled on two trains, two buses, a ship and a taxi to get there.

"Yes. I'm sure."

I was distressed to learn that the operation would not be performed there and then. It would be the next day at a clinic a couple of miles away. This was just a reception point. I'd have to venture inland on this foreign soil, and with my illegal tender. Oh God!

I was to stay at a guest house that night which was in the same street as the clinic. The receptionist assured me it wasn't far and I could change my money at any bank. I set off reluctantly, armed with addresses, phone numbers and bus information. I had to buy sanitary towels and a sanitary belt so I gritted my teeth and went into a chemist's where an old man served me without curiosity.

The guest house was a big gabled building and there was an arrangement whereby girls like me could stay in the attic bedrooms prior to the termination. The elderly couple who ran it seemed kind. He smiled at me and she brought me up tea and toast in the early evening. They asked me to take a pair of slippers back to a man in Cork who'd forgotten them. I read and reread the leaflet I'd been given. Nothing to eat after seven o'clock that night. Be at the clinic at seven the next morning.

The first thing I saw when I walked into the clinic was a woman with a big round belly. She was wearing a dressing gown and I wondered if there was a maternity unit here too. But . . . but there couldn't be . . . This . . . this was an abortion clinic! Suddenly, with a shudder of horror, I realised she was going to abort a baby – not a small collection of cells but a baby, big enough to have her belly swelling out like a melon. Even though I was there for the same purpose, I was absolutely appalled. I couldn't understand how it was allowed. I was naive and totally ignorant of the circumstances that might force a woman to abort at that late stage.

I put the whole thing firmly out of my mind and watched from my hospital bed as two porters hoisted women onto a gurney and took them to theatre. A radio was playing pop songs and they whistled at their work, like warehousemen humping sacks of potatoes. A nurse came to check my blood pressure and told me to take the sanitary belt with me when I went. I got it ready. The women cried when they came back and the ward was filling up with the sound of it. I asked a passing nurse why and, without breaking stride, she said it was just a reaction to the anaesthetic.

Finally, it was my turn. I stuffed the belt down beside me, hoping the porters wouldn't see it, and kept my eyes shut tight as we trundled along. We came to a stop and didn't seem to be moving again so I opened them and found a smiling face looming over me. A needle went into the back of my hand and I blanked out.

The next thing I knew someone was calling my name. I felt a towel between my legs and the tightness of the sanitary belt. Soon the whistling boys came and loaded me onto the gurney and took me back to the ward where they dumped me onto the bed. I scrambled under the covers and curled up tightly on my side, waiting for tears to come. And pain. I'd seen the nurses giving out painkillers like smarties. But nothing happened. I was all right.

A nurse tried to make me get up and walk around but I refused. She shrugged and went away. Good. I knew of old that, when you were in bed, curling up on your side was the only response to bad things. If I stayed like that, I'd be fine. Eventually, though, I was forced to get up to go to the toilet. As soon as I was upright – O Sweet Jesus, help me! – a torrent of purple blood gushed down my legs. I watched, transfixed with horror, as an inch-wide flow ran down my thighs and reached my calves and feet. I stood there, immobilised by the sight, my legs apart and shaking and let out a sort of deep animal cry: "AAAAH . . . AAAAHHH . . . AAAAAHHHH!" Then I was reaching out with words: "HEEELLLP . . . MEEE . . . PLLEEEEZE."

A nurse came running and barked at me to get back into bed. A doctor appeared who looked at my notes and massaged my abdomen deeply. While she did so, she spoke to me:

"Okay," she said, "you've had a little haemorrhage. Have you been exercising?

"No," I admitted guiltily.

"Oh. Well, the blood's collected like in the u-bend of a toilet. You *have* to get up and walk around to drain it all out. Do you understand?"

"Yes," I answered meekly.

She pulled back the curtains and watched as I took my first steps. I walked up and down the ward, through a valley of eyes, while my sheets were changed and the floor was mopped. Pain came like red hot pokers and it was so bad that it bent me over and I shuffled up and down like an old woman. When I'd had sufficient exercise, I crawled back into bed and lay there undisturbed until evening.

I looked around. There was a young girl opposite me whose mother had been with her and holding her hand all day long. She had Lucozade and grapes and teddy bears as if she'd been having her tonsils out. I tried to imagine my own mother there with me. The sheer implausibility of it made me laugh bitterly inside but evening restored calm and order. There were magazines to look at, a fry-up followed by apple tart and a mug of tea, and then *Dallas* on the television.

The next morning, I was up and ready to go at seven o'clock. There was breakfast before I left: tea, toast and a big bowl of hard-boiled eggs. Bowls of eggs. I was reminded of Midleton. I stared at the eggs, really wanting one. All I had to do was put out my hand and take one, but I couldn't do it. Not even a humble hard-boiled egg. I was sure someone would tell me to keep my dirty Irish hands off them. Instead, head bowed and silent, I had a nibble of toast and a sip of tea, and then I left.

I ticked off the stages of the journey home; the clinic to the ferry port, Liverpool to Dublin and finally Dublin to Cork. Dear old Cork. It seemed like a lifetime since I'd been there and I was dying to get back. I vowed that I'd never leave Cork again. It was my little fortressed world, within which there was everything I needed. By lunchtime that day, I was on the train leaving Dublin. Cork was getting nearer all the time and I was feeling safe and sleepy with the clackety-clack of the wheels on the track.

I thought about Gerry – the cowardly bastard! I still couldn't believe that he'd given his dinner priority over me. A meal, a fucking *meal*, for Christ's sake! The knowledge that he was tucking into his festive treats while I was going through that nightmare in Liverpool made me feel sick. I remembered the intractable way he'd refused to come to Dublin. There'd been no persuading him. In that case, for the sake of my dignity, couldn't he have lied and made up something with a bit more gravitas – like his father was dying or his house had burnt down or something of that order? But no. He couldn't come because of the special Christmas cake! I should have left him. If I'd had any self-respect I would have but, in truth, I didn't care how he'd treated me. It was only what I deserved. I could *see* the ignominy of how he'd behaved, the sheer pig-ignorance of it, but I couldn't *feel* it. I didn't *feel* angry. I didn't feel anything but an intense relief at not being pregnant any more. Like an animal that had wriggled out of a trap, I'd escaped. I'd surfaced. I was still alive. I'd been reprieved from death by pregnancy.

For the next ten months I hardly went out. Gerry's student grant paid the rent and while he did his post-graduate teacher training I stayed at home and read. I had an insatiable need to open a book and fly away from reality. I read only the best and had a variety of destinations: France with Zola; Russia with Tolstoy and Dostoyevsky; England with the Brontës, D.H. Lawrence, George Eliot and many more. I didn't want to know the outside world at all. I went shopping once a week in the same place and quickly bought the same things. In the evenings we went drinking when we could afford it and I got drunk as quickly as possible.

Gerry qualified as a teacher and then he dropped his bombshell. He was leaving me. He was going home to Wexford where he'd got a job at his old school and he was moving back in with his parents. It was all planned and I was so engrossed in myself, I hadn't seen it coming. There was no argument. We both knew that was the end. I didn't want to go to Wexford and he didn't want me to come.

The landlord discovered there were two of us instead of one in his bedsit and he wasn't pleased, so I had to move out immediately. In my haste I took the first place that came along – a cold dark back room in an old house down by the river. There was a little cast-iron fireplace which was pretty and anaglypta wallpaper, yellowed with age. I imagined an Edwardian family living there, the father with a starched collar working as a clerk in the city, coming home at tea-time with kippers and the *Evening Echo*. The window looked out onto a small yard that abutted the railway embankment. I had a bed, a table, a chair, a Baby Belling cooker and a single-bar electric heater.

I didn't miss Gerry but I was lost without someone to hide behind. I hated being on my own but now I was alone all the time in this old, crepuscular room. I was frightened by the cold and the dark and the silence. There was no one in the house during the day. Everyone else was out at work. The gloom put bad thoughts in my head. I was haunted by my childhood. Scenes of horror came to me in flashback, and I saw and felt the blood running down my legs in Liverpool. Sadness and guilt choked me up and made me crawl into bed and curl up in a tight, foetal ball in the middle of the day when everyone else was about their business. I'd just been made a Bachelor of Arts with a degree in Double Honours Applied Psychology, but you'd never have guessed it. I had no plans, not even for the next day. I simply stared out the window at the embankment wall and became what I would remain for many years – a person with no self-worth moving here and there, from one rented room to another, like a leaf blowing around in the wind.

The winter came and I turned on the electric heater. I sat right in front of it on the floor but I still felt cold. I longed for a proper fire in the little cast-iron hearth. One day I noticed a bag of coal in the yard and took some. Tip-toeing in, my heart in my mouth in case a door flew open and I was caught, I laid my booty gently in the hearth. Excitedly, I crumpled up an old magazine and pieces of orange box that I found under the bed and placed the coal carefully on top. Then I put a match to it and turned off the light. Before long, there was a tongue of orange flame and though it was dark the room danced with shadows; then another and another until I felt the first glorious waves of heat.

I sat as close to my little fire as I could get, right in the hearth, and stared into its glowing core for a long time, feeling cheered and encouraged by the flames. I had a bar of chocolate in my bag and I ate it in celebration of my improved mood. The next evening, I did the same, plopping the lumps of coal gently into the plastic bag so as not to be heard and pilfering just enough for the evening. When I went back on the third night, the game was up. A short, pithy note had been pinned to the coal sack, which read: "Get your own, thief!"

I blushed hot and scarlet in the dark and scanned around to see if I was being watched. It was impossible to know. I hurried back inside and locked the door. I was mortified. The shame of it – being caught nicking coal! I could see the headlines: *Local Graduate Steals Coal!* I fretted and waited for an angry knock at the door but none came and after a while I calmed down.

In order to pay the rent I had to get a job so I went back to the factory of my college days. The light and noise were a Godsend – a welcome distraction from that depressing little room. The smell was the same and it was still warm and friendly but everything else had changed – Ali had left to get married; Jean had got her office job; and the sisters had retired.

However, I made a new friend, a woman called Yvonne Newley, who was working at the factory while she did an MA in History. She told me about her life. She had a young daughter, who lived with her parents in County Galway and I marvelled at the story of her birth: how she got pregnant by a Turkish waiter; how her parents hid her and the baby in their remote farmhouse; and the lengths to which they went to keep the baby secret – never taking her into the town, going miles out of their way to buy nappies. When Yvonne moved to Cork to go to university, they cared for the little girl themselves, to let their daughter get on with her studies. They did all this because they loved her. In my perversely loveless world I was fascinated by this couple and their parental love. It seemed exotic and peculiar to me. It was unconditional love that spurred them into action and this emotion was mythic to me, a chimera. I'd certainly never experienced it and never expected to, not with my violent, name-calling father and indifferent mother.

I could not understand why the Newleys didn't punish their daughter for having an illegitimate baby. Mind you, they'd lived in England for a long time and I reckoned that made a difference. Things certainly seemed to work differently over there. They weren't Catholics. They had no truck with priests and nuns. Everyone was free. I compared Yvonne's pregnancy with my own, the one that had ended in a bloody abortion in Liverpool, and deep down I was intensely jealous. My bitterness made me two-faced. While on the surface I was her friend, secretly I wondered what was wrong with her stupid parents. Why hadn't she been punished? Why hadn't she had an abortion? Shouldn't she have suffered in some way for having an illegitimate baby? No. Yvonne's parents loved her no matter what she did and that was that. They even bought her a house to live in while she studied, a funny little place that clung to a ledge on a steep hillside and could only be reached by a long set of steps. It had a flat roof and looked like a cardboard box that had blown there in the wind.

Yvonne introduced me to her English cousin Simon

and we went on a date. It didn't matter that he pinched my fingers with battery clips and made them bleed that first night. I didn't know what his intentions were when he told me to close my eyes and hold out my index fingers. Innocently, I thought he had some rings for me. Jesus, the pain! My eyes flew open and I saw the awful metal things clamped on me. He was giggling hysterically. I screamed at him to get them off and when he saw the blood he apologised profusely. I forgave him and put it down to first night nerves and the pain soaked away into my reservoir of numbness. Neither did it matter that he kept a motorbike at the end of his bed, or that we'd nothing in common. He was handsome in a teen-magazine sort of way and I was smitten. When he asked me to come with him to his home town, Birmingham, I said yes. It's not that I really wanted to go to England; in fact I was downright afraid. I'd seen documentaries about English cities in the 1950s with notices that said *No blacks. No Irish.* They didn't like us over there, I knew that much. Now it was 1981 there were stories of Irishmen who had been attacked at work, wrongful arrests and Irish goods being taken off the shelves because of the IRA. Simon assured me that nothing like that ever happened where he lived and with nothing to keep me but that cold little room down by the river, I went.

We caught the ferry to Fishguard and on the other side the police stopped us. I was horrified. My worst dream was coming true – they were going to arrest us as Irish terrorists. The British police were so different from the Gardaí, who we laughingly supposed played cards and drank tea all day. Sirens blazing, they pulled in sharply in front of us and told us both to get out. Impassive and business-like, they informed us that one of our brake lights wasn't working and that Simon's old Escort van was overloaded. One constable made him open the back and take everything out while the other turned his attention to me. He fired these questions at me:

"What's your name?"

"Where are you from?"

"What are you doing in England?"

All these questions were asked in such a cold and hostile tone that I came out in a sweat. My mother's Gaelophobia bloomed up in me like a poisonous fungus as l stood before him, deeply ashamed of myself and my origins. I was so filled with self-loathing that I couldn't speak. I didn't want him to hear my brogue. He mustn't hear that – it was awful. My mother said so. Even though I didn't want to, I *had* to speak because he wanted answers, so I mumbled through a dry mouth and several times I had to repeat myself because he couldn't understand me. Finally, it was over. They let Simon go with a warning and we got back in the van. I was so embarrassed that I wanted the ground to open up and swallow me.

I divided that incident with the police into before and after. Before, I'd been un-self-conscious. Back home in Cork we all sounded the same and I'd spoken freely, with never a thought to my accent. My mother's critical voice was drowned out by the homogenous mass. After, I was alone with my Irishness and I became painfully aware of every sound that came out of my mouth. My brogue became a focus of my self-hatred, and I was always vigilant about the way I spoke among the English, convinced that the few racist jokes I heard on television in Birmingham were representative of the attitudes of the whole population. Simon was no help. I was shrinking down inside myself just as he started laughing about what a lark the police thing had been.

Damn my mother! Why was it that she seemed to hobble me at every turn? The dubious merits of the Irish was a line of debate she'd kept up throughout my childhood and it had seeped into my consciousness, separating me from my own people. It would be years before I appreciated it for the nonsense it was. She believed the Irish were stupid. Did that mean that we, her children, were stupid? Our language was a joke. But I knew through Eamon that it was not a joke, rather it was a pure and venerable tongue. The Irish had no culture. But we had a vast and ancient tradition of music, literature and art – our museums were full of it. My mother admired the English for their civility. But they'd abused us savagely, notwithstanding their good manners. Hadn't they taken our food away and let us starve to death?

Years later in a heated argument I put it to my mother that she'd doomed my life in England with her hatred of Ireland. I shot this at her:

"I went to England with a terrible inferiority complex about being Irish, thanks to you!"

"No, you didn't," she fired back obtusely, "you went with Simon."

I behaved like a convict on the run in Simon's house. I stayed indoors as much as possible and hid from view whenever anyone came to the door. The landlord and his wife wanted to meet me but I resisted.

"Why? What do they want?" I asked suspiciously.

"Nothing. They're nice people and they just want to say hello."

"NO!" I shouted, barricading myself in the toilet. "They won't like me! I'm Irish, remember!"

Simon couldn't relate to this twisted logic and it frightened him. Slamming doors and banging things down, he shouted: "You *have* to meet them! They own this fucking house and they only live two doors away, for fuck's sake!"

I'd never seen him so angry, so I gritted my teeth and went to Beverly and Tom's for tea. And they were nice people. Beverly had two canaries and she'd baked a cake specially; Tom had been a prisoner of war in Burma and hated the Japanese.

Oh. The Japanese.

So it was the Japanese who'd get it in the neck here, not the Irish. I relaxed immediately and started to enjoy myself. Shyly, still guarding my brogue, I told them about my family, minus my father and Cork and how I'd met Simon. The cake was delicious – a very lemony sponge – and Tom gave us bags of his home-grown tomatoes and onions to take home.

Simon wanted me to get a job but I categorically refused. I was so predisposed to abuse that I was afraid of the local people. I was convinced that if I engaged with them I'd be ridiculed or, worse, attacked just for being Irish. Whenever I spoke among them, which wasn't often, I caused a ripple of curiosity. Sometimes, when queuing at the shops, people openly turned and stared when they heard the brogue. Others, more slyly, glanced around wide-angled and took me in on the sweep. There'd be no smiling countenances, only some shuffling of feet before the queue settled down again, and I was tolerated in it, like a foreign body.

I hated it. I wanted to be invisible yet I stuck out like a sore thumb. The only thing to do was to remain silent whenever possible. I tried to explain my fears to Simon but he didn't understand. He thought it was bizarre that an attractive young woman should want to hide herself away like that. His solution was to avoid me. He stayed in the garage while I watched television or wandered around the city on my own. He had lots of records and I played the same ones over and over and it drove him crazy.

He asked his friend Arthur to come and visit us and he agreed. He was coming for the weekend. I didn't want him to. I'd never met him and I was nervous about his visit. He'd be in the house and I'd have to speak to him. I could hardly avoid him without being downright rude. What did he want anyway? Hopefully, like Tom, he hated some other race and the spotlight would be off my Irishness. Simon tried to reassure me.

"Arthur's not like that, Coley."

"Okay . . ." I allowed tentatively.

Arthur had famously been on the dole for eleven years and during that time he'd shared this house with Simon. He was a night owl. He stayed up all night and slept all day and he had the biggest collection of records Simon had ever seen. When the doorbell rang, Simon was in the garage so I went to answer it and when I opened the door, there on the path was a tall thin man with a halo of fuzzy brown hair. He was standing neatly with two little feet together, holding an overnight bag and smoking a cigarette. We looked at each other and I felt a jolt inside me. It was his eyes. They were hazel and wolfish and he stared at me with the most penetrating gaze, as if some unearthly creature was looking out. Nervously, I went out onto the doorstep rather than moving back to let him enter.

"Are you Arthur?"

"Yes. You must be Coley," he said with a deep languorous voice, addressing me sardonically by the nickname Simon used. When I stepped back, I stumbled. *Stupid cunt!* He walked with a mincing sashaying gait like a woman on a catwalk and followed me to the kitchen. I could still feel his gaze on me. He sat down and smiled as I put the kettle on and went to get Simon from the garage. "Is he gay?" I whispered on our way up the garden. Simon assured me he wasn't.

We drank beer and smoked cigarettes at the kitchen table. They remembered their days together in the house: the cat that got lost; the vegetables Arthur grew and unearthed to check their growth; other house mates, like Christian who'd shake a pan of boiling oil like a castanet to hasten his chips, or Mark, marooned on a table by a mouse. Confidence flooded into me, golden and smelling of hops. I laughed at their reminiscences and Simon was his old self again, burbling with jokes and local gossip.

He had a night job in the post office and later before

he left for work he warned me to be on my guard with Arthur. "What do you mean?" I asked curiously but he wouldn't say anymore, out of loyalty to his friend I supposed.

"Just be on your guard," he said again, as if repeating himself explained everything.

Then he was gone and Arthur and I were alone. He turned the heating up in the living room until it was stifling; he didn't like the cold. He turned the television off. I felt powerless to protest. He sat opposite me and stared at me unblinking. I felt that jolt again as I looked into the strange ethereal eyes. No one had ever done this to me before and my heart picked up speed. I felt that he knew me in the very depths of my being and my hurt, neglected self cried out to him for recognition. But was I mistaken? There was that strange walk, so light and girlish, at odds with the powerful presence. And the eyes; were they just mocking me? I looked at the ground and I could feel those eyes burning into me. Christ! Why hadn't Simon told me about them and not the records and the dole? I forced myself to meet his gaze.

He was smoking a joint and asked, "Are you in love with Simon?" blowing out smoke that hung around his head like ectoplasm.

Stumped, not knowing much about love, I squirmed in my chair without an answer. He let me off the hook by moving onto another question: "Why did you loom out at me on the doorstep this morning?"

*Loom out.* It sounded like something adrift in the fog.

"I don't know . . . I was glad to meet you," I answered, hot with embarrassment.

142

"Why? You don't know me."

True. I felt foolish and stared at the floor again.

"Why are you ashamed of being Irish?" So Simon had told him, the bastard.

". . . I don't know . . ." I answered, flushed with discomfort and confusion. I traced the pattern of the carpet to his little feet but couldn't drag my eyes from the floor.

"Why don't you have sex with Simon?"

Jesus! Was there anything he hadn't told him. More discomfort. No answer.

"Have you ever had an orgasm?"

"No."

I gave this answer readily but miserably, like a patient hoping for a cure, tears welling up inside me, about to plop out.

Then he did something that astounded me. He held out his hand. I stared at it and tentatively took it. Gazing intently at me, he pulled me onto his lap, cradling me firmly there like an adult would a child. I couldn't believe where I now was – sitting across his thighs, this man whom I'd only met that day, my head against his chest. I closed my eyes and tried to relax but my heart was pounding. Was I too heavy?

"Tell me about your childhood," he said.

Nobody had ever asked me that before. I recounted the facts: the squalor, the violence, my father's botched suicide. It was easy to talk about these events and my father's shortcomings but more difficult to describe my mother with her neglect and her inner and outer circles of children. In any case, guilt stabbed me into silence where she was concerned.

Arthur cradled me in sympathy for a long time and then we had sex on the floor, after which he told me to go to bed and I did, like an obedient child. He stayed up all night smoking pot and I heard him talking to Simon on his return in the early morning. Arthur went home that day and I was bereft when he left. I daydreamed about him constantly and went over and over that evening, not quite believing the way he'd pulled me onto his lap and listened to my story. I wanted more and I blatantly pined for him.

Poor Simon. He couldn't stand it. He wanted rid of me. He rang Arthur and they talked for a long time and when he put the phone down Simon told me to go to him. He was happy for me to go. Whatever Arthur had said to him, he really wanted me to go. He even helped me pack and gave me a bag of grass to take with me.

I bought a one-way ticket from Birmingham to Hereford. As the train sped southwest out of the Midlands the landscape changed. There were huge fields of wheat that ran up to wooded hilltops. Silver streams shone under blue skies. It was beautiful. Although I hardly knew him, I was sure that Arthur and I would walk in fields like that. We'd hold hands and in the evenings we'd go home and make love. We'd have friends and go to parties and I'd catch his eye across crowded rooms. There'd be nights of sitting on his lap and finding there all the love and protection I'd ever need.

I felt elated and even loved the little train that was taking me nearer to him. Finally it arrived in the pretty Victorian station. I climbed the hill that led to his home with a fluttering heart and I was breathing hard when I rang the doorbell of his flat, thinking that with this ringing doorbell my life was starting again.

But there was no answer. I rang again and again but he wasn't there. I couldn't believe it. We'd spoken on the phone so he knew I was coming, but he wasn't there. He definitely wasn't there.

The ground dissolved under my feet. I paced up and down but I seemed to have no legs and I bit my cheeks really hard with anxiety. I tried to consider reasonable explanations. Maybe he'd been up all night and had fallen asleep or maybe he'd gone out to get some milk. These were logical possibilities. However, irrational thoughts held greater sway. He didn't want me after all and he'd gone out to avoid me. Simon said he was not to be trusted. Now I wondered what he meant. Had I angered him? Did he think I was a whore for having sex with him that night? Yes! Yes! That was it! I was a whore and he didn't want me. No one did. My mother didn't, my father didn't, Simon didn't, now Arthur didn't. *I was bad, bad, bad!*

The colour drained from my face, my mouth filled with bloody saliva and cold sweat trickled down my back. I stepped back from the building and looked up. I knew his flat was on the top floor. The windows were too far up to throw a stone at so I screeched his name out loud but only silence came back. I felt abandoned and descended into panic. Crying started and soon I was out of control. You stupid cunt! What are you going to do now? I walked unsteadily down the hill and out of the town.

Without thinking it through I devised a course of

action – I'd stop a car and beg the driver to take me back to Birmingham. Yes. Yes. This was all a mistake. I had to go back. Poor Simon! What had I done to him, mooning about another man under his very nose? I sat on a grass verge and when I heard a car coming I stepped out onto the road, startling the driver, a woman, who swerved and honked her horn. I went back to the verge and bit my fingers and nails, which hurt terribly and started bleeding. Another car came by. This time it was a man, who stopped and wound down his window. Through my tears, I implored him: "*Please* take me home! *Please!* I beg you! *Please*!"

I made to get into his car but the door was locked. When I told him where I wanted to go, he was aghast.

"What?! Birmingham? But that's miles away!"

He looked at me for a long minute, crying and ringing my hands, released the lock and told me to get in. Keeping a keen eye on me, he turned the car around and headed back into town. "This is where you should be, love," he said, stopping outside the police station. He made to yank me out of the car as if he expected me to resist. On the contrary, I went inside with him as meek as a lamb and he explained to the duty officer that he'd found me at the side of the road, clearly distressed. A policewoman took me to an interview room and brought me a cup of sweetened tea. I was weeping inconsolably and I couldn't stop. The crying woman at the psychiatric hospital my father was taken to flashed into my mind.

Questions began.

"What's your name, sweetheart?"

"C . . . C . . . Cora." I remembered how my self-consciousness had begun with a policeman but I was too far gone to care about my accent.

"Cora what?"

"C . . . Coleman."

"Where do you live?"

"I . . . don't . . . know."

"What do you mean you don't know?"

"I . . . came here . . . to live with Arthur . . . but he's not here."

"Who's Arthur?"

"He lives at the top of the hill but he's not there. I want to go back to Simon."

"Who's Simon?"

"My boyfriend. I want to go back to him."

"Has he got a phone number?"

I stumbled through it while rummaging in my bag for a cigarette. Suddenly, right at the bottom, I felt the bag of grass. Touching it sobered me up like a cold shower. I saw the Birmingham police going round to Simon's to talk to him about me and discovering his marijuana plants. I calmed right down and came back to the present. I stopped crying, lit the cigarette and took a gulp of the tea.

The police rang Simon, who told them not to worry; I was just highly strung. Arthur had gone to the train station to meet me and we'd missed each other on the road. That was all. Such a simple explanation! Oh happy days! He wanted me after all. He'd actually gone to the station to meet me; how great was that?! Of course, I should have realised he'd be at the station. Any other woman would have expected it.

I backed slowly out of the police station, apologising

for wasting their time and thanking them for their help, put a note on Arthur's door and went to wait in the pub. Each time the door opened, I thought it was him – and finally it was. He looked wonderful in a blue denim shirt and blue jeans, like Marlboro Man, until he moved and then he was Marlboro Woman. He was holding my note, fists clenched in mock anger, eyes laughing.

Once indoors, he cradled me in his arms as he'd done in Simon's living room and I told him everything that had happened. He was full of deep, rumbling laughter at the whole episode: my panic, my stopping of the cars, the police ringing Simon and the pot in my bag. We smoked some of the grass and he asked me more questions: Why didn't I orgasm? Did I hate men because of my father?

We got high and he told me about himself: how he believed he could read people's minds, how they couldn't hide from him. He saw good and evil, fear and anger, sadness and joy in everyone he met, even in strangers that he passed on the street. He saw beams of light passing between lovers and the subtle weapons they used when love went sour. His favourite subject was women and their sexuality. He'd managed to stay on the dole for so long by seducing women at the dole office, in thought, if not in deed. But he liked men too and told me about the unconscious drives and deeper motivations of those he knew. Simon, for example, was driven by guilt that his mother had died after his birth, which had left his father heart-broken.

He spoke plainly about sexual functions in a way that was devoid of shame. He described his past sexual experiences in detail: girlfriends and what they did together, women who screamed when they came, other women who got very wet. His fascination with the power of the female both shocked and thrilled me. It was catching and through his eyes I saw women as possessors of dark sexual secrets and powers. He loved *The Chrysalids* by John Wyndham, a science fiction story involving telepathy, and he believed that he would have a telepathic relationship with the woman of his dreams and they would have a daughter and call her Petra, like in the book. High on pot in that flat perched at the top of the hill, I thought he was some sort of shaman.

"Are you a magician?" I asked naively. He just laughed and cuddled me closer.

Now it was my turn to speak and I told him about the abortion. Suddenly, without warning, he set me down hard. For the second time that day, I sobered up very quickly. He lit a cigarette and smoked it pensively while I sat where I'd been dumped, at the far end of the sofa. Long minutes passed. A clock ticked and he wouldn't look at me. I waited, mystified and anxious for his verdict on what I'd done. Feeling as though I was on trial, I pulled myself to the very edge of the seat, as yet not free to relax.

Finally, he smiled. I was pardoned. Thank God, it was a thumbs-up! He'd forgiven me the sin of abortion and beckoned me back into his arms. I scampered in and we smoked more grass and drank some wine. Later, when the sky went dark and we seemed to be the only two people in the world, he turned the full power of his intense gaze on me and ordered me to heal.

"HEAL!" he roared.

I stared at him plaintively, knowing it wouldn't

happen but trying to feel something, like a constipated child trying to have a movement to please a parent.

Later, in bed, he ordered me to come.

"COME!" he commanded.

But I didn't come and we were both disappointed.

In the clear light of day, he frightened me with his talk of telepathy and his shock tactics and homespun psychoanalysis. Furthermore, he'd shown me some strange gothic pornography that he wanted to interest me in. With big man's hands but the gestures of a woman, he delicately turned the pages, his face a picture of lustful desire. Was he joking? Why did he think I'd be interested in pornography? Hadn't I told him about my father? He had dirty books that made my father's stuff look wholesome by comparison. It was all under his bed. I realised I was having my lovers' tryst on top of a pile of filth.

It was a cold grey morning and the wind had changed. I decided to go back to Simon.

"Simon doesn't want you!" he snapped.

"Yes, he does!" I countered with hurt pride.

"No, he doesn't. You frighten him."

"No, I don't."

"Cora . . . listen to me. Simon didn't realise you were so . . . damaged. You have too many problems for him. He thinks you're nuts."

"No, he doesn't!" I shouted, stung now by Simon's betrayal.

"Yes . . . he . . . does. He wrote to me in desperation. That's why I came to see you."

"No, he didn't!" I countered.

"He did!"

"I don't care. I want to go back!"

And I did. As suddenly and abruptly as I'd left Birmingham, I returned. But Arthur was right, Simon didn't want me any more. All that time in the garage had given him an idea for a business and, like something that was in the way, he packed me off back to Cork.

It was a beautiful morning as the boat came into Cork Harbour. The early morning sunshine made the tops of the buildings glow and the ferry cut through water that was liquid gold.

I borrowed a room from a friend of Yvonne's and went straight to bed. I howled for Simon – someone I didn't love and who didn't love me. A spring in the bed scratched my back painfully but I was too upset to get up and turn the mattress over. The truth was I was howling because I was back where I'd started, in a cold dark room on my own. I'd failed in England and guilt was a sword hanging over my head. It would only take a visit to my mother to bring it down. I avoided her for that reason – but the news from home was good.

She'd finally left *him*. The house I grew up in had been sold and *he'd* gone back to live with his mother. With some of the proceeds and a mortgage, she managed to buy her own home, an old house in the middle of Cobh. The bedrooms had interesting titles. There was: Mammy's Room, Grace's Room, Peter's Room and the Big Room. Grace, who hadn't lived at home in years, had a room of her own but Sarah, who was still a minor, had none. She slept in the Big Room and had only visitor status, like the rest of us.

My mother's refinement rose like a phoenix from the

ashes of her marriage. This was a house where there'd be no pornography, no Frank Sinatra, no cigarettes, piss buckets, mouldy newspapers or foul language. She and Grace went shopping for furnishings in Cork and together they chose the wallpaper, curtains and carpets. Although she knew I was back, we never met up. They'd browse the department stores, have coffee and cakes and go home as if we were in parallel universes.

Nevertheless, things started looking up for me. Through an old college friend, I got a job in a language school teaching English as a foreign language. After a short training course, I went straight into the classroom. I was lucky because my first student was a Dutch psychiatrist who smiled at my faltering attempts to explain English grammar and was happy to let me practise on him. With such help, I slowly improved as a teacher. I moved from the room I was in to a beautiful old flat on a hillside in an elegant part of the city. It was so high up that you could see straight out to the bluey-green hills in the distance and right down to the river where ships came and went twenty-four hours a day.

In the evenings, I drank, often after work at five o'clock with other teachers. I wouldn't go home until closing time, making do with a sandwich or some chips, raised unsteadily to my lips during slurred conversations. The alcohol often connected with the anger inside me and I was a nasty, insulting drunk, which shocked my new teaching friends. I had no dignity when I was inebriated. One night, while pissing on the street, I fell into a pile of dogshit and got it all over my hands and knees.

The weekends were awful because I felt profoundly and painfully alone and I did various things to kill the time. I made a duvet cover by hand; I altered my clothes in pointless, painstaking ways; I paced the flat, desperate for company, for someone to come and claim me. I was hungry for something that I couldn't name but feeling paralysed in the depths of my being, completely unable to reach out to other people. By day, I watched the ships docking and hauling anchor. By night I stared at a certain set of traffic lights down in the city, watching them turn green, amber, red, over and over; knowing that down there were young people going to the cinema, the theatre, restaurants and clubs, enjoying life and having fun.

I turned to the library for comfort. I read voraciously and if I had a good book on a Saturday night, all was not lost. I could escape from myself and my indeterminate gnawing hunger for a few hours at least. I grew interested in London and preferred to read books that were set there. I was drawn inexorably to that city. I found myself studying maps of London in the library and watching films and TV programmes simply because they were set there. I built up a romantic, post-hippy picture of London as a Mecca for artists, full of booze, drugs and entertainment, a sort of majestic throbbing organ whose constituent parts were millions of happy, confident people. I felt that *I'd* be happy and confident there too. I knew lots of young people who were going, for the sheer excitement of it. A delicious frisson of fear and excitement went through me when I considered taking the plunge.

Then I met Danny, who was English. We were drawn

together by a shared love of books. It turned out that he'd been in London several times because his brother lived in Earl's Court. I wrung information out of him about the city. Earl's Court, eh? What was that like? Full of Aussies, wasn't it? His brother an artist, eh? How amazing! I was a bit of an artist myself. I thought of some of the famous places on the old Monopoly board at home. Had he been to any of them? What were the pubs like? Amazing probably. He'd been at a gig in Hyde Park. Wow, what was that like? I thought about Mick Jagger in 1969 in his dress shirt, releasing all the butterflies. I imagined sixties-type girls floating around London in a sort of time warp.

He wanted to go back for good and asked me to go with him. Not as a couple, just so we could help each other out and share expenses. I wanted to so much but I was reluctant as well. I was established in Cork by now. I had my lovely flat, lots of books and plants and my job as an English teacher. On the other hand, the loneliness I felt was like a physical pain. I cried myself to sleep with it, I drank myself into a stupor to escape from it. I was bewildered by it. I couldn't understand why I felt so deeply alone but I did. So before the opportunity passed, I gave away all my things, said goodbye yet again and off I went to London.

A truck driver I hitched a lift with knew the city and he warned me not to go to London. He said I'd be eaten alive there. Simon said it was beyond human scale. Someone else said I was too innocent. These forebodings only served to increase its mythic status in my mind, the size and sense of danger adding to its majesty. Ironically, the facet of London which would affect me most was something I hadn't even thought of – the anonymity. I became a tiny fish in a huge pond. It was like the darkness I embraced as a child. No one knew who I was and that made me feel like I couldn't be seen. When I couldn't be seen, shame was less of a burden, and with the lifting of that burden, I felt free.

I escaped the strictures of provincial life and found myself another kind of darkness: I had my second abortion in London, got my criminal record there and was badly beaten there many times. It was in London that I found men who'd satisfy the hunger I'd always felt but couldn't name. It was a need to experience violence, to know what my mother had felt, to be vindicated and have proof of what I believed: that all men were violent bastards.

The one with the bruises isn't always the victim. Or, at least, not the victim in a straightforward way. The cloak of anonymity let me go so low as to goad men into beating me. I look back now and I feel sorry for those men. They were unlucky to have met me at that time and might never have touched a woman if I hadn't come along. I hardly recognise myself from those years in London. I look back and see myself – ugly and drunk, demented with hatred and mistrust, picking at men's wounds and faults, shouting: "COME ON! LET'S SEE THE REAL YOU", until they finally exploded.

My descent into that horror started like this.

In July 1984, Danny and I went by ferry and coach to Victoria Station. I read all the way but closed my book as soon as we reached the outskirts of the great metropolis. The Smoke. I loved that sobriquet. It was so evocative of the history and character of London. I imagined fog, the Blitz, Sherlock Holmes and Eliza Doolittle. I wanted to see it all, even the stuff on the outskirts: the industrial estates; the tower blocks, pale monoliths on the horizon; even the grimy little houses that bordered the busy roads. I drank in the passing scene, not missing a detail, until we reached the fabulous West End, which unfolded all around us like a beautiful flower.

At Victoria we took the Underground. It was my first time and I'd rehearsed the route: the Victoria Line north-bound to Oxford Circus. Change to the District Line. The District Line westbound to Danny's brother's home in Earl's Court. Nick had a tiny flat that he shared with his girlfriend, Sally, and he twitched nervously as we plonked our bags in his hallway. I knew immediately that he was an artist – his paintings were everywhere, all on the same theme: beautiful young women striking erotic poses, like soft porn glamour models rendered in oils. He was anxious to know what Danny's plans were.

"You'll be looking for somewhere straight away, right?" he asked with a nervous little laugh.

"Of course, Nicky," said Dan with a grin, confident that his older brother would always look out for him.

So Nick turned to me. I knew the score. I was the extra one, the one who was causing the crush so it was incumbent upon me to make things happen. I got a job at a language school almost immediately and found us a place to live in the East End. I took it sight unseen, so strong was my feeling that Nick wanted us out of his flat as soon as possible. My new home was the ugliest flat I'd ever seen. It stank of sick hemmed in by the pong of stale air freshener, and none of the rooms was square. There was a blanket with a thick, plate-sized blood stain, which we threw out. A plastic garden set served as our table and chairs and to add to the strange outdoors effect, the dirty sticky carpet was lawn green.

Outside, however, it was a glorious summer and I embraced the overheated city with a sense of awe. I loved the new smells, and one in particular – a cocktail of cooking oil and spices from the ethnic restaurants, melting road tar and exhaust fumes. There were major roads behind and in front of the flat and my hair was soon stiff with grime, which got up my nose and in my eyes. But I didn't care. I was a metropolitan chick now, buzzing on the enormity and energy of this beast of a city. I couldn't believe how big it was. Danny and I studied a map of London, as I'd done in the library in Cork, and my head spun with the knowledge that the long, broad road we lived on was an infinitesimally small dot. We celebrated our successful move with cans of Special Brew – in spite of our hideous surroundings, we'd made it! In any case, most weekends we went over to Earl's Court.

Sally was kind. She fed us and then we four would go for a stroll, often a couple of laps of Brompton Cemetery, which was at the end of the street. One evening, in the pub, Nick grabbed my hands and told me he loved me. I was astonished and didn't know what to say. I'd had no idea that he had any feelings for me. In fact, I thought he disliked me, since he'd wanted us out of his flat so quickly. I stared at him, gobsmacked, and he stared back, twitching and miserable. *I* certainly didn't love *him* although I did feel a shy affinity with him because of the art. I had to rescue my hands from his firm grip before the others got back, so I pulled them free and lit a cigarette just as Sally emerged from the Ladies and Danny came back from the bar.

"All right, Cora?" he enquired, grinning, face shiny and eyes bloodshot from the alcohol, but I just nodded, stunned at the guilty secret I now had with his brother. I glanced at Nick and he was staring balefully at the ashtray on the table.

By the end of the week the cat was out of the bag. When Nick told Sally he was in love with me, she was distraught. She screamed and cried and wouldn't believe it. Danny gave him a black eye, denounced me as an evil bitch and went to keep Sally company in Earl's Court. Nick came to live with me in the East End and just then I discovered I was pregnant by Dan.

Another abortion? Yes, it would have to be. We couldn't let a little problem like that get in the way of our great love affair. And I knew it was a great love affair because Nick kept telling it was. I was only too happy to agree. I was completely caught up in the drama of what was happening. An intense and talented young London artist wanted *me*. He was miserably love-sick over me, was turning his life upside down because of me. He told me that I was beautiful and irresistible. Starved of attention, my poor impoverished ego simply couldn't resist. And we had a great soundtrack – Bob Dylan. There was a Bob Dylan song for every occasion and I worked my way into every one. Nick was Bob and I was the girl: alternately the good girl, the bad girl, the girl who broke his heart, and the girl who saved his life, depending on the song. I didn't care about Sally and Danny. They'd get over it. I didn't feel any guilt about them. It was just a bit of unpleasantness. I'd known worse.

The termination happened at the Mile End hospital, a short walk from the flat, and I had no qualms about that either. I still didn't want a baby. Let alone Danny's baby. I was with his brother the artist now and nothing was going to get in the way of that. I was only just pregnant and I promised myself that I'd never have another abortion and that absolved me from any guilt. In fact, my only concern on the day was that I hadn't shaved my legs. This time there was no haemorrhaging, no crying and no pain; and the next day I modelled for a pornographic magazine.

It came about like this. One day, when I got back from work, Nick had great news – he'd landed some photographic work for a national magazine.

"National magazine! Which one?" I was as excited as he was.

"It's, ehh . . . it's . . ." he began with little nervous laughs. "Emm . . . it's a *gentleman's* publication."

"You mean a porn mag?" I said, my voice deflating.

"Yes. But a really *big* one."

He told me the name but I'd never heard of it. His pictures would illustrate stories about the sexual exploits of various women. The first was about a florist who does men in the back of her van at the early-morning flower markets. The stories would get a prominent position in the magazine and pictures would be very tasteful, rest assured. But there was a problem – he didn't have a model for the shoot and he couldn't afford to hire one.

"How much would it cost?" I asked.

"Too much," he answered, sitting down heavily on a plastic chair. "Anyway, that's not the kind of woman I need. She has to look real. It's supposed to be about the adventures of real women."

"How much?"

"About five hundred pounds," he answered, opening a can of beer and quaffing deeply. He didn't have it and neither did I but if he didn't get a model, he'd lose the job. Long seconds went by, during which he was rolling a joint, and then I offered to do it.

"Oh, fantastic babe!" he exclaimed, getting to his feet and showering me with kisses, "thank you, thank you, thank you!"

I couldn't refuse. I felt I owed it to him, being the cause of his break-up with Sally. I was the scarlet woman. What right did I have to morals? He was so relieved and I was delighted with the power I had to bestow favours. It felt great. We smoked the joint and discussed the shoot.

The day after the termination dawned bright and beautiful. Nick told me not to wear underwear as the marks would show up in the photographs. He'd borrowed a van and drove purposefully through the early morning streets. It was fascinating to see how it all joined up: Mile End to Whitechapel to Holborn to Oxford Street, down Park Lane and along Knightsbridge to a florist's in South Kensington where we had the keys until opening time. Inside, the air was warm and moist with the intense perfume of exotic flowers. I was to arrange blooms and stare dreamily out the window while he clicked away with his camera. Then we went to a courtyard in Chelsea where he produced some coke which we snorted before he photographed me in various poses and states of undress.

When I saw the pictures I blushed. It didn't look like me. Thanks to the cocaine and Nick's encouragement, I looked much saucier and more voluptuous than I did in real life. When the magazine accepted them, I felt great. He couldn't have done it without me and we celebrated with a pub crawl. I was on top of the world. I'd never felt so beautiful. But my moment passed and he moved on to his next assignment. I think the next model was his pot dealer's wife.

Nick's family were united in hating me because they all loved Sally. Their mother was dead and Sally assuaged that loss with her warmth and tenderness. Our relationship was also a scandal among his friends. He took me to a birthday party once where no one would speak to me. The men just wanted to see what I looked like and the women openly despised me. Naively, I went up to the glaring birthday girl to wish her well.

"Happy Birtday," I said awkwardly. Oh God. It's bir*th*day not birtday. I could have kicked myself. Where'd my "th" gone? The brogue had escaped its fetters and I blushed a deep crimson.

She pounced on it straight away. "Tanks," she sneered in an ugly stage-Oirish voice. My heart was pounding as she continued, "Ah, sure, yer sorry aboush Sally aren't ja? An ya didn't mean ta hurt no one, did ja? Don't tell me. Yer deeply in luv wit Nicheles, aren't ja?"

Idiotically, I nodded at everything she said and when she finished, she turned her back on me while those within earshot tittered. I cringed to my very core and looked around for Nick. There he was in the corner, skinning up and laughing with his friends, completely oblivious to me. I should have left but after the birthday girl incident I saw myself as they did – a scheming bitch and a stupid Paddy – and I stayed for more humiliation. My answer was to get very drunk and make a fool of myself and then everyone *really* wanted Nick to go back to Sally.

Edwin, Nick's best friend, sidled up to me. Sally had invested so much time in him, you see. Seven years. I had to agree. With my track record, seven years with the same man seemed like a lifetime. When I told him what Edwin had said, Nick got angry and kicked the doors and punched things in frustration. They didn't *understand*! He didn't *love* her any more. He never really had. She was older than him. She'd been more like a big sister. He didn't want to grow old with her – or with any woman for that matter, although he didn't say this. He didn't want to stay with Sally so his brothers could have a mother figure. It was so frustrating for him. He couldn't go back to his studio until she left the flat in Earl's Court and she seemed to be in no hurry to do so. He dug his heels in and we soldiered on in the East End.

Shortly after the photo-shoot, I got my first black eye from Nick. I don't remember the circumstances because I was too drunk. I know it was a big black shiner and Dan smiled when he saw it. The problem was the drinking. Nick and his friends favoured super-strength lagers and I followed suit. When I was on the lagers, jealous anger engulfed me. I was so insecure I never felt sure of Nicholas. His head was so easily turned by a pretty girl. I felt that any minute now he was going to move on to someone younger, like he'd done to Sally. Dead drunk, the real Cora emerged – bitter and wounded, intent on proving to herself that men were feckless, unpredictable bastards. I focused all of that on Nick and provoked him from every angle. I criticised his art, his looks, his love-making and his treatment of Sally. Anything to get a rise out of him. Fighting became a regular thing for us. After the first one I never seemed to be without a black eye, always seeming to have a fresh one before the last one was quite gone. I didn't care. My mother couldn't see them and that was the main thing.

In October 1985, he wanted me to go New York with him. He and Sally had been invited and he wanted me to take her place. Filling her shoes like that seemed crass to me so I refused and kept refusing until one night, in a pub in Mile End, he lashed out, shouting at me: "YOU *WILL* COME OR ELSE I'M OUTTA HERE!" With that he swept everything off the table and disappeared out the door. Glasses, bottles and a full ashtray went flying and crashed to the floor. The pub went quiet and everyone looked at me as I bent down to pick up the cigarette butts and broken glass. The barman came out from behind the counter to help me.

"Wot's 'is problem, ven?" he asked.

I was mortified and couldn't even look at him, never mind give him the answer that the whole place was waiting to hear. He told me to leave the mess so I picked up my bag and went after Nick. When I got home, he wasn't there. What did he mean *I'm outta here?* Was he going to leave me? I realised I'd have to go to New York with him or the relationship was over and I dreaded the thought of being left in that ugly, smelly place on my own. I saw no other alternative. In that city of a million bedsits I thought there was nowhere else for me but that awful place, so I went.

We were met at Newark Airport by our gay host, Don. It was clear from the start that Don wanted Nick. Inviting the girlfriend was just a necessity to get him there. He had an apartment in Manhattan that was full of nooks and crannies and the two of them played cat-and-mouse. I heard scuffling and giggling and lips smacking, always just around the corner, just out of sight. I was superfluous and on my own until Nick would come back to me all flushed and mock-guilty, like a naughty child to his mother. I regarded him coldly, thinking how much better suited Sally was to this treatment, given her maternal nature.

Out on the street, Don insulted passers-by with his acerbic wit. The old, the fat, the crippled and the ugly – they were all fair game. His victims simply stared at him open-mouthed as he scuttled past. Through peals of laughter, Nick warned him not to try it in London or he'd get his head kicked in. Secretly, I hoped he would.

One night, we went out without Don and found ourselves in a lesbian bar where we sat in a booth and watched some women playing pool. I was fascinated by them: the way they swaggered around the pool table owning the space like men, chalking their cues and smashing balls into pockets. These weren't just lesbians, they were New York lesbians and I admired the supreme confidence they exuded. Nick wasn't comfortable, however. He didn't like lesbians. Lipstick lesbians yes, the kind that featured in male fantasies, but these big hairy ones? No. Homosexuals were fine as long as they were men. We got a turn on the pool table and he couldn't play. He was trembling and I beat him hands down. I was drinking whiskey chasers and thinking about the whole trip. I'd endured the humiliation of coming here in another woman's place because he'd forced me to. And for what? To watch him playing hide-and-seek with that nasty faggot. Probably laughing at me behind my back, the pair of them. How dare he! Sally might have put up with it, the stupid bitch, but I certainly wouldn't. Look at him! Going to pieces because he's in a lesbian bar when I've had to put up with his poncey shenanigans all week. The more I thought about it, the more I boiled on it. I was so drunk that when we left I could hardly walk straight. Out on the street I exploded, taunting him mercilessly, calling him a fucking hypocrite over and over as we headed for the subway.

We went down the steps and onto the platform. I was still shouting and he was imploring me to be quiet. The more reasonable he was, the more he incensed me. That morning he'd bought me a pair of pink fishnet tights that I'd admired and now in my drunken rage they symbolised the exploitation of women everywhere. I brandished the tights and screamed:

"I SUPPOSE YOU WANT ME TO MODEL THESE

THINGS IN YOUR FILTHY, FUCKING MAGAZINE, YOU FUCKING BASTARD!"

With that I threw the tights onto the train tracks and Nick, who was also drunk, got down onto the tracks and rescued them. Seconds later a train came hurtling into the station and we boarded it. All the passengers looked like murderers and that quietened me down. We hurtled along in silence: me red in the face, him pale and intense, our breath snorting and both reeking of alcohol, until we got to the Eighty-Third Street stop. As soon as we got off the train, I felt a tremendous pain on the side of my head. It was Nick and he was hammering me with his knuckles for all he was worth. Clout, clout, clout. I'd heard that sound before – my father's fists on my mother's head. This was what it felt like. Enormously painful. A pain that echoed through your whole being and left you dazed and confused. We went up the steps and onto the street like that, conjoined in violence. Him with his arms going like pistons and me crouched to protect my head. Outside, someone tried to drag him off me – "HEY BUDDY! LEAVE DE LADY ALONE!" – but he was unstoppable and they backed off.

We got into the apartment and in the bedroom he attacked me with absolute savagery. He pounded my face over and over and over and I could hear Don in the doorway cautioning: "Not on her *face* Nick, not on her *face*."

He paused at Don's interjection and that was my chance to hit back. I landed a blow on his shoulder and we toppled together onto a bedside lamp which caught fire. That's what appalled Don. He ran into the room with a wet tea-towel to put out the flames, just as Nick was dragging me onto the floor by my hair, all the while knuckling my face with his fist. Don hovered by the door and when it was over, he led Nick away and I was left alone in the bedroom where I fell into a drunken sleep.

I woke in the early hours to a world of pain. I was shocked when I saw my face. It was sort of hexagonal and twice its normal size. My eyes were swollen slits and there was a fist-sized swelling on my forehead that made me look like a Klingon. My body ached in all the places where he'd kicked and punched me. I hid in the bed as long as I could and when Don looked in, he too was shocked at what he saw. He retreated and I could hear his voice through the wall – serious, advisory, no doubt telling Nick how to deal with the situation when we got back to London. He assumed I'd go to the police, which I should have done. A normal woman would have. But what was I talking about – a normal woman, unused to horror, would not have been there in the first place.

Nick was truly shocked by what he'd done. He just stared at me, on the verge of tears. I think he wanted to leave me but I took all the blame on board and by so doing we stayed together and I avoided the one thing that I absolutely dreaded – being left on my own.

We came home early and I went to the airport with my face hidden behind a scarf and dark glasses. I stayed off work for a while and tried not to drink. Nick and I didn't fight when we were sober but drinking was like lighting a fuse in both of us and a few weeks after coming back from New York, when the last of my bruises were healing, we had another terrible row. We were on the

Special Brews and talking about two small metal chairs we'd brought back from New York with us. He said they were his and I brooded on this. His. Not ours. He obviously didn't see us staying together. Rather, he saw a future without me when he'd abscond with his precious chairs. Yes, that was it! The little shit was going to abandon me. Probably when he got his precious flat back from his ex-girlfriend. He was going to leave me in this shit-hole knowing I hated being alone and after what he'd done to me in New York! Oh, the fucking bastard! He was only using me until she was gone. I wasn't good enough to take over to Earl's Court, I suppose. This poisonous bile found its way out of my mouth accompanied by a stream of name-calling. I called him a prick, a pornographer, a woman-beater, a misogynist, a faggot and much more. He tried to ignore me but I wouldn't let him and I went on and on until he snapped.

He jumped up from his chair, toppling the drinks on the table, and came at me, his face contorted with violent intent and his fists clenched. Fizzing pungent beer spread out and dripped onto the floor. The next minute I felt his awful knuckles on my arms and face and his boots on my legs. I shouted at him to stop but he was out of control. He picked up one of the New York chairs, shouting: "HERE'S YOUR FUCKING CHAIR, YOU STUPID CUNT! IF YOU WANT IT, GO AND GET IT!"

He hurled the chair at the big old window and it went through it with a crescendo of breaking glass, followed by the clanging sound of the chair hitting the ground way below. Cold night air rushed in through the huge jagged hole. The window was destroyed. All twelve panes of glass had shattered and the wooden frame had fallen to bits. I wailed at him drunkenly to stop but he punched me in the face and then turned on the flat, kicking over the plastic table, pulling the cooker and the fridge to the floor. Pots and pans crashed and the kitchen floor was a lake of milk and broken eggs. It looked like there had been an earthquake with the window destroyed and the cooker and fridge pulled from their moorings.

Suddenly there was a knock at the door. It was the two men from the flat above us. They'd heard the noise and were concerned. About Nick. He brought them in and they were stunned at what they saw. They led him out to the hallway, one with his arm around his shoulder while the other one insisted: "You don't need this, mate. Just walk away. You don't need it. Walk away, mate, because you don't need it."

High on the adrenalin of the fight and stung that they were ignoring me, I shouted:

"GET THE FUCK OUT OF MY FLAT! IF YOU WANT TO TALK TO THAT BASTARD, DO IT OUTSIDE!"

The three of them retreated, one with his arm still around Nick's shoulder while the voice went on in a loop: "You don't need it, mate. Just walk away. You don't need it. None of us do. It's not worth it. Just walk away, mate."

Nick returned ashen-faced and the steam went out of both of us after that. Weeping, I lit a cigarette and he went down to get the chair. I looked at the remains of the window. How much would it cost to replace? We were skint. My face was swelling and I knew I'd soon have another black eye to explain away, if not two.

I felt utterly miserable. I was getting heartily sick of this. I had my proof by now. Men were bastards. There was no doubt about it. So wasn't it time to leave? Surely being on my own couldn't be worse than this? I wanted to walk away too but I was sure there was nowhere to go. The truth is, I was addicted to the highs and lows of all that violence. Incredible as it seems now, I preferred this to being alone. I always got so depressed on my own and deep insecurity, instilled by years of my father, wouldn't let me rest. So I clung to Nick and the bitter lessons he taught me about the nature of men.

Eventually Sally moved out of the flat in Earl's Court and we moved in. Nick slipped back into the life he'd lived before. While I was at work, he pottered around his studio, smoking joints and making phone calls. His friends and family came round and were a bit more polite to me now, except for one woman, whose name was Cassandra. She was an old friend of his from art school and one Saturday she called but he was out. Deciding to wait, she sat in the kitchen in silence. I offered her a drink but she refused; I tried to start a conversation but she turned her haughty face away and studied the messages and doodles on the wall. I tried again but she cut me off in a cold voice: "Look, I've come here to see Nick, not you. I'm only interested in Nick. Not his women. Okay?" The "Okay" was angry and she went back to studying the wall.

I retreated to the bedroom and soon after, Nick arrived. Dylan went on the stereo. I heard the sound of beer cans cracking open and I could smell hash. The bastard! He was doing *our* things with another woman, whose tone was soft now, her laugh warm and seductive. A few days later she needed his help and he went to meet her.

While he was gone, I drew a cartoon of him sitting in a pub with a bottle of beer. It was a good drawing by anyone's standards, so I stuck it on the kitchen wall. When he came back, he drew over it and said: "There, that's better."

"DON'T DO THAT!" I wailed and before I knew what I was doing, I'd thumped him hard on the arm. He came at me with a dreadful ferocity, his face black with hatred. The knuckle hammer was going like a piston. Knock, knock, knock on my face. Within seconds he'd battered my nose so hard it was pouring blood and my lips were split. He was kicking and punching me down the narrow hallway towards the bathroom, when, suddenly, he disappeared into the studio. Why? Maybe he was going to calm himself down. Maybe he'd be out in a minute to apologise. I staggered towards the bathroom, stunned, my nose and lips pouring blood.

Then he was back, marching purposefully towards me, holding a can of red paint. When he was near enough, he flung it straight at me. My heart missed a beat as the paint swept into my eyes, ears and mouth, splashed up my nose and soaked down to my scalp and skin. I got into the bathroom, choking and snorting to clear my airways, and locked the door. He pounded for a while, calling me a cunt and a whore, telling me to get out of his flat, and then with great relief I heard him leaving. I waited by the locked door for a few minutes until I heard the front door slamming shut and was sure he was gone. In the silence that now surrounded me, I stared at myself in the mirror. I looked at the cap of red paint on my hair, the mixture of paint and blood on my face, my swelling eyes and nose, and the paint and blood dripping down my neck and shoulders. My nose and lips were still bleeding and I watched the blood ooze out without intervention. I was numb. I just stared at myself, as if someone else, a creature from a horror film, was staring back. My nose was broken. That was obvious. It was so swollen that the skin was stretched tight and greeny-white across it.

Eventually I showered and got most of the paint off. Then I took a bottle of wine and a packet of cigarettes and holed up in the bedroom. I drank and drank but didn't get drunk. I sucked at the blood-stained cigarettes with my split lips. I should have phoned the police but I couldn't. I'd thumped him first, hadn't I? And just because he'd scribbled on my drawing. Who was I to be drawing? There was room for only one artist in this relationship and that was Nick. Day turned into night.

At ten o'clock the phone rang. It was his friend Edwin asking me to leave the flat so Nick could come back:

"Look here," he began, "we're down in Sloane Square and he's smashing up phone boxes and he's going to get himself arrested if you don't get out."

At long last, anger roared up from my guts and took me with it. I shouted at Edwin:

"FUCK OFF, WILL YOU! HE'S BROKEN MY NOSE! I HOPE HE DOES GET ARRESTED! TELL HIM NOT TO COME BACK HERE TONIGHT OR I'LL PHONE THE POLICE MYSELF! IF HE COMES BACK TONIGHT, I'LL WRECK HIS PRECIOUS FLAT . . . AND HIS STUPID FUCKING PAINTINGS!"

With that, I put the phone down. My heart was pounding and all my sore places were throbbing but I must have made an impression on Edwin because Nick didn't turn up for several days.

When he did, the epicentre had passed. The swelling on my nose had gone down somewhat and I could feel the break. It was on the bridge, right between my eyes. The bones clicked when I pressed them. I got it fixed at the Whittington Hospital in Highgate, where there was peace and nurses who came and asked me if I was all right and meals brought to me in bed. Then Nick came to take me home. I was still woozy from the anaesthetic on the bus journey back to Earl's Court. I thought I'd have to get off near Hyde Park because I was going to be sick. Christ! Couldn't he have stretched to a taxi? Fortunately, the nausea passed and soon I was propped up in bed clutching a can of Special Brew. The TV was on in the bedroom and as Nick watched it, I watched him. I was haunted by that vision of myself in the bathroom mirror. He did that to me yet he hadn't even apologised. His conscience was clear. You could see it on his face. He looked happy and contented as he watched his programme and skinned up his joint. It was entirely my fault and it would always be like that. The next day, I went to stay with a work colleague, Barbara, and never went back to Nick.

I drifted downwards. Work was the only thing that kept me in touch with normality. At night I wandered around on my own, not around the West End but into scraggy parts of London. I walked along by train tracks and canals and across industrial wastelands.

A stranger approached me once and, uncaring, I didn't even flinch at his sudden presence by my side. He fell into step with me and made to whisper something in my ear. I expected filth but what he said to me was this:

"What are you doing out here on your own? A young one like you shouldn't be out here on her own in the dark. Go home, girl."

I hardly even looked at him.

When I look back, I see a naked man clutching a carving knife. I was alone with him in a squat with broken window panes. No front teeth and he was lisping threats to kill me.

"You don't frighten me," I said.

It wasn't true but I was numb from alcohol.

I see a man in a doss-house telling me I was all he could get now that he was broke. Another one telling me I was over the hill at twenty-nine.

I see myself drunk in a pub in Notting Hill setting fire to my hair and face while trying to light a cigarette.

When I was a child I was always gazing at horizons, dreaming about the good things beyond them. Between the twin headlands that enclosed our harbour stretched the impossibly straight line of the horizon. It cut my world in two – the known and the unknown. The ocean washed up to foreign shores where, in my mind, there were always blue skies framed in roses. There was a farmhouse on the crest of a hill with huge banks of sky spreading out above it. I imagined Texas, gingham dresses, warm winds and horses. A new man to me was like a horizon. I approached each one with the same sense of promise and anticipation, like a child on Christmas morning. I was incorrigible. No amount of abuse could discourage me. No matter what happened with one, I approached the next with the same sense of wonder. And each one took me a little bit further down.

I had a friend at work called Rebecca. She was funny and made me laugh. One evening, after work, we were in a pub near the school. She was bemoaning the fact that some wealthy students had given her a packet of biscuits as a leaving gift and we were laughing at the meanness of it.

I didn't notice Mathew at first. It was Rebecca who saw that he was chuckling at the biscuit conversation so she stretched across and offered him one. Laughing, he put his magazine down and took it. In return for the biscuit, he bought us a drink and I was attracted to his good humour and taste. He drank brandy, not beer, and smoked cigars, not cigarettes. The magazine was about antiques, not cars or football. He wore a blazer and well-polished shoes. While he was at the bar Rebecca said she had to go.

I panicked. "No! Please don't go! Don't leave me alone with him!"

"Don't be silly. He's all right. Just talk to him." With that she drained her glass and left.

Just talk to him. I couldn't just talk to a man. I had to be drunk first. So I got drunk and, encouraged by his laughter, my mouth ran away with me. He laughed at every stupid thing I said and didn't give a damn about my tee haitches or my brogue. I even sang a bit of a rebel song and he grinned indulgently without a trace of embarrassment.

The next thing I remember is waking up naked on a

floor in Turnpike Lane with Mathew naked beside me, our modesty preserved by an old velvet curtain. I sat up, searched for my clothes and found them, all except my knickers. Knickerless and hung-over, I got dressed and was about to leave when Mathew woke up and said something funny which made me laugh. He urged me to quieten down:

"Sssshhh . . . or we'll wake Jason," he whispered.

"Who's Jason?" I asked.

"My son."

"What?! Are you married? Is this your home?" I really wished I'd found the knickers.

"No. Yes . . . I mean . . . no. Jason lives here with his Mum. I gave her the house when we split up. I just crash here sometimes."

We met again a few days later in a bar in the West End. He had my knickers. We both laughed as he handed them over. He had a tablet with his beer and I thought he had a headache. The pupils of his blue eyes were as tiny as pin pricks. We walked up Tottenham Court Road and he seemed to know a lot of people. What a popular man, I thought, as we turned left and went to a little Italian restaurant in Soho. When he told me about his heroin addiction he never used the word junkie. He hated it. It wasn't how he saw himself. Junkie meant hopeless druggie, whereas he was an antiques dealer and prided himself on his appearance. He shined his shoes every morning and always had a good haircut. He undid his shirtsleeve and showed me his arm. No tracks, but a strange little hole near his elbow. He assured me he didn't do heroin anymore, just the methadone that he got on prescription:

ampules and needles for a weekly fix and the linctus that was his mainstay. Out of curiosity, I had a swig of the thick green liquid, which made me feel sick.

He told me about his antiques – the things that he found and sold to accommodating dealers. By "found" I mean that he scoured the streets for old houses that were abandoned or boarded up and broke in when it was dark to see what was left. Victoriana, particularly, was at a premium since Londoners had woken up to the wanton destruction of the modernist 1960s.

We moved in together and when he went out at night, all in black, he was like a cat, deft and quiet. He never got caught. He'd come home in the early morning, smelling of the night air and, bubbling with excitement, spill his haul – door handles, light fittings, decorative tiles, oil lamps, old rugs and much more – onto the bed. He knew his stuff and occasionally turned up something really special. Three things come to mind: a Louis XVI marquetry table that someone had painted blue; a seventeenth-century apothecary's jar, broken and glued together with Evostick; and a rare Afghan rug with a hole in the middle – things the house clearance men had missed or didn't want. I didn't think of Mathew as a thief – he was just picking up old things in empty houses. If anything he was rescuing them and I listened with rapt attention to the stories he told of the strange things he'd seen – like the ghostly old man in the nightcap who came out of a bedroom as Mathew took the stairs three at a time in an effort to get away, or the four-poster bed with the watches and clocks nailed all over it.

I wanted to join him in this free-wheeling lifestyle so I gave up my teaching job and started going out with him at night. He told me to wear dark clothing and soft shoes and to walk on the balls of my feet. The best nights were moonless because it was dark, and windy because the wind muffled noise. It was thrilling. I imagined various contexts: I was a child in an Enid Blyton adventure, other times I was a special agent on a secret mission with the SAS, or I was a sleek black panther padding silently through the sleeping city. Old windows gave easily. A small crack and we were in. I wasn't afraid because I liked the dark and trusted Mathew utterly. We felt our way around in inky blackness, reading the walls like Braille, feeling for any bits of Victoriana, torches only when necessary, our footsteps echoing in the cavernous empty rooms.

Most Fridays we went to the West End where he sold half his ampules to junkies in Tottenham Court Road. Transactions happened so fast I hardly noticed and when they were done we went to Selfridges in Oxford Street where I bought coffee and cakes and he had a fix in the toilets.

We were happy with our nocturnal life but then the winter came and everything changed. There was a dearth of antiques and I wasn't working so we were always short of money. The weather depressed me and I started nipping at his methadone. One day he noticed and went mad:

"WHAT THE FUCK'VE YOU BEEN DOING?" he shouted, his eyes wide in disbelief at how much was missing. He got his big hands around my throat and, squeezing hard, he threatened:

"DON'T YOU EVER TOUCH MY GEAR AGAIN OR I'LL FUCKING KILL YOU! D'YOU HEAR ME?"

I nodded but it wasn't enough.

"D'YOU HEAR ME?" he shouted again. I nodded vigorously and he let me go. My throat hurt for days and from then on we sat at opposite ends of our little room, wishing the other one would go out for the day and come back with some money. I thought it should be him and he thought it should be me but neither of us did it. Then he started staying out all night and one day I felt so alone and frightened that I used my giro to get the ferry back home.

I went straight to my mother's. It was morning when I arrived and I was exhausted by the long journey from London. My mother's first question was always the same: how long I was staying? I assured her it wouldn't be long, went up to the Big Room and fell asleep. An hour later, I woke in a panic. Oh Jesus! I was sweating. The bed was too hot. The Cathedral bells, just down the road, started booming out the hour. One o'clock. Dinnertime. My mother was downstairs getting a stew out of the oven for herself and Joseph. I could hear them chatting. I felt like a ghost. A presence that they were unaware of, that didn't belong. The bells tolled. BOOM for guilt. BOOM for failure. BOOM for not belonging.

I shot out of the bed, my chest heaving in the grip of an anxiety that I couldn't name. All I knew was that I had to get away again. It was a mistake coming back here. I didn't belong. I had to get back to Mathew in London. That's where I belonged now. What would he do without me? He'd be missing me and I hadn't even left a note. I left that evening, making some excuse that I can't remember.

Back in London, I found Mathew asleep, an empty syringe by the bed. I watched him as he snored softly. Look at him, I thought angrily, off in some junkie's paradise. Why couldn't he go out on the prowl, like he used to? Coming back bright-eyed and loaded down with lovely old things that we could sell. I could go with him; we'd be happy again. But the balance in him had changed, weighted now in favour of the junkie and not the antiques man. I didn't understand why. I looked for the methadone bottle but he'd hidden it.

When he woke up he was glad to see me but I'd hardly say he'd missed me. He was incredulous when I said I'd been over and back to Cork since I'd last seen him. I made us a cup of coffee and he said he had a plan. We'd quit the room, doss on some floor and come back for the housing benefit cheques. Why, of course! What a good idea! Why hadn't I thought of it? I commended him on his inventiveness and we moved out the next morning.

The following Monday, giro day, we duly knocked on the front door and it was opened by the old lady who lived on the ground floor. Mathew was spick-and-span and at his most charming:

"Good morning, Mrs Bottomley, and how are you? Well, I hope. Could I possibly check the hall stand for some post?"

"You can check but it's not there," said Mrs Bottomley flatly.

"What's not there?" asked Mathew, the charm leaking from his voice.

"The giro. That's what you're after, isn't it? I sent it back because you don't live here any more," she gloated.

We were stunned by her interference and what it meant to our circumstances, but Mathew recovered quickly. "Do you mean to say," he began in a low, measured tone, "that my personal correspondence . . . has been intercepted . . . by a little SACK OF SHIT like you?"

She went to close the door but he held it open and roared:

"Do you mean to say that you've been STICKING YOUR FUCKING NOSE IN *MY* BUSINESS?!"

Mrs Bottomley, appalled by his language, found extra strength and managed to close the door, which Mathew kicked repeatedly. Then we stood outside, homeless and penniless. Eventually, we walked away and just kept going, in the direction of the West End. We arrived in Hyde Park at midday and I fell down on the grass and went to sleep. Mathew read the paper.

I woke up with my ear to the ground and felt the dull roar of the traffic on Bayswater Road and Park Lane. The grass had made a red grooved impression on my face and I had dribble on my cheek. Oh, how different Hyde Park seemed now from when I'd dreamt of it back in Cork.

When evening drew in we started walking again, northwards this time, through Camden, Harringay and Southgate. When we were tired, we looked for somewhere to sleep. Mathew noticed an empty house on the North Circular Road. We went round the back and the moon shone down on luminous white flowers and apple trees. The back door opened with a push and inside there was a most wonderful smell – clean and fresh like warm, dry laundry; and a thick carpet underfoot that I'd gladly have slept on. Feeling our way upstairs, we found a bed, collapsed onto it without a word and slept until morning.

In the daylight we saw that we were in an old lady's bedroom. There were plastic flowers and rosy wallpaper, rouge and talc on a dressing table. We left as soon as we woke up. On the way out I noticed a parcel on the kitchen table. It was heavy and had a label which read: *Enfield Crematorium* and *Mrs Elizabeth Goodison*. The package was dated July 1985 and it was now October 1986.

We spent another night in Mrs Goodison's house but the following evening the curtains looked different and we couldn't go back. Damn it! We both wanted her big, soft bed more than anything else in the world. Further along the road we found another empty house but this time we slept on bare floorboards. Mathew couldn't afford a fix and he was in withdrawal. He moaned all night about the pain in his hands:

"Oh my hands! Oh my fucking hands! Oh dear Jesus, my fucking hands!" Early the next morning he borrowed some money and went to the West End. When he came back, he'd had some gear and he was himself again.

We couldn't go on like that, with nowhere to live, so we went to the DSS in Wood Green, who found us a room in a hotel in Highbury and it was there that I had one of the worst experiences of my life. It started as an argument, the course of which I don't recall until I called Mathew a junkie at the top of my voice, knowing that he hated it and that the walls were paper thin:

"JUNKIE! JUNKIE! JUNKIE!" I screamed, as loud as I could.

I knew I'd gone too far when I saw the murderous look on his face. As I backed away, apologising, hoping to get to the door, he growled:

"FUCKING BITCH!"

He lunged, getting his hands around my neck and squeezing.

"FUCKING BITCH! . . . FUCKING BITCH! . . . FUCKING BITCH!" he snarled, slowly and deliberately.

With each expletive he tightened his grip and I was terrified that he was going to kill me. When I was almost blacking out, with my tongue swelling and my arms flailing, he let go. But it wasn't over because then he grabbed my hair tight enough to pull it out and yanked my head back. I tried to pull away but it was like trying to get out of a vice.

"DON'T YOU EVER CALL ME THAT AGAIN, YOU FUCKING CUNT!" he roared into my ear.

My head hurt so much I was begging him to let go, but he was impervious to my cries. He dragged me across to the wash basin and got my nail varnish remover. Then he dragged me back to the bed where he clamped the bottle between his knees and opened it.

"Don't you ever call me that again!" he whispered into my ear and, yanking my head right back, he splashed the solvent liberally into my eyes.

"YOU'RE NOTHING! D'you hear me?" he shouted. "You're NOTHING!"

"STOP IT! STOP IT! I CAN'T SEE!!! OH GOD, I CAN'T SEE!"

Oh dear God Almighty, I'd gone too far and now I was blind! All I could see was a greyish-pink blur. I wanted to close my eyes so he couldn't put any more in but I was afraid if I did, I'd make it worse. I needed water to splash my eyes. I had to get to water and with such urgency that a fierce energy rose in me which was greater than his. Hardly feeling the pain of the ripping hair I jerked my head free of his grip, all the while blinking furiously, trying to dispel the solution. Now that I was free I made for the door and shot this at him as I went through it:

"YES, I'M NOTHING, YOU STUPID FUCKING BASTARD BUT AT LEAST I'M NOT A JUNKIE LIKE YOU!"

I sprinted to a bathroom along the corridor, locked myself in and splashed my eyes for all I was worth until my sight was restored, him banging and kicking furiously at the door and shouting obscenities. The receptionist arrived and threatened to evict us. We promised to stop but I stayed in the bathroom for well over an hour until I was sure Mathew had calmed right down. While I waited I thought bitterly about what he'd said. At long last, someone had said it. It was out in the open. YES! YES! YES! You're right, Mathew, I'm nothing. Why has it taken you so long to say it, you stupid bastard?

Now that we'd crossed the Rubicon, it happened again. The next time, he smashed me in the face as we were driving along. One eye on the road and one hand on the steering wheel, he whacked his fist into my mouth, which split my lip and made it bleed profusely. I screamed at him to stop the car and jumped out. He drove on but doubled back. When I saw him I darted between some houses and ran away. Once, on the street, he placed a fat roll of banknotes on a window sill, all the better to take a swing at me, and forgot about them. Another time, he locked us both in a room and threatened to set light to a can of petrol. I thought, being a junkie, he might well do it, so I got down on my knees and begged him to let me go.

Ironically it was Mathew who left me. He met another girl and moved on. I was lucky too and good things found me. Like 21 Toulouse Avenue. It wasn't another room but a lovely little council house, warm and light, with wooden floors and white walls. I didn't have to pay rent but it was due for redevelopment and I knew that eventually I'd have to move on. But for now it was mine and I lived there alone.

I was on my own for the first time in years. There was no one to kick me or punch me or call me names. I got a little black kitten and peace seeped up through the fear of being by myself. I was blessed with a sort of solitary happiness and I definitely didn't want to see any more violence. I'd seen enough.

Art came back to me. I went to classes at the City of London Poly where I had a wonderful teacher who said he couldn't teach me anything. He invited me to his home in Wales and while I was there, I was struck by the purity of the air, the blackness of the night and the brilliance of the stars in the sky, things I'd forgotten, living under the grey-orange sky dome of London. He was concerned for me and wanted me to stay in the nurturing countryside, to put down roots and make a better life for myself. But I had no roots to put down in Wales. I was bored and lonely there, standing on the periphery of his family life, inadvertently excluded. Before long I was back in the Smoke.

A new man came along. He was called Samuel. He had a handsome gypsy face with velvet brown eyes and when he turned the charm on, I was putty in his hands. One day in the pub, with all his mates listening, he asked me to help a friend of his, a young artist whose girlfriend was pregnant. They were scraping the money together for an abortion and had nothing left over for food. He had a credit card and if I'd just go to the supermarket and get some stuff with it, it'd help them a lot.

"But how can I use your credit card?" I asked.

"It's not mine," he explained.

I looked at the card for the first time. It had a woman's name on it. Danielle Brewer.

"But that's not me." There were titters all around.

"Yes, I know," he said evenly. "You're going to *pretend* to be her."

I stared at the card, finally realising what he wanted me to do. I felt hot and queasy. I'd never done anything illegal before. Yes, I'd smoked pot and broken into old houses, but that didn't count. This was fraud. All his friends were watching me. If I went ahead, they'd be *my* friends too. I'd belong. If I didn't, he'd dump me. It was as simple as that.

Sensing my reluctance, he pressed on: "Don't worry sweetheart, Danielle won't lose much. After the first fifty quid, the bank picks up the tab."

The way he said "sweetheart" made my heart melt. He kissed me and squeezed me tight.

"I'll be waiting outside. If it comes on top, I'll put my hands up to it. All right?"

"All right."

There were sounds of approval. Someone bought me a drink. I practised Danielle's signature a few times and off we went.

At the supermarket door I stopped and his face fell.

"What's wrong?"

"Where's the shopping list?"

"There isn't one. Just get plenty of booze . . . vodka, whiskey and brandy . . . and . . . I dunno . . . some bread and milk, I suppose."

I went in. With a racing heart, I got exactly what he said and went up to the till. When the items were totted up, I packed them and proffered the card. It went through and the cashier produced a slip for me to sign. I signed and she filed it away with hardly a glance. I picked up the carrier bags and left the shop. Samuel was beaming at me, giving me two thumbs up. What a gal!

We crossed the road to the gang and cracked open the bottle of vodka to celebrate. What cheek I had, nicking it and drinking it right across the street. I was on top of the world, the girl of the moment. The bottle went round and spirits were high. The one with the pregnant girlfriend was laughing loudest of all.

On the strength of my success, Samuel and I used the card again in two off-licences and a restaurant, where we got caught. He was telling me how beautiful I was when the waiter approached and said the card was stolen.

They'd already phoned the police. We were taken to Tottenham Police Station where I spent the night in a cold, dirty cell that reeked of urine.

I didn't sleep but spent the night thinking about how stupid I'd been and worrying about what would happen next. Would I go to jail? I'd been finger-printed. Oh, the shame of it! I met Samuel outside the next morning – not the dashing gypsy now, more like a miserable little boy. We were both clutching pieces of paper with court dates on them. He trailed after me to the bus-stop, wanting to come home with me, but I told him to go away.

He did *put his hands up to it* and it was clear to the authorities that I was just a silly girl in thrall to a handsome rogue. The judge gave me a probation order and I had to see a probation officer once a week for six months. He was a kind man and we talked about art and books. When I told him about my childhood, he said I should get some therapy.

But what did I need with therapy when I found my solace in public houses? One night I met Oliver in a pub in Finsbury Park. He was wandering around in a long black coat and work boots, his hair stiff with cement and brick dust. He had a swagger about him and I caught his eye. He bought me a drink.

He said he was Canadian but actually he was Northern Irish and went to live in Canada when he was a child. He spoke so poetically about that country that I could almost smell the pine trees and taste the snow. He told me that he had a plot of land in the Rocky Mountains and some day he was going to build a cabin on it. He knew how to survive in the wild, scare off grizzly bears and pluck fish out of streams with his hands. All that was missing was the right woman. As I listened, I was enthralled by the images he conjured up and I saw myself there, living a romantic life far from civilisation.

In my rapture, I blurted out: "Oh Oliver, that'd be wonderful! That's exactly how I want to live!"

I got this in response: "Hey hey, whoa! . . . no bitch is hitching a ride to the Rockies on my back! Let's just wait and see what happens, shall we?"

I was stung by his coarseness but couldn't shift the image of us together in a cabin in the Rocky Mountains. What a horizon this was! We arranged a date for the following evening and I arrived at the appointed place and time, excited and looking my best, only to find him drunk and in his working clothes.

The first thing he said was: "You'll have to take me as you find me because I'm too fucking tired to put on a show."

That was okay. I didn't expect a show. Ignoring his crudeness, I pulled up a barstool and sat down beside him. He didn't buy me a drink so I bought my own. He was looking at me blearily and then he beckoned me closer with his finger.

I leant in close to him and he whispered, "Cora, can you answer me something?"

"Yes. What is it?"

But he kept it going. "No, no. Come closer."

And I did so until our heads were touching. "What?" I was really curious now.

"Are *you* really a woman?" he hissed, not a Canadian

ranger now, but a mean Ulster peasant. "Did ja hear me?
Are ya *really* a woman?"

I was riveted to the stool with shame. I couldn't even
lift my eyes from the counter. I was aware of the door and
how it would take just a few strides to be out of there and
away from him, but I didn't move. Any other woman
wouldn't have been seen dead with him but shame didn't
affect me like other people. For me, it wasn't a reason to
get up and walk away. His ugly black heart resonated
with my own sense of badness and I was hooked.

"Yes," I replied, with a meekness that was absurd.

His evil whispering continued: "Are ya sure? Did ja
hear me? Are ya sure?"

"What do you mean?" I asked tightly, forcing myself
to look him in the eye.

He was indignant at my countering, angry even.
"Sure, ya *look* like a man, that's what! Where're yer tits?
Look at ja! Ya haven't *got* any!" And then his *coup de
grace*: "From the side you look like a man!"

I remained on my barstool as I lurched downwards,
unable to let go of that dream of the good man in the
mountains. Sooner or later he'd say something nice. I'd
stamp down on my hurt and wait for that. In the
meantime, he talked about himself and his family, his
language and tone now respectful. His sisters were all in
Canada, both brothers were in England and he was the
youngest. The parents were dead. They'd owned a farm
in South Armagh but that place had been sold long ago.
He soon became self-pitying. He didn't feel at home
anywhere. When he was in Canada, he longed for
England and when he was in England he longed for

Ireland. But he never went back there, now that the farm was gone.

We left the pub and walked along Blackstock Road to the bus-stop. He was coming back to my place. Suddenly, without warning, he broke away from me and shouted: "WATCH THIS!" With that he dived out into the roaring traffic. I screamed and there was screeching of brakes and honking of horns as he dodged among the cars, laughing his head off and banging on car bonnets. I should have melted into the crowd and disappeared, but I didn't. When he got to the other side of the road, he beamed back at me, so pleased was he with his prank.

We got on the bus and went upstairs where he fell asleep on my shoulder. I felt sorry for him with his thick, calloused hands and his hair matted with cement, working so hard that he was asleep by ten o'clock. I was drunk so I kissed him on the head as a mother might kiss a child. He elected to sleep on my sofa that night, in homage to his old-fashioned morals.

I woke up in the early morning and remembered his words. *Are you sure you're a woman? . . . No tits . . . You look like a man from the side*. I looked at myself in the mirror, wanting desperately to see the femininity that I'd always seen and not the masculinity that he saw. I craned around to see my profile. Did I look like a man from the side? I looked down at my breasts. They were small but they *were* there.

He was on the stairs with a cup of tea. Quickly, I hid the mirror. He was meek, remembering nothing about the night before, apologising but not knowing what he was apologising for. We arranged a date for the Friday night but even I had my limits and I didn't turn up. I didn't think he'd find his way back to my house but he did and a few weeks later, I was pregnant.

I couldn't take it in at first. I had a shocked, unreal feeling as I looked at the pregnancy test. We'd only had sex once. I knew in my heart that this time there'd be no abortion. I was sure of that. My sisters had started having babies and I wanted one too. I needed a baby. I needed love so badly and in my life I'd found so little that I decided to make it myself.

I stared at the little blue line and the magnitude of the situation hit me. In a few months' time I'd have a baby to take care of. This would be a child, my child, and he or she would be completely dependent on me. If I won, he'd win but if I lost he'd lose. For the first time in my life I had a sense of purpose. I had something to fight for.

My family were happy for me, albeit in a qualified sense. I was unmarried, after all, and there was no sign of the father. I'd be on my own with the baby but that didn't bother me. I didn't think I was doing anything wrong. I didn't see fathers as good but bad. My father was and I felt sure that Oliver would be too. I saw my baby's fatherless status as a plus. My mother said the baby would be a bit of company for me. I laughed at this quirky announcement. How right she was! My baby *would* be company for me. I'd never really be alone again. From now on there'd be two of us and we'd be bound together with the strongest ties of all – those between mother and child. This realisation astounded me. It was a sort of epiphany. It changed everything. My aloneness was gone with *two of us.* I repeated it. Two of us. Two of us. Two of us. I'd never be alone again.

I didn't tell Oliver I was pregnant even when he came round one evening, all cleaned up, and asked me to go to Canada with him. I politely declined. He eyed me suspiciously, not understanding this new reserve and in spite of himself his coarseness broke loose.

"Well . . . aren't you the smug slut?!" he began, about to launch into a bitter tirade about the ingratitude of women, but I cut him off:

"NO!" I shouted, my voice reverberating around the room, "I'M *NOT* SMUG AND I'M *NOT* A SLUT!"

Silence followed, during which he sized me up again. I had to get him out of the house or I was going to blurt my news out, so I suggested going for a drink. We went to a small pub in Wood Green and on the way he did his traffic-stopping thing again. More horns and screeching brakes and when he reached the central reservation, another triumphant smirk. He had a pint of Guinness and I had an orange juice. He was getting back to the subject of smug sluts when I surprised him by banging my glass down hard on the table and getting up to go. I'd got him out of the house. Mission accomplished. In a voice cold enough to freeze hell over, I told him not to come round again and he didn't.

I had a wonderful pregnancy in the spring and summer of 1989 and I was so happy. I still had my little house in Wood Green and I spent my time getting it ready for the baby. I foraged among the charity shops and car boot sales for all the things I needed and got a cot, a pushchair, a sling, a changing mat, babygrows, blankets and lots of other bits and pieces. I ordered coal and got a big rug for the floor boards.

As I busied myself, I talked to my baby, tiny still. I caressed my bump as it grew and ate the best food I could afford. I attended the North Middlesex Hospital in Edmonton for the ante-natal check-ups and I was fine, a strong healthy female with a perfect foetus. Now that I'd allowed myself to have love, I was in heaven and my happiness was undisturbed – except for one awful incident.

One day, when I was seven months pregnant, I joined a bus queue where a group of teenage boys and girls were mock-fighting and shrieking with laughter. One of them, a big black boy, pushed me and I lost my footing. I protested but, hardly missing a beat, he shouted at me to fuck off.

I countered: "No, I won't f- off." I'd stopped swearing for the sake of the baby. "How *dare* you speak to me like that!"

With his face inches from mine, he snarled, "I said FUCK OFF or I'll PUNCH YOUR FUCKING FACE IN!"

Confident that he wouldn't hit a hugely pregnant woman I had another go. "DON'T speak to me like that!"

The next thing I knew – BANG – a big man-sized fist ploughed into my right cheek. I reeled as my brain wobbled with the impact. A woman screamed, "God Almighty!" and the queue went quiet, not quite believing what they'd seen; a taboo broken in their midst. I staggered backwards to stop myself from falling, trying to catch up with what had happened. I was stunned and disbelieving but I could see him now, his angry face swearing at me and threatening me and the fist coming at me way too fast to avoid it.

Chaos filled the vacuum of my disbelief. Somehow my purse was gone, my hat was on the ground and one of my shoes had fallen off. The bus driver wouldn't let me on without the fare, although he'd seen everything. He pulled away from the kerb with his grey impassive face. The screaming woman was on the top deck shouting at me through the window: "Call the police! Call the police!"

The boy-man was long gone and I was alone at the side of the road. Picking up my hat and putting my shoe back on, I searched around frantically for my purse but I couldn't find it, so I started the long walk home. I started crying and was just unable to stop. I was hysterical and couldn't contain the huge sobs that broke out of me.

Then I started to have strange cramps all around my bump. Dear Jesus, I thought, is there something wrong with the baby? Maybe my distress was going to make me miscarry. Oh God, please don't let that happen! I saw a bench, eased myself down and made a huge effort to calm myself, breathing deeply like I'd been shown in the antenatal class. I could feel a swelling under my eye and I longed to get home.

After a while the pains stopped and I started walking again. The walking soothed me somewhat. It was all right. I was fine and the baby was fine. I was sure of it. I just needed to get indoors where I wouldn't be gaped at. Passers-by were staring at me. To be fair I must have looked a sight. Seven months pregnant in a long purple dress, obviously distressed with a rising black eye. Plenty of people looked but no-one stopped to help. I suppose a crying pregnant woman with a swollen face just spells trouble.

I finally reached Toulouse Avenue, went in, locked the door and rang the police. A police constable came and we had a cup of tea together. She took a description of my attacker – young, black, with big fists. He had a sort of spiral design shaved into his head and I thought they'd be able to find him with that but she didn't hold out much hope. Like looking for a needle in a haystack, she said.

I went into labour on the morning of September 20th 1989. It was a glorious autumn day. The pain started innocently enough – a bit like being prodded with a steak knife, whereas by midday it was like being impaled on one. I was out of my mind with agony and screaming for an epidural. Literally screaming. The maternity staff were overstretched and I felt that asking politely would not get me what I needed. The pain was blurring my vision, driving me out to the edge of reason and I screamed every time I had a contraction. I heard contemptuous whispers about a low pain threshold. It went on for so long that the nurse on duty, an Irishwoman, lost her temper, shoved me into a wheelchair and took me down to the delivery room, which was blacked out and empty.

"Ha! There you are!" she announced triumphantly. "You wanted to get down here for your epidural and there's no-one ta give it ta ya!"

With that she turned on her heel and left me there alone to clamber onto the solitary gurney in the gathering dusk. I had no one with me, but there was a phone number at the bottom of my bag. It belonged to Alexandra, a girl from Argentina whom I'd recently met at the art school. I rang it between contractions and, bless her, she came and stayed with me for the rest of the labour. Then a wonderful West Indian midwife called Christine appeared and soon after that I got my epidural.

Jack was in no hurry to be born and eventually made his appearance at five past midnight on September 21st. Christine raised him up in her big black hands and as she did so everything seemed to stop. I could hear and see nothing but my baby. What I remember most from the moment of his birth are his eyes. I thought babies' eyes were screwed up closed when they were born but Jack's eyes were wide open as he scanned the room in an elemental need to find me.

Christine's voice came back in, rejoicing at his arrival with these words: "Welcome to the world, little man!"

He must have cried but I've forgotten. She weighed him, whooped at his size, 9lbs 10oz, and plopped him onto my stomach. He looked stranded there, all wet and slimy with mucus, like a little sea creature with the tide gone out. I picked him up and cuddled him into my chest. I felt I knew him already from talking to him in the womb and feeling his kicks and now I couldn't take my eyes off him. Later, back on the ward, I watched him constantly. I couldn't quite believe he was mine.

When I'd discovered I was pregnant, I'd wondered how I'd feel when I gave birth. I hadn't known what to expect. I knew that mothers loved their babies but I'd also heard of mothers who had suffered post-natal depression and rejected them. I thought of one woman I'd heard of who kept putting her baby in the dustbin and had to be hospitalised. Also, I'd had two abortions. I wasn't sure of my maternal instincts or if I'd have good parenting skills. What would I do if it was a boy, considering how I felt about men? I had one hundred and one doubts but now that he was here, a feeling rushed through me which swept all that aside. I was stunned and overjoyed.

Alexandra went home so I could rest but I watched him instead of sleeping. He was like an angel, serene and beautiful, all cleaned up now and cosy in his blankets. Even when he was hungry he didn't screech like the other babies. His voice was deep and resonant and when I put him to the breast he sucked and got milk straight away. I loved being a mother from the very start. My bond with Jack was immediate and magnetic. I actually felt myself physically pulled towards him, as if the umbilical cord was still there and he was tugging on it. He was flesh of my flesh, for whom I'd move mountains if need be. It was the power of love. Romance was nothing compared to this. Although my life had conspired to starve me of it, at long last I knew what love felt like and I felt it deeply. Love had come, even to me, and come to stay. I didn't venture far with him once I got him home. My favourite things were to have him in bed beside me where I could gaze at him, or downstairs in the evenings with the fire lit. I preferred to take him out in a sling but it hurt my back so I started using the buggy.

One Saturday in October when I was wheeling Jack down Wood Green High Road, on my way to Sainsbury's, two black men were walking down the hill behind me. As they passed, the air was filled with beer fumes and one of them shouted at me: "WATCH IT OR I'LL KICK YOUR FUCKING PRAM OVER!"

I jumped. What was it? What about the buggy? I looked at the one who'd shouted and he was glaring at me, his face twisted with hatred. I didn't know what he was talking about. Up to that point I'd thought I was alone on the street. It seems that the path of the buggy was veering slightly in their direction and he was blaming me in advance for the accident he might have had. I dreaded to think what he'd have done if the buggy had in fact tripped him up and he'd fallen. I tacked off double quick in the opposite direction.

As with the bus stop incident, I struggled to shut this ugly experience out of my mind. The punch to my face was like a phantom wound. I still felt it. It was the random violence that got me: the threat to my baby in the contractions I'd felt that day; and now the vision of the buggy, with Jack inside it, being kicked aside like so much rubbish.

When Jack was six weeks old, I got a phone call from Arthur. I was stunned to hear from him and my instinct was to ask him how he'd got my phone number. He'd rung my mother and she'd given it to him. She could have asked me first. It seemed like a lifetime since the days in Birmingham and Hereford and we recounted the changes. He wasn't on the dole any more. He was working as a lab technician in his home town, living in the house he grew up in. We chatted about various things – Simon, London, Cork – and then I told him I had a baby.

"Oh. Is the father around?"

"No."

"Oh."

Why the second "Oh"? What was he thinking? He was always thinking something. Did he think I was bad for having Jack on my own? I told him I'd fallen out of love with London and he invited me to go and stay with him. I didn't need to think about it. I'd just had notice to quit from the council so I accepted unreservedly. He came up to collect us and I gasped inwardly at how much he'd changed in the few years since I'd last seen him. He looked so thin and old. No longer the wolf-man who'd taken my breath away. The eyes that had mesmerised me were feverish and shadowed. He'd lost most of his hair and his pate and high-domed forehead shone greasily like some strange helmet.

It was a long drive to his home town and he questioned me on the way: Had giving birth changed me? Had it changed my attitude to men? The same old Arthur – always probing beneath the surface. Yes to both but it was hard to articulate those changes. I couldn't find the words to describe the tenderness that came over me when I looked at Jack's little penis and started to discover the vulnerability of manhood.

When we arrived, night had fallen. He pulled up outside a little semi and, wrapping Jack up warmly, I got out. The air was smoky and there was a clanging and banging way off in the darkness and the whoosh of a giant chimney stack as it flared up in the night sky.

"What's that?" I asked as Arthur was putting his key in the door.

"The foundry."

My father, with his sweaty vests and chronic resentment, flashed through my mind. The hallway had the desolate smell of stale cigarette smoke and a naked bulb shed a yellow, waxy light.

"I'm done in, Arthur," I said in a voice made small by tiredness, "where can we sleep?"

He took me up to a little bedroom which was piled high with cardboard boxes and other bits of storage. There was a bed with no legs propped against the wall and a fireplace full of rubbish. I had Jack in my arms and I nearly crumpled on the floor with exhaustion. Why wasn't the bed made up? Of course, I thought, blushing. He assumed we'd be sleeping in with him, like an instant family, but the thought hadn't even entered my head. He went in search of the legs and I looked out the window at the smelting plant, lit up like a Christmas tree, right at the end of the garden. He read my face accurately when he came back because he turned his intense eyes on me said, "Don't bolt, Cora."

The next morning dawned clear and blue. I went downstairs, unlocked the back door and went out. There was a sharp breeze. The hot summer was cooling down for autumn. It was quiet now and the air was clean. I gazed up at the blue sky and it gladdened my heart. Maybe it wouldn't be so bad down here after all. I went round to the front of the house. There was a small park across the road, more houses and then a hill that rose up steeply, covered in gorse and neatly planted fir trees. I went back inside and my spirits dropped. It was that smell again, stale cigarettes – the scent of my father. Arthur's family had all smoked and they'd been doing it in that little house for years and years. I went into the back room. Tobacco yellow. There was Arthur's precious Bang and Olufsen stereo and a slimmed-down collection of albums. The furniture was modern, all smooth and plastic but tired, bought by his father in the sixties with the confidence of a man who had a job for life at the foundry.

Finally Arthur got up and we had coffee and cigarettes. I asked about his parents. His father was dead and he told me matter-of-factly that he'd forced his mother out by booby-trapping the house. The bedroom I'd slept in, for example, was full of cardboard boxes so she couldn't get at the immersion switch in the corner. He showed me the front room. It was piled high with household goods still in their packaging: kettles, toasters, foot spas, digital clocks, electric razors, hair dryers and much more. There was a gas fire but you couldn't see it for all the boxes. She'd never have settled in there. He said he'd collected it all with me in mind, hoping that one day we'd be together. I started to sweat. He didn't know I'd had a second abortion yet. Remembering his reaction to the first one, I decided not to tell him.

I put on a wash and he told me I'd have to wipe the soot off the line before I put my clothes out. Then I fed and changed Jack and we went to look around the town. It was a drab place with the foundry at one end and an oil refinery at the other. There was a beach where slack washed up in long drifts and fog was always rolling in. My heart sank. After our tour, Arthur stopped at a supermarket and parked in front of a high stone wall. I stayed in the car while he went in.

In his absence I groaned deeply and felt grim. Life was

just like that wall – cold and hard, something to get round or over somehow. I didn't like this town at all. But what choice did I have? At least I was out of London. I felt homesick and thought about my beloved Cork, overlooking the loneliness I'd felt there. Coincidentally, I was facing west, so Cork was straight ahead. I stared through the stones and in my mind's eye I saw the corners I loved: the River Lee, the Mardyke, Shandon and Sunday's Well, every one of them a graceful place, not like this grimy, foggy hellhole. But if Cork was great why didn't I go back there? I thought about it but I was afraid on my own.

Arthur and I spent the evenings talking. With the insight of a woman and the instincts of a man he was still thrilling and slightly dangerous to engage with. When I'd been there a few weeks, he wanted to know why we weren't sleeping together. I didn't want to sleep with anyone apart from my baby. I told him I was sick of men and underlined my feelings by reminding him of all the beatings and the humiliation I'd received in London, but it only bored him. He found my story predictable. Of course a woman with a violent father would seek out violent men. What he wanted to know was how much longer it would take me to overcome my childhood. He couldn't wait forever. There were other girls.

"Oh? . . . Like who?"

"Sharon."

He hadn't had any trouble getting *her* into bed. He even taught her to enjoy oral sex but in the end he couldn't prise her away from her boyfriend.

"Was that when you rang me?"

"Yes."

"And all the stuff in the front parlour – was that for Sharon as well?"

"Yes . . . no . . . I mean, it's for my wife, whoever that might be. I've been driving around, by the sea mainly, looking for my princess."

"Your princess," I echoed.

"Yes," he said, smiling shyly.

"By the sea . . ." I trailed off, visualising him with a mermaid.

"Yes. The villages down there are beautiful."

"So you hadn't been saving it all for me."

"No."

"You lied to me!"

"Not really. You could be my wife. It's up to you but if you won't sleep with me, what am I supposed to think?"

"Give me time. I've just had a baby."

However, mention of this Sharon made me jealous and I moved into his room that night. I didn't want to – I'd come to live with Arthur as a friend but I should have known better. He could never just be friends with a woman. Later, in bed, he compared us: I was slimmer, she had pinker nipples. There was always a sexual element, whether it was with me or Sharon or whoever. Once, I'd seen him caressing the legs of a ten-year-old girl, while her drunken parents looked on impassively.

One night, the spotlight was on my sexual history. We were halfway through a bottle of cider when he said:

"Exactly how many partners have you had?"

204

"A few," I answered tentatively.

"How many?" he demanded.

"Quite a few . . . I suppose."

Looking at me in disgust, he repeated mockingly, "Quite–a–few–you–suppose." He took a drag on his cigarette: "HOW MANY?"

On trial, I blushed and started to sweat. My throat was dry. I felt like a worm wriggling on a stick. I gulped some cider for lubrication and, trembling with apprehension, I divulged name after name. The tally grew. When I hesitated he demanded that I go on. Finally, I found my anger and in a cold voice I shot at him: "You have no right to do this to me! I don't do it to you!"

But he just boomed back, "GO ON!"

"No! Why do you want to know anyway?"

"GO ON!" he ordered, like a hanging judge, pate shining, eyes burning.

"NO!!!"

Pointing at the ceiling, he glowered at me: "Calm down! You're upsetting your child."

Wearily, I climbed the stairs to check on Jack but he was asleep. I went back down with a heavy heart. Would he forgive me the sin of fornication, as he had done the sin of abortion all those years ago? If not, what would I do? Where would I go? I wished now that I hadn't left London. I could have dug my heels in when Toulouse Avenue went back to the council and they'd have been obliged to rehouse me. Downstairs, I found him cogitating on the data I'd provided but he hadn't finished so I lit a cigarette and waited for the verdict. Critical seconds passed. The clock ticked loudly and then he cracked a smile. Oh thank God! It was another yes! A thumbs-up! He was prepared to forgive me my past. What a blessed relief!

When Arthur was at work and Jack was asleep I sat in the back room and listened to the clanging and banging of the foundry. I wiped the line down before I put my washing out. I took Jack across the road to the little park or put him in the buggy and wheeled him into the centre of town just for something to do. It was patently obvious that any spark between Arthur and me had died. After all his efforts to get me into bed, he said that sleeping with me was like sleeping with his sister, so we stopped and he helped me to find a flat in the town. When I settled in there, I was happy again. It was just me and my baby and when I closed my door on the world I was peaceful and contented. I had gallons of breast milk – so much so that it used to spray out when Jack was feeding and sometimes his whole face would get showered in it and he'd laugh delightedly. I lived frugally on benefits and was so happy I even finished a set of pictures that I'd begun at the art school in London. I called them "My Home Town". Meanwhile, Arthur went back to scouring the seaside for his princess.

I went over to Cork in July 1990 and the circumstances of my visit were auspicious. With Rose's help, I'd secured an exhibition of "My Home Town" at the university and there was an artist-in-residence stint to go with it. Imagine: Cora Coleman – artist-in-residence. Arthur, who knew I pined for Ireland, thought I should stay there. I had the opportunity to go home and re-invent myself as an artist and he helped me plan it: stay with your mother until you get your own place, push forward with the art, get on local radio to promote the exhibition, get a piece in the local paper. It was so exciting that I was giddy with anticipation! A new and wonderful chapter in my life was about to open. I was going to take my beautiful son and my art, go back to Ireland and draw a line under my sordid past. As far as Arthur was concerned, it was a full stop. I was saying goodbye to England, intending never to return and he didn't expect me back.

He didn't reckon with my mother, however. As usual, she eyed my luggage suspiciously and, in a roundabout way, she checked my travel plans. Was it just the three weeks that we'd be staying? Would I be going back to England then?

"Eehh . . . yes."

She sensed the lie. Never mind, that could wait. In the meantime, I was driven. I divided myself in two – artist and mother. Apart from Jack, all my energy went into the exhibition and the residency. My pictures looked amazing in the huge gallery space. Huge yellow and black images against a white background. The piece for the residency was on the theme of emigration, and that would be semi-abstract, green and black, a mixture of oils and charcoal. I was bemused standing there drawing and getting paid for the privilege while students came and went, occasionally nudging each other about the one in the corner, drawing.

I took Jack with me some of the days. Other times Sarah or my old friend Ali from the factory looked after him. I did what Arthur said and got a promotional piece in the *Cork Examiner* – "Artist Returns Home" – and a slot on the radio. My mother didn't listen to it. Neighbours who did said she must be proud of me. She didn't want to see the exhibition either but she forced herself and one day before it ended my mother, Sarah and I caught the train to Cork, and she walked out to the university in belligerent silence, like a prisoner on the march to her execution. When she saw my pictures, Sarah was impressed. I think they were bigger and better than she'd expected. She praised me with genuine feeling but my mother was unmoved, said nothing but made it clear she was ready to go after five minutes.

When the three weeks ended and I asked her if we could stay, my mother's face turned ashen and the word that had been waiting in her guts for weeks finally had its moment: "NNNOOO!"

"Why not?" I asked plaintively, already feeling defeat. She wouldn't discuss it with me. Instead, she brushed past me and holed up in her bedroom until Sarah came home. I sat in the kitchen, stunned by her refusal, then I put Jack in his buggy and went out.

I sought out the back roads of Cobh and eventually came to White Bay. It was deserted so I sat on the old sea wall and listened to the water lapping on the shingle. The tide was going out. Maybe she just needed time to get used to the idea, I thought hopefully. There was plenty of room after all. Jack and I could have one room and Sarah and her baby could have another. I went back feeling better, positive that she'd got used to the idea and was ready to help me. But when I got back, it was worse. Sarah had returned and my mother had galvanised her against me.

NO, NO, NO, was all I heard.

"That poor child will be called a bastard!"

"Times have changed," I countered, although I was thinking more of England when I said this.

"What will you live on?"

"I'll manage."

"Where will you stay?"

"Here?"

"NO!"

I got Jack ready for bed and we stayed upstairs in Peter's room until the following morning. As soon as he woke, I fed and changed him and we left the house. It was early and there wasn't a sound except the birds and the clackety-clack of the buggy's wheels on the old roads. I avoided the town but, around lunchtime, I went to see a woman my mother knew with property to rent. She saw me coming. More no's. I wandered the island for another day or two and then came the show-down. I was in the kitchen, feeding Jack, when I was waylaid by an angry Sarah.

"Look, Cora, we have to talk about this," she began.

"I don't want to talk about it."

"Well, we *are* going to talk about it because it's upsetting Mammy!"

My mother had slipped in and was hiding behind her. I could see one guilty brown eye. Her presence fired Sarah up and, baring her teeth in a grimace, she shouted:

"YOU *CAN'T* STAY HERE! YOU *HAVE* TO GO BACK TO ENGLAND! JACK WILL BE CALLED A BASTARD IF YOU STAY HERE! IT'LL BE AWFUL FOR HIM!"

"You're not married. Won't your son be called a bastard?"

"THAT'S DIFFERENT!"

"How?"

"I'M with TONY!"

"Really? Where is he?"

"That's none of your business . . . we . . . we're getting back together soon."

We could have gone on like that for a good bit longer. I could have said Tony was a waster, not good father material. I could have run upstairs like a cornered rat and squatted in one of the bedrooms. I could have put up more of a fight but my mother's complete rejection of me – myself, my son and my artistic talent – took the steam out of me. No. Worse than that. It crushed me. I had no stomach for attacking Sarah, my youngest sister. She was only doing her mother's bidding, after all. I knew she felt guilty about my mother too. But I was puzzled. When I'd arrived she was welcoming, really glad that I wanted to stay and now the wind had changed and it seemed that she wouldn't rest until I was gone.

It was years before I unearthed my mother's skulduggery; how she'd sat Rose and Sarah down and told them – no, *warned* them – that they weren't to help me. She painted a pernicious picture of the damage it would do Jack if we stayed. I wasn't to be allowed to do it to him. Her Dickensian vision touched a nerve with my insecure sisters and their fears were made worse by me. They'd watched my downward spiral with bewilderment and apprehension: the wasted degree, the violent boyfriends, the two abortions, the broken nose, the criminal record (I think I even bragged about that and I can still see their unsettled faces as they shrank from me), and now a baby on my own. What next, they must have wondered, and with good cause.

Ironically, the self-destructive Cora that they feared was gone and I was on the brink of a new life. I'd stopped the juggernaut of self-harm and was emerging from my turbulent years as a mother and an artist. People outside the family were supportive. A carpenter offered to frame my pictures for nothing, an artist with a baby told me it could be done. She showed me a studio where I could paint and when I baulked at the difficulty she pushed me on with these words:

"You hold the baby with one hand and a paintbrush with the other."

Ali implored me not to run away, to hold tight, adopt a siege mentality and it'd all come good.

But my mother's rejection was too much. I couldn't brush it off and it knocked me back to the bottom of the ladder, into a hellish place. My own mother didn't want me. What did that tell you about me? My own mother was prepared to throw me out on the street along with my baby. She'd give shelter to one daughter with a baby but not another.

Why not? Why not me? WHY . . . NOT . . . ME? WHYYYY . . . NOT . . . MEEEE!!!??

There was plenty of room.

WHY NOT ME? Why did I have to go away? WHY? WHY? WHY?

She hated me, that was why. She couldn't have done it otherwise. I was Bad Cora again, trying to cling on where I wasn't wanted. She knew I was bad and she hated me for it. She hated me for the reproach that was implicit in my self-destructive history and my precarious circumstances. Bloody bitch, landing myself over here and causing trouble. Stupid fucking cunt!

Having a baby was proving to be a lot more difficult than I thought. My dreams of a new life was a tower of cards and it came tumbling down. I went to buy nappies one day and kicked them the last fifty yards to the house in frustration. Who did I think I was? I didn't deserve studios or paintings or exhibitions. Who was I kidding?

There was only one thing to do. I surrendered to my mother's rejection.

"All right. I'll go."

The relief was palpable. Tense, angry faces relaxed. We could all be friends again, now that was decided. No one enquired where I'd go or what I'd do. I was going and that was all that mattered. Hard as it'd be in England on my own, it'd be easier than this. I spent the rest of the time outdoors, with Jack in his buggy, staying on the country roads, avoiding people. I felt uncomfortable now in the house and I only went in at meal-times and to sleep.

Once, I came to the edge of the town and sat on a bench looking out at the orange sun setting on the harbour, its deep familiarity soothing my anxious mind. I didn't know what I was going to do. I had a contact in London, Clare, and I was going to her initially, but beyond that I didn't know what the future held for us. I didn't want to go back to Arthur. I could still see him pawing that child's legs and I recoiled from him. I looked at my Jack, plump and beautiful, asleep in his buggy, oblivious to our emergency. No matter what, I had to protect my child, but that wasn't going to be easy, with no money and no home. Nevertheless, despite my fears, grim determination filled my veins. I stared out at the dear old water and vowed, like a soldier on the eve of battle, that I'd fight for all I was worth and we'd survive.

This is what became of us:

A few days later, on a foggy evening, I went back to England on the ferry. I had a berth and when we went to bed, I dreamt vividly of my mother. She was smiling at me and begging me to forgive her, imploring me to come back. We reached London the next day. Clare was sympathetic but realistic. If I wanted to stay in London, I'd have to take my chances on the housing waiting list, and it was notoriously long. I didn't want to be in London any more. Not after the bus-stop assault and the buggy incident. The truth is, I didn't know what to do. I'd gone over to Cork on a wave of happiness and come back trembling with fear. My confidence in myself and in life was gone. I felt there was nothing behind me but a black hole and the way that made me feel was indescribably bad. It was a deep, terrifying feeling and I felt that the only person who'd understand it was Arthur, so I rang him. He listened in silence to what had happened with my mother and reckoned that if we kept coming back to each other, it was fate. We should start living together again and we'd just have to work through the lack of chemistry. I could have argued that a flat in the town, like before, would do. I just needed his help for a while but my mother's unequivocal rejection echoed balefully in my mind, reinforcing my sense of badness. I'd do whatever Arthur said. He knew best.

I caught the train with a heavy heart, knowing that sex was inevitable, a duty on both our parts, a prerequisite of our new departure. He met me at the station and we drove back to his house in silence. I put it off for as long as I could – a couple of weeks I think – but eventually he nudged me up the stairs and into his bedroom. Lying there cadaver-like with my eyes closed, he loomed over me and forced himself into me. I peeked at him briefly and he was grimacing, teeth-clenched, with effort. The vision made me snap my eyes shut and then he came with a series of long deep groans that made me cringe.

We went on like that for a couple of months, forcing ourselves into bed together. It was absurd and before long, I had morning sickness. Oh God no! Please God no! Don't let it be true! Please don't let me be pregnant! He didn't always wear a condom because he didn't like them. I wanted him to wear them but he always promised to pull out in time. I should have insisted. Why hadn't I insisted? I was afraid to. If I was difficult *he'd* throw us out too. If my mother could do it, anyone could. Then what would I do?

In spite of my fears, I should have been stronger and insisted on condoms. I knew he wanted a child. Not just a child, a daughter. It had to be a daughter. I got so sick every morning that I couldn't hide it from him. When I told him I was considering another abortion he banished me to the spare room, where I rocked back and forth in distress, nibbling dry biscuits in a vain attempt to stop the nausea.

I went to the local doctor for confirmation and, sure enough, I was pregnant. When I told Dr Ellis who the father was, his face fell and he implored me to have a termination and get away from Arthur. Shocked, I asked him to elaborate but he wouldn't say any more. Just that it'd be better for my son and me to leave him. Get out of the town altogether. I walked back home, my head reeling with dark imaginings. What the hell had he meant? It must be something awful for a doctor to talk about one of his patients like that. Arthur's sister-in-law wanted me to go as well. She whispered that she'd never left her children alone with him. Oh God. I imagined the future – me out at work, Jack at school, Arthur at home interfering with our child. I looked down at Jack's beautiful blond head as I wheeled him along and I imagined the tragedy of him growing up with an abused sister. And what if it was a boy? What then?

The atmosphere was terrible. I stayed out all day and spent the evenings in the front room with all the gadgets, trying to keep Jack quiet until bedtime. He was in the back room with the door shut out against me, playing loud rock. I didn't dare tell him to turn it down. When Jack was in bed, I went back to my rocking.

Then a little thing happened that moved me on. One day, after a terse shopping trip, we were unpacking groceries and Arthur was checking each item against the receipt, as was his custom. It didn't add up. The bill was thirty-five pence out and he wouldn't let it go. Although we'd just put everything away, we'd have to check it all again. Frantic about the thirty-five pence, he barked orders at me to take all the shopping out of the cupboards and put it on the floor for inspection. It was demented. Nervously, I slammed the fridge door shut and he snarled at me to be careful with his things. Sitting neatly on his heels like a long, thin woman, he checked everything again and again to find the missing thirty-five pence. I watched him – head-helmet shining, eyes flitting wildly from item to item, and I was trembling with fear, all for the sake of a few pence.

Suddenly, something deep inside me unlocked and I made a decision – I'd have to get away from this man. For good. We had a brief unhappy exchange.

He said sourly, "It appears I've made a mistake."

To which I replied, "Yes. A big one."

Now I was able to act. I went back to the doctor and he helped me to arrange the termination. After that I went to my former landlady and begged her for a room. Arthur had one last go at coaxing me into going ahead with the pregnancy but my resolve to end it was unshakeable. Before I left he was nasty and foul and his parting shot was about Jack. He condemned me for having him on my own, insisting that a child needs a father and if it wasn't going to be him, it'd better be Oliver. Guilt twisted my heart but I had to put it on hold.

The termination was a few days later. I got up at six o'clock one morning and stole over to the General Hospital on the first bus. Jack was about sixteen months old and I had to take him with me because there was no one I could leave him with. I had a room to myself and a nurse brought a cot in for him. I left Jack in the care of this nurse while I was away having the operation. I hoped he'd be all right. When I came back there was an empty feeding bottle beside him and he was asleep. I needed a sanitary towel from the bag over by the wall so I got up to get one. As I did so, blood plopped from between my legs onto the floor. Not like Liverpool, just drops. My door was open and a little man sitting in the hallway was shocked at what he saw. I closed the door on his stunned face, got the sanitary towel and went over to look at my son. He was sleeping peacefully, the little angel. We went home that afternoon.

After the abortion, I sat and stared. I didn't see what I was looking at. I was turned inwards, taking stock of the fact that I'd had not one, not two, but *three* abortions. I was shocked at myself. One abortion was sad, two was unfortunate, but three was sick. It was sick and I'd done it. Outwardly I was very still, hardly moving a muscle, just looking out at the grey-white sky or at the TV screen. But inwardly a bomb had gone off, alarm bells were ringing and I was in the grip of a new sensation – the realisation that something was terribly wrong with my life.

Furthermore, I knew that it wasn't my father's fault or my mother's fault or anyone else's fault. *I* had got myself pregnant and I'd chosen abortion *three times*. And I'd had one of them since giving birth to Jack. Not only that, I'd had to take him with me when I'd had it done. How sick was that? Clearly, the maternal feelings I had for Jack didn't extend to my latest foetus. Why not? Was I so callous? But I'd been forced into it, hadn't I? No. Arthur was unquestionably strange but the fact remained that *I* had chosen to have a third abortion. My thinking went in a never-ending loop like this: I should have been on the pill, I should have put my foot down about the condom, I should have left the town, I should have gone on the run from him, but with two children, where would I have gone? Then, back to thinking I should have been on the pill.

I was sick of life. I wanted it to end. I thought about suicide constantly. I knew I'd never do it because of Jack but I thought about it all the time. Imagining everything ending brought me some relief. Eventually, cold and low, I got up from my chair and carried on. I remembered what Arthur had said about Jack needing his father so, looking for some way forward, I got out Oliver's phone number in Canada and forced myself to ring him. I had to go to a payphone after midnight to catch him at a good time in Alberta, leaving Jack asleep on his own. I was desperate but tried not to show it. He was surprised to hear from me, suspicious even.

"Why now?" he asked.

The answer to this was crucial. I couldn't mention Arthur, the abortions, the turn-out with my mother or any of the other things that were driving me. I'd drafted and practised a plausible response to this question and now I delivered it:

"I've always regretted not telling you I was pregnant. Jack looks so like you and he should be with his father. I think for his sake we should give it a try."

Long minutes passed and then he said: ". . . Okay . . ."

He wasn't surprised to learn he had a son. I wasn't the only woman he'd got pregnant in England, he told me with laddish pride.

I asked him if the offer to go to Canada was still open. There was a hesitation and then: "Sure."

"Really?"

"Ah, sure, why not?"

"What if it doesn't work out between us?" I knew it wouldn't and I clutched the handset as if my life depended on it.

"Ah, never mind. I'll help youz to stay here anyway."

"Oh thank you, Oliver, thank you. I'm so sorry I didn't tell you about Jack," I repeated, although I wasn't.

"Ah, never mind. These things happen. Send me a photo."

And I did, choosing the one in which Jack closely resembled him.

I was as high as a kite after that first phone call. I was under the auspices of a man again and he was going to change our lives. I was going to start a new life in Canada. Wouldn't that be a great thing to tell my mother? She would have a daughter in Canada! I was euphoric with relief. In spite of my three abortions I'd edged back into the human race. I couldn't sleep that night with excitement so I got out of bed and walked all around the room several times. I had an atlas and I looked up Alberta. It was a big rectangular region with strange, romantic place-names like Grande Prairie, Medicine Hat, Lac La Biche – names to conjure with, and all in the shadow of the Rocky Mountains. By the next day I'd calmed down a bit and saw things more realistically. He hadn't offered to help with the airfare for myself or his son. Where did he think I was going to get five hundred pounds? In the end I begged it from my father. I heard on the grapevine that he was regretful about the past, "especially for the girls' sake". I scoffed bitterly at this. Did he think his sons were immune? We were all swill. I hated doing it – sending a begging letter to a man I loathed – and kept putting it off. How was I going to begin it? *Dear Dad.* The word was as strange written as spoken. As with Oliver I gave him a heroic spin on things: I'd decided to do the decent thing and join Jack's father in Canada. I'd be forever indebted to him if he could give me the airfare. To his credit, he did – with the proviso that I wouldn't ask him for any more.

It was the early wintry days of 1991 and there was a long wait while documentation was sorted out. I had to get a passport and put Oliver on Jack's birth certificate, which involved solicitors and letters going back and forth between England and Canada. While I waited, I occasionally bumped into Arthur, whose face bore a look of such demonic contempt that I thought he was going to assault me. When I thought about Oliver, I strangled the memories I had of him in London and the doubts I had about his character with palliative thoughts like this:

*He's probably a nicer person in Canada;*
*London had a bad effect on him;*
*Now that he's got a son, he'll be a better person.*

I booked a flight for May 10th and went over to Ireland once more to say goodbye. This time my mother was happy to see me and when we were out she introduced me to people with pride.

"This is my daughter Cora and her son Jack. They're emigrating to Canada, you know."

I met Rose and Peter in London the day before the flight. When we finally parted I hugged them goodbye and mounted a bus. Rose burst into tears as the bus was pulling away. She thought she'd never see us again. The next day we took off from Gatwick, bound for Edmonton, Alberta. Jack was twenty months old and I hoped he'd sleep on the flight, which he did. Ten hours later, as we were nearing Edmonton, I gazed out of the window. The landscape was a patchwork of huge rectangular fields and when the airport came into view it was like a huddle of condiments on a chequered tablecloth. Now that we were nearly there I didn't want to land. It was so nice up in the air, suspended between the sky and the earth, safe from strife. I clung to the promise that Oliver had made to help me stay in Canada. That was what had compelled me to come. That was the only way forward for me as far as I could see and as soon as we landed I'd have to start fighting for it. But, Jesus, I was tired. Down to the very bones. I prayed that this would be it, that good fortune would carry me to some little corner of this huge country where I could make a decent life for myself and my baby.

The plane descended and landed with a hard, grinding bump. We went through customs and there was Oliver, in the arrivals lounge, unwashed and unshaven in dirty old clothes but, weirdly, holding a single red rose. The rose was at variance with his sweaty, unkempt appearance, as if someone had dumped it on him at the last minute and run away. His eyes darted suspiciously all over us and came to rest on Jack. He looked at him for a long moment but didn't address him. He shoved the rose at me and made a comment about how I'd lost weight. Then he led the way out to the car park.

Outside, it was hot and sunny and in the dusty car the smell of body odour was overpowering. Oliver held a running commentary about the cost of living in Canada. Everything was expensive. Cheese, for example, was a terrible price. Buying a pound of cheese was like buying fillet steak. He warned me not to expect "a cake walk" because he wasn't working and he had no intention of doing so. He'd spent his last Canadian winter on the building sites and money was tight. I wanted to sympathise – I didn't expect him to flog himself to death on our behalf – but I saw the angry bunched-up set of his features and I remained silent. It wasn't just the harshness of his words but the way he said them, like a warning shouted from behind a barricade. What had happened to the nice man from the phone calls? He'd gone, evaporated. It was easy to be nice when your problem was thousands of miles away but now we were here in the flesh and he didn't seem to like it one bit. I held Jack close and cursed Arthur. How could I let someone persuade me that I needed this nasty little man? It had all been a big mistake. He'd never help me to immigrate. I knew that as early as the drive from the airport. I bit my cheeks hard to stop myself from crying. Oh God! I wanted to go home, but the big black hole behind me yawned cold air and there was nowhere for me to go except forward.

Oliver lived in a complex of low-rise apartment buildings in landscaped grounds. To my eyes, it was salubrious but it was what North Americans call a "project" – in other words, a ghetto. The people who lived there were all disadvantaged in some way. There were one-parent families; Native Americans, the red Indians of my childhood, complete with plaits; and unemployed people like Oliver. His one-bedroom apartment was spacious and well-equipped but it was a mess and smelled bad. Flies buzzed around a full rubbish bin in the kitchen. Dirty laundry lay in piles on the floor.

Jack was tired and so was I but, ignoring our pressing need for sleep, Oliver picked up his guitar and, strumming it lightly, started on about Jesus. I didn't remember this religiosity from London. Plucking the guitar strings, he sermonised, rambling on with little quotes from the Bible like, "Judge lest ye be judged."

He said it several times like that, without the *not*, until I interjected mildly: "It's 'Judge *not*, lest ye be judged', isn't it?"

He stopped strumming and stared at me. Then, in a tone of utter disdain, looking me up and down with his blazing Ulsterman's eyes, he shouted: "WHO D'YOU THINK Y'ARE? YER NOT HERE FIVE MINUTES AND YER LAYIN' DOWN THE LAW. DON'T YOU BE CORRECTING WHAT I SAY, D'YA HEAR ME?"

Jack stirred and cried in his buggy and, in an attempt to appease Oliver, I produced a bottle of Cointreau that I'd picked up at Duty Free. It was a drink he liked in London but now it only made matters worse. He got up and stomped around, kicking things in his path, upbraiding me for my arrogance and the sin of intemperance. Jack started crying and I put it down to tiredness.

Oliver had three sisters who lived in Edmonton, all well-established Canadians and he referred to them like that: *The Sisters*. I was reminded of the Valkyries or the Furies and wondered if they were behind his compliant attitude during our phone calls. He'd said they were "over the moon" about Jack. I suddenly realised that it must have been The Sisters' idea for us to come to Canada, not his. I could see that quite clearly now. That's where he got the rose as well, no doubt. He must have been earning kudos from them for taking us on while I was getting kudos from my mother for going. One of them had given him a cot for Jack and I could see it stacked in the corner, forgotten. I took Jack into the bedroom, changed and fed him, laid him on the bed and curled up around him. I was too tired to care about Oliver and in a detached, exhausted way I heard him resentfully banging the parts of the cot together.

We rubbed along for a couple of weeks: me mollifying him with flattery and good food, him quoting the Bible and strumming his guitar. Encouraged by my apparent servility, he confided that he wanted to go to college and become a profe*sh*er. He kept saying profe*sh*er with that mispronunciation but I thought better of correcting him. I wondered what he meant. What was a professor in Canada? Was it like a teacher? Surely he didn't mean professor, as in the head of a university department?

There was no intimacy between us; quite the contrary. He took delight in quoting something he'd heard on a building site and wrongly attributed to Robbie Burns which described the vagina as *a slippery, slimy slit half an inch from shit*. He called me Nurse Ratched, after the monstrous character from *One Flew Over the Cuckoo's Nest* and when I took Jack outside to the play area, I knew he was watching me from the shadows.

I hated every minute of being with him but I gritted my teeth and soldiered on because, against the odds, I'd managed to get him to contact the Immigration Office. Before long, however, we hit a major obstacle. In order to continue with my application to stay in Canada, we had to be married and he had to have a job. This was bad news. We really didn't want to be married to each other and he really didn't want to work. Nevertheless, The Sisters, particularly Anne the eldest, persuaded him to go back on the building sites and a couple of weeks later we were married at her house.

I looked awful. My hair was standing on end and my cheeks were hollow. Oliver referred to me throughout as The Witch and guests who watched us exchange our vows could see that we didn't even like each other. Afterwards, I drank too much and had to lie down. I felt bleak. My wedding day, something every girl dreams about, had been an awful sham. The groom had been strong-armed into it. He'd insulted me and so had his fat nephews: they said in reference to me that he'd "lucked out". I didn't even have a wedding dress. I was wearing a blue pleated thing that I'd borrowed. I looked like an old-fashioned air-hostess. The only pleasure I had all day was right then – the little bit of solitude in that spare bedroom. Oh, Jesus Christ, help me! I wanted to take my son, now being feted by his aunts, and disappear off the face of the earth.

That night Oliver and I had perfunctory sex and I got cystitis. I had no medical insurance so I tried to ignore it but it got worse and worse. Finally, I went to see a doctor who jokingly called it the honeymoon bug, common in women who hadn't had sex before or not for some time. In an unguarded moment I told Oliver that he might have given it to me. What a mistake! It was like stepping on a pus-filled carbuncle, which burst and splattered all over me.

"HOW DARE YOU, YOU DIRTY FUCKING WHORE!" he exploded, "I'M CLEAN, D'YA HEAR ME? I'M CLEAN!"

His outrage increased exponentially: "YOU'RE THE DIRTY ONE!"

Scandalised and disbelieving, he continued: "HOW DARE YA? . . . HOW DARE YA?! . . .YER NOTHING BUT A DIRTY WHORE! COMING OVER HERE WITH YER TONGUE HANGING OUT FOR SEX!"

I blushed with shame. Jack had heard him and, although he couldn't understand the words, he was crying at the ugly, violent tone. He was in my arms and I turned him away to protect him from the sight of his demented father, in high dudgeon now, eyes popping with a big bruised ego bulging right behind them.

He went on: "MY MOTHER SAID YE'D NEVER MEET A GOOD WOMAN IN A BAR AND BY GOD SHE WAS RIGHT! THAT WAS A BAD NIGHT FOR ME, RUNNING INTO A TRAMP LIKE YOU! FINSBURY PARK!" he spat out, "SURE, EVERYONE KNOWS FINSBURY PARK'S FULL OF WHORES."

I wanted to explain what the doctor had said but he wouldn't let me. I took Jack and locked myself in the bedroom until he calmed down.

Married and back on the building sites, Oliver became more and more unbearable. He demanded expensive roast dinners in the sweltering heat, wouldn't let us watch television because it offended his Christianity, or talk to the neighbours because they were single-parent "tramps".

I had a return portion on my air ticket and he desperately wanted me to use it. His behaviour worsened as the departure date drew near. He assured me that he wouldn't be helping me any further with immigration. He knew about the fraud and threatened to expose my criminal conviction. I clung to the ledge but he was doing his best to push me off. I was rocking myself like a mental patient again in an effort to calm down but I couldn't. My insides were permanently filled with a gas cloud of anxiety.

I was close to breaking. He told me to keep Jack quiet and smacked him so hard on the face one day that he screamed in pain. Closer.

One very hot day, Oliver was stomping around looking for his cigarette papers while doing the usual – that is, shouting at me to go back to England. I was rocking on the sofa and Jack was on a tricycle. Suddenly he changed tack and in a sweet voice he wheedled:

"Come on everyone. We're going to help Daddy look for his cigarette papers. Oh where can they be? Mmmmhhhh . . . maybe they're on the sofa . . . but I can't see past Mummy's BIG NOSE!" With that he forced two thick fingers into my nostrils and yanked me up.

Pain and humiliation mobilised me and I spat at him and swore: "GET THE HELL AWAY FROM ME YOU SICK, STUPID BASTARD!"

Just then, Jack collided with his father's leg and Oliver spun round and kicked the tricycle from under him so that he was thrown from it and banged his head on the floor. In an instant, I had my screaming baby in my arms and, grabbing my bag, I was out the door. I hurried down the stairs and out of the building. I stood at the entrance for a long time, not knowing what to do.

An old lady asked me if I was all right. "Fine, thanks," I lied, flatly. I bit my cheeks. I knew I'd never go back to that apartment, but what was I going to do? I didn't have the price of a phone call and who would I phone anyway? I walked up and down outside and then sat on a step, Jack asleep in my arms. Dusk descended. Then I saw a girl who lived in the basement, one of the single-parent "tramps". She smiled as she approached and, on the verge of tears, I asked her to help me. She gladly took us in for the night and told me about a women's refuge on the other side of the city.

I went to the refuge the next day with nothing but the clothes I stood up in. I didn't even have Jack's buggy. It was another hot day and twice he nearly slipped from my sweaty grasp. By the time I reached the long white house, my arms ached terribly. The door was opened by a big smiling woman who brought me in and passed me on to a counsellor. Jack played with some toys while I was interviewed. The first questions I was asked were about my health. I said I was fine but the counsellor raised an eyebrow and said doubtfully: "You look real stressed to me."

She noted my gaunt, lined face and the pouches in my dress where my breasts used to be. Only a few weeks earlier, in England, I'd filled that dress to bursting. Now it hung off me like an old coat on a scarecrow. I told her about the fingers up my nose, the verbal abuse, how he was trying to force me to go back to England. We moved onto questions about Jack. I described in detail how Oliver had abused him, the vicious slaps in the name of discipline and the tricycle incident. She made copious notes which I hoped would get him into trouble.

After the interview, the smiley woman took me on a tour of the house. First stop was the lounge where there was a huge television switched on at a very high volume. A clutch of teenagers were draped across three large sofas watching MTV. Two enormous glass sliding doors focused the strong sunlight indoors so that it was oppressively hot. Beyond these doors there was a scrubby garden with a sand pit and a slide for the children.

Next, the kitchen. It was full to bursting with women and children having lunch. The air reeked of burgers and fries.

"LISTEN UP, EVERYONE!" shouted the counsellor. Oh no! Don't draw attention to me, please, I thought, as everyone turned to look. "This is Cora and her son Jack. They're going to be staying with us for a while."

I looked at the ground. Someone asked me where I was from. Painfully shy, I whispered: "I'm Irish."

"Irish?" said a thin little woman with bleached blonde hair and a haggard face. "I HATE THOSE BASTARDS! They're vicious, cowardly bastards! I hate them! Look what one of them did to me."

With that she lifted her tee-shirt to reveal big, plate-sized bruises on her front and back.

"That was with his work boots!" she added, as if his fists would have been a lesser crime. I was ashamed of my race and I felt my brogue draw in. I knew that I'd only speak when I was spoken to.

We went upstairs to a room at the end of a long corridor. It was clean and bright with a cot and a single bed. She told me where I could get milk, feeding bottles and nappies; what time dinner was; and that I could get a voucher for the St Vincent de Paul shop from the office. I put Jack down for a nap and sat on the floor beside the cot. The carpet looked brand new. It was a soothing beige and before I knew it I was flat out on it, asleep. But it was just the micro-sleep of the very anxious and I woke up minutes later, shocked and disorientated, my heart banging like a drum. I could hardly breathe as I tried to find the present moment, my mind flicking through a myriad of images – fingers rammed into my nose, Jack banging his head, Rose crying, Arthur's face, Jack slipping from my sweaty grip, the taxi-ride to a long white house – and then I was back in the room. My breathing slowed and I went over to look out the window. It was a pretty neighbourhood. I could see other houses similar to this one, flowerbeds, lawns and an ornamental pond.

As soon as he woke, I fed and changed Jack, took him in my arms and went to the charity shop. The streets were deserted. In every direction there were sprinklers on perfectly manicured gardens; a car purred by occasionally and turned into a driveway where electronic gates glided open. The only sound was the rat-tat-tat of a construction site in the far distance. I walked up to the highway, which was empty of traffic. The St Vincent de Paul shop was on the other side, at the back of a shopping mall. The word *mall*. I remembered embarrassing one of The Sisters in front of her friend when I pronounced it "mall" as in "pal" rather than "mall" as in "hall". I got as much clothing as I could carry for both of us and when I got back to the refuge it was dinner time. More burgers and fries. The little blonde woman came into the dining room, narrowed her eyes and sat with her back to me.

Oliver's sisters found out what had happened and they were aghast. We met and for the first time they spoke about him honestly. He was the youngest and their mother, God rest her soul, had spoiled him rotten. He was a spineless waster and a bad influence on his nephews. He'd once pushed his aged father down the stairs, so angry was he at getting the strap as a child. He'd been at a strip club the night before we arrived and the sisters could not understand what a woman like me was doing with him. I was moved by their kindness and support and, because they wanted to help me stay in Canada, I told them about my criminal record. I thought it best to tell them before Oliver did. But they dropped me like a hot brick. I rang Anne and begged her to meet me to let me explain further but she said they were sick of clearing up Oliver's mistakes and not to ring again. I was on my own.

But that was good. In the context of the refuge I was at a distinct advantage. Most of the women there were on the run from men who'd kill them if they found them. Guns were common and the women were in fear of their lives. The staff were nervous too because their worst nightmare had already come true when a man had located the refuge and shot his wife dead. A case worker had taken her out for lunch. They were in a car park when someone shouted, "BITCH!" The women cast around frantically but it was too late. A single shot rang out and she slumped to the ground, fatally wounded in the chest.

In spite of the pain, there was laughter. Some nights we sat around the kitchen table and chatted and I was reminded of my mother and those other women in Midleton all those years ago, huddled around the stove in the convent. Women with broken ribs and split lips laughed even though it hurt. A woman rolled cigarettes from a communal tin and handed them out. Teenage sons hovered around their mothers like bodyguards. There were sedatives for anyone who couldn't sleep and I was always first in the queue for those.

The maximum time you could stay at the refuge was three weeks. After that you had to find your own accommodation. If you had no funds, City Hall would provide you with an apartment like Oliver's but that option wasn't open to me because I wasn't a Canadian citizen. I was a visitor and I couldn't move on in the usual way. The refuge didn't know what to do with me. Then someone suggested the Sisters of St Claude, an order of nuns in the city centre which sometimes took people in. I didn't want to go at first. I'd got used to the refuge and my knowledge of nuns was based on the Irish model but I had no other choice so one afternoon I packed all our belongings into a bin bag and a case worker drove us downtown.

St Claude's Priory was a big two-storey building, covered in ivy and surrounded by huge old oak and pine trees. I stood at the front door quaking in my boots, held Jack's hand and rang the bell. The door was opened by a middle-aged woman in a short blue habit. With her smiling face and unveiled hair, she wasn't at all like the Sr Jocelyns of my childhood. Her name was Sr Madeline and she welcomed us and gestured for us to come in. We stepped tentatively over the threshold into a cool dark interior that smelled of beeswax and flowers. I brought the bin bag in and she gestured for me to leave it by the door. Then she led us down a long corridor and out into a bright, sunlit garden. Under a spreading oak tree there was a long table and six figures sat around it, three in blue habits: there was Sr Ruth-Anne, who was the prioress, Sr Corinne and Sr Louisa. There was also Edie who cleaned and cooked; Judith, a reformed alcoholic; and Clara, a devout Native American Christian. The table was spread with plates of mouth-watering food: bowls of salad and pots of soup, baskets of bread, cold meats, cheeses, tomatoes and lots of fruit. Madeline introduced us and everyone said hello. Ruth-Anne considered me sternly and my stomach closed up under her steely gaze. I took the only free seat, right beside her, but she ignored me and resumed a conversation she was having about a man who was working for the diocese. "Top-notch" she said of him. I felt excluded and squirmed with self-hatred. I was bottom-notch, a bottom feeder scrounging charity and although I fed Jack, I couldn't take any food for myself, so I sat there starving and miserable.

After lunch, Madeline took us to our room. We went upstairs, along another long corridor, to the far end of the building. There was a yellow cot waiting for Jack, with an orange teddy bear sitting on the pillow. There was also a buggy, a bag of nappies, a box of toys and a potty underneath the cot. Through the window I could see a blue sky, trees and the kitchen garden. Louisa and Edie were out there in sun hats picking vegetables for that night's dinner. Madeline left us to get settled in. I thanked her profusely for everything but she said they were just glad to help. Ruth-Anne's stern face flashed through my mind and I couldn't believe *she* wanted to help me. I put Jack down for a nap and sat on the narrow monastic bed. I was transfixed by the cloistered atmosphere of this house, coming straight after the noise and stress of the refuge. The perfume of flowers filled my senses. It was beautiful. For a while I couldn't move. Then I got up and unpacked my bin bag into the waiting chest of drawers.

As this was an Anglican community, there were services every day in the chapel. When Jack woke up, I took him and the teddy bear downstairs for Vespers. The evening sun streamed in through a huge stained-glass window illuminating the altar and the small collection of pews. I sat in a chair near the door but Madeline gestured for me to come closer, which I did. Ruth-Anne gave a sermon. It was about compassion and understanding. I watched her solemn face and felt reassured. Surely she didn't exclude me from that. I felt myself relax a little and my attention shifted to the shafts of sunlight washing everything in delicate shades of blue, orange and green; the vases of flowers; the heads bent in supplication.

After Vespers it was time for dinner. The little congregation moved to a spacious dining room, where we ate at a long polished table. Everything gleamed with loving care. It was Corinne's job to wheel in the hostess trolley loaded with the food that Edie prepared before she went home. Ruth-Anne sat at the head of the table and dished up. I didn't sit beside her this time, but as far down the table as I could get, with Jack beside me in a highchair. I found myself opposite Judith, who pulled funny faces that made Jack laugh. That night there was Swiss chard and squash – vegetables I'd never heard of – meatloaf and an unusual dish, tomatoes in aspic.

No one asked me any questions. We were simply accepted and this time when I was offered food, I took it. Afterwards, I excused myself and went back upstairs. When Jack was asleep I went next door to a little sitting room where there were lots of books, mostly religious, but I found some Agatha Christies and started one of the Hercule Poirot mysteries. Not for the first time, books came to my rescue. I could still read a story, whatever my circumstances, and be completely absorbed by it. Later I had no difficulty going to sleep, but staying asleep was a problem. I tossed and turned all night, waking at four o'clock fretting about the future, in a sweat and unable to get back to sleep. At six o'clock, I got up and all my muscles ached so I ran a hot bath and lay in it for as long as I could.

After Matins and breakfast I had the morning to kill so I took Jack out in his new buggy and wheeled him around the neighbourhood. It was a joy not to have to carry him in my thin arms. There were no sweeping lawns or electric gates here. The Priory was downtown, amidst the poor, in Edmonton's red light district. There were fridges and washing machines in the front gardens and old rusty cars abandoned beside the cracked weedy pavements. A couple of streets away, half-naked women strolled up and down, waiting for kerb-crawlers.

On the third day, I had an interview with Ruth-Anne. She needed to know more about me in order to help me.

She was concerned for us and really didn't know what would become of us. If I couldn't stay in Canada, where would I go? Did I really have no one who could help? She needed to be in possession of all the facts so I girded my loins and prepared to tell her about the fraud. I was nervous. How would she react? Like The Sisters? In a moment of weakness I considered not mentioning it but in the end I pushed out the truth, albeit through a dry mouth and flaming hot cheeks. I sat there red-faced, waiting for her judgement, but she said nothing for a while, and then:

"Is there anything else?"

"No."

"Do you want to stay in Canada?"

"Yes."

She didn't think that one minor offence was such a terrible thing. She told me that Louisa counselled women in prison who'd done far worse things and she promised to discuss my case with the Diocese of Edmonton to see if they'd sponsor my application to stay. My heart leapt. A future in Canada suddenly became real again. I very possibly might be able to stay. My imagination took flight and I saw a cabin in the woods, not too far from St Claude's, with a pot of coffee on the stove, a log fire going and an old truck out the front. I couldn't drive but I'd learn. Anything was possible in this vast country. Ruth-Anne said she'd put the wheels in motion that very day. How wonderful! I would have hugged her but her august demeanour forbade it.

Meanwhile, Jack needed other children to play with and there was a free day nursery that I took him to three mornings a week. To get to it I had to wheel him through the heart of the red-light district and there was always a sense of it being the morning after the night before – only me striding purposefully and the rest of the world out cold. There weren't any prostitutes around at that time but I saw native people lying unconscious in hedges and gutters, their faces obscured by their long blue-black hair; people with the shakes waiting for the off-licence to open; men with bloody faces who were still drunk; and musty drifters in jeans and baseball caps.

I dropped Jack off in the safety of the nursery and went back to the Priory to help with the chores. Then I went to collect him and after lunch we went to the playground across the road. Then it was Vespers, dinner and bed at ten o'clock. That was our routine for the next few weeks. The order and serenity of the Priory soothed and comforted me and I thought less and less about the future. Mealtimes were great. Our food was simple and lovingly prepared and we ate like a family, chatting and passing this or that dish up and down the table. Jack was a great hit and after meals he loved to run around the table and end up on Madeline's or Ruth-Anne's lap, pulling at their faces and saying funny little things that weren't quite sentences. I was happy to live within the confines of the day, safe in the knowledge that Ruth-Anne and the might of the Diocese were working on my behalf.

I even went on a day-trip. The nursery organised outings for mums and toddlers and one such trip was to Fort Edmonton, the original settlement which had been moved, timber by timber, to a location outside the city.

On the bus, I sat beside a beautiful Dutch girl who, like Oliver, had moved to Canada as a child. She hated it and wanted to go back to Holland. According to her, everything Canadian was rubbish. The people were fat and lazy and had fat, spoilt children. The food was disgusting – fries with everything and vegetables in jelly, for God's sake! There was no art, no literature, no theatre, just barbecues and SUVs. She wanted her son to grow up a Dutchman, at home in Holland, not a fat immigrant stuffing his face with junk food. She couldn't leave because her mother, who lived in Toronto, was ill. I wanted to put the case for Canada, to draw her attention to the opportunities, the space and the majesty of the landscape but her home-sickness was so deep and resonated so much with my own that I just sat beside her limp and motionless, in the grip of a powerful longing for home. Holland, eh? Maybe I could go and live there. I was so far from home that Holland seemed like a stone's throw from Ireland. The Dutch were nice people by all accounts and they spoke English. I'd be near enough to visit but far enough away not to be a problem.

Fort Edmonton was surrounded by teepees and I was surprised by that. I didn't realise that the white man and the red man had lived so close together. The fort and the teepees seemed huddled up together, as if united in the face of a common enemy – the winter, perhaps. I'd been warned about the terrible winters in Alberta, when the snow would be knee deep and the wind chill from the North could be as low as minus seventy. On those days you couldn't go out with your skin exposed because it would burn. If you did go out, you had to have a car. I couldn't even drive. I gulped and thought about Jack and our few thin clothes and I simply couldn't imagine what would happen to us once the summer was over. The soldiers' quarters had low ceilings and dirt floors. Everything was built from logs and everywhere you looked there were bearskins: on the beds, on the chairs, on the floors and at the windows. I could feel the ghosts of the people who'd come out here all those years ago and dug a toe-hold in the savage wilderness. There were one or two old photographs on the walls – weathered faces rendered stupid by the flash of the camera. I looked into the camera-stunned eyes and wondered what had happened to those men and women. Had they stayed in the newly founded Province of Alberta? Or had they gone over the Rockies to the milder climes of the West Coast? Had they lived long lives or met untimely deaths? I was inspired by their sheer tenacity. If they could endure their hardships and overcome their obstacles, surely I could do the same. Ours was the tourist route through the fort and a rope gently guided us towards the café and gift shop. With no money, I didn't linger but took Jack outside for the picnic lunch laid on by the nursery.

When I got back to the Priory, Madeline and Ruth-Anne were agitated. There'd been bad news. A lawyer had rung to say that my case had been rejected. Not only that, he'd advised me to leave Canada as soon as possible. On paper, Oliver looked the better candidate for custody of Jack. He had a home, a job and an affluent family while I, on the other hand, had nothing. And my visa had run out. I was illegal. If I stayed on and ended up being deported, Jack could be taken away from me. There was no room for argument and no more avenues to try. I'd have to go and go quickly.

When they told me all this, I was in shock. The end had come so suddenly that I couldn't take it in. I'd got used to the Priory. We'd been there nearly three months and we were part of the family by now. I'd found love of a kind there and I didn't want to leave. I was so upset, I couldn't catch my breath. Ruth-Anne and Madeline stood over me. I looked from face to face and their expressions were pained as they watched me gasping for air like a fish on a river bank.

"Oh, Cora," said Madeline, her voice heavy with compassion.

I couldn't believe it. After all I'd gone through – the lonely wait in the shadow of Arthur, begging the airfare from my father, enduring the detestable Oliver, the tense overheated refuge, the weight loss, the anxiety. I'd endured it all, hoping that it was leading somewhere. Now it seemed it was all for nothing. I was like the fly eternally crawling up the side of the glass only to slide back down. And I was afraid. I knew there was nothing back there for me but I'd have to go back all the same.

When I'd calmed down sufficiently, Madeline and I discussed what to do. The obvious thing was to go back to London. It'd be a starting point. But where in London? I had no money, not a bean, and there was no-one who could take us in. I thought of Rose, who would help, but she shared a flat. She didn't have a place of her own. Slowly and reluctantly, it dawned on me – I'd come to the Priory from a refuge and, if all else failed, I'd have to go back to one. That was it then. It was decided. We'd go to a refuge in London.

We did some research and found a women's shelter in London called Haven, and as soon as it was nine o'clock in the morning there, we rang. Madeline explained who she was, how I'd come to the Priory and why I had to leave Canada. They agreed to take us without a moment's hesitation and even said there'd be someone at the airport to meet me. It was a great relief. At least now there was somewhere to go.

Later that morning we went to the travel agent's where the Diocese paid for our tickets to Gatwick. Jack's second birthday was coming up so we had an early birthday party for him. Edie made a cake in the shape of a lamb and stuck little plastic frogs all around it. It was September and Edmonton was cooling down fast. Icy breezes cut through my summer dress and I went to another St Vincent de Paul shop to get some warmer clothes. It was busy with poor people bent to the task of preparing themselves for the cold. Like the Fort, there was fur everywhere and huge baskets of long johns and thermal vests. I got warm pants, socks, bootees, a coat, a hat and some jumpers for Jack and some jeans and jumpers for myself.

As the departure date approached, I cried constantly. I'd been running from the black hole all this time and now I had to turn around and go back into it. The thought of another women's shelter was cold comfort indeed. I spent the evenings with Madeline and she reassured me and told me that doors would open when I needed them.

We left after lunch on September 16th. Everyone gathered around the front gate to see us off. There were hugs and kisses and then we got into a car. As soon as I closed the door, it pulled away and sped up to the top of the street. I couldn't look back. I didn't want to see my kind friends getting smaller and smaller and disappearing from my life. We turned left and were gone.

There was a stopover in Toronto and, as arranged, I rang Ruth-Anne. She was deeply sad that we had to leave, with nothing waiting for us at the other end but a battered women's refuge. I was too tired and scared to cry. She gave me words of encouragement and we promised to stay in touch, no matter what. Then, under a starry sky, we boarded the flight to London.

# Part Three

## Kitchen Devil

We arrived in Gatwick at seven o'clock in the morning. A woman called Adele was picking us up. She said she'd be wearing a pink blouse and a blue skirt and after customs I saw her immediately, the pink and blue shining like a beacon in the fog. I smiled recognition and she came forward, hugged me and took my luggage so I could push the buggy with both hands. She clutched the wayward trolley with fingers bedecked in a dazzling array of silver rings. We made our way to the car park and it took us a while to get all of my stuff into the boot of her little green Datsun. Then we headed into London under a beautiful blue sky, going up through Croydon, Streatham, Clapham, and finally we were crossing Hammersmith Bridge.

On the way, Adele warned me about the refuge: "It's not the Ritz, Cora," she said, more than once.

Haven had three sites – the original house where the organisation was founded in the 1970s and two other properties, acquired later with the help of donations. Adele took me to House No. 1, where the main office was, to have my details registered, and then to one of the other houses. On the way, she said again, "It's not the Ritz." What exactly did she mean? The house we'd just been in was all right – clean and quiet – so why did she keep telling me that? We pulled up outside a large red-brick house at the end of a street, with a sycamore in the garden shedding its leaves and pretty black and white tiles that led up to the front door. It looked lovely – typical London elegance.

Adele led the way and once over the threshold I could see what she meant. It really wasn't the Ritz. In fact, it was the dirtiest, noisiest and smelliest place I'd ever been and the intense atmosphere came out and hit me like a gas cloud. The founder of the refuge believed that women should not be forced to do housework when they were sheltering there and she'd been taken at her word. It wasn't that the residents were dirty; it was that no one wanted to clean up for the common good. All the communal areas had a heavy patina of grime. The once-white walls were grey. The carpets were sticky and there was a smell of vomit and excrement. Adele introduced me to a case worker and left. Then I was taken upstairs and I was so exhausted that I was glad to have a room, dirty or not, and I collapsed onto the bed with Jack beside me and fell fast asleep.

When I awoke, I saw the sycamore right outside my window. The sun was shining through its red and orange leaves but I had that jarring surreal sensation of feeling very bad on a beautiful sunny day. I couldn't breathe properly and I jumped up. There was Jack on the bed, but where were we? I was in a cold sweat. This wasn't the Priory? Where was Madeline? What had happened? I shot out the door and tore down the stairs to the office. The case worker was busy with a queue of women but I wanted attention straight away. I went straight up to the desk and interrupted her conversation, insisting that I had to get back to Canada. She eyed me coldly and told me to wait my turn so I paced the room wringing my hands and keening hysterically. Women nudged each other and looked at me but I didn't care. I sat down and rocked myself back and forth, trying to calm myself down but it didn't work.

Eventually the social worker turned to me but all I could say was: "I have to go back to the nuns." I keened this over and over in rhythm with my rocking. Adele was sent for and when she arrived I burst into tears. I wailed as I threw my sweaty arms around her. I was so desperate, I thought magic could happen. I wanted to be with Madeline, Ruth-Anne and the rest of them and I thought kind, beautiful Adele could make it happen.

"You might some day, Cora, you never know," she said gently and drew my attention to Jack, who was alone on the bed upstairs. Thinking about him calmed me down somewhat and she persuaded me to get dressed and go shopping with my emergency DSS payment. We went to Sainsbury's but my mind was blank. I stared at her beautiful rings and imagined the charmed life she must have and wished I could go home with her.

Adele nudged me along. "What are you going to have for tea today?"

"I don't know."

"Do you want to cook or just put something in the oven?"

"Oven."

"What about Jack?"

"I don't know."

"What does he like?"

"Ehhhh . . . chips."

"Anything else?"

". . . Fish fingers." He'd never eaten fish fingers before, being used to squash and meatloaf, but I remembered how much I'd loved them as a child.

"Right. Let's get some oven chips and fish fingers. What do you want for breakfast?"

I just shook my head.

"What does Jack normally have?"

"Weetabix."

"Okay, cereals are in the next aisle, I'll go and get some. Have you got enough nappies?"

"No."

We went on like that until I had a basketful of shopping. I queued at the check-out feeling faint while Adele stood behind me with the buggy. Then she took me back to the refuge, dropped me off outside and waited until I went up to the front door.

I swallowed hard and knocked. The door was opened by two beaming faces. They were Alice and Julie, best friends since meeting at the refuge. Alice reminded me of Hannah. She took my shopping while I manoeuvred the buggy over the step. It was nearly tea-time and beyond them in the hallway there were children screaming and shouting and women hanging up jackets and taking babies out of buggies. Someone was swearing and trying to close the cupboard under the stairs, which was full to bursting with donated clothing. I followed Alice and Julie into the kitchen and they showed me where I could keep my groceries and insisted on making me a cup of tea. It was customary to do this for a newcomer and I was touched and grateful for the gesture.

Bryan Adams came on the radio and everyone groaned. "TURN THAT FUCKER OFF!" shouted a girl sitting at the table feeding her daughter, and Julie obligingly changed the station. I was shocked to hear a mother swear like that in front of her child. I never did in front of Jack because I knew so well that foul language was a violation of innocence. I asked Alice why no-one liked Bryan Adams and she told me that he'd been at number one in the charts for twelve weeks and everyone was sick of him.

A loud clamour of activity went on around me. There were two big gas cookers but that was barely enough for the number of families at the refuge. Mothers jostled and vied for oven trays, oven space, pots, pans and hotplates. Fridges opened and slammed shut. There were peals of laughter and voices raised both in jest and anger, the strings of words held together with various obscenities. Above all of this was the screech of pop music from the radio. Rubbish bins filled up quickly with all sorts of packaging because nobody cooked a meal from raw ingredients. With a queue pressing in behind, there simply wasn't time or space. For me as a newcomer there was another ritual – I was given an oven tray. I hastily covered it with oven chips and fish fingers and disappeared upstairs.

My room was big compared to others but it was L-shaped and in the alcove there was a single bed so I knew that at some point I'd have to share. That first night I got into bed with a Bible I'd been given at the Priory. I didn't read it but clutched it to my chest as a talisman. I had some muscle relaxants, which I finished off and drifted off to sleep. My dreams took me away and I was happy but when I woke up I felt another electric shock of reality. It was not as bad as the day before but still I cowered in bed and had to force myself to get up to tend to Jack. I changed and dressed him but waited until the children went to school and the house emptied out before I went downstairs. The kitchen was like a bombsite but I found a clean bowl and a clean mug, gave Jack some Weetabix, made a mug of tea and went back upstairs as quickly as possible.

I was frightened of the other women. They were loud and forceful and there was some resentment that I was a newcomer and had been given the big room. Marcia, a mixed-race woman with a hard expression confronted me with all the politeness she could muster: "The fing is, you're new 'ere. Yo the last one in, an' you 'ave the biggest bleedin' room!" I pointed out that, yes, it was big but it had to be shared and she was welcome to swap rooms if she liked. No one wanted to share so the subject was dropped.

I kept my head down and tried to be as unobtrusive as possible. I thought some woman here might also have been beaten up by an Irishman like in the refuge in Canada so I kept the brogue to a minimum. I spoke only when I was spoken to. A vicious circle developed because I didn't speak much. The other women thought I was stuck up and that caused anger which frightened me more and made me less keen to communicate. I used the kitchen off-peak, stayed in my room or went out with Jack. I just pushed the buggy around all day and eventually we ended up in the local park. As soon as I passed through the gates and smelled the earth and saw the trees, I felt better. There was a long avenue of tall smooth-skinned beeches and their majestic beauty filled my heart with gladness. Golden and russet leaves swirled all around us. There were some flowers still in bloom and a pond with ducks and swans. It was still warm enough to have picnics so every day from then on I'd take some food and sit on the grass in the mild sunshine.

While Jack slept in his buggy, I started reading a self-help book that I'd been given in Canada called *You Can Heal Your Life* by Louise L. Hay. This book was flying off the shelves so I surmised that my experience of life was far from unique. Lots of people felt lost and alone. In a strange way it was good to know that other people felt like me. I had a community of sorts; in a sense, I belonged somewhere.

A basic premise of the book was the need to challenge negative beliefs about ourselves. The repetition of positive statements or affirmations about ourselves would alter our thought patterns and reprogramme the mind with self-esteem. Chief among the affirmations that I repeated were: "I am beautiful and everybody loves me" and "I love and approve of myself". These words meant nothing to me at that time but I recited them anyway and the repetition itself was comforting. While I was engaged in this chanting, I couldn't be fretting about anything else. I must have told myself that I was beautiful and that everybody loved me a million times as I wheeled Jack around and especially on my way back to the refuge, my stomach tightening with apprehension, because I knew that, far from loving me, nobody there even liked me.

I broke the tension around the room in a way that benefitted everyone – I cleaned up. There was a rota for housework but it was ignored so I bought a pair of rubber gloves and washed up after every meal and even mopped the kitchen floor. I took a bucket of hot bleachy water and went over everything until all the black grimy smudges were gone. I washed out the fridges and cleaned the windows. I even washed the walls in the kitchen, which took four buckets of scalding hot water. I needed to, it's what I'd have done in my own home and the sight of order and cleanliness made me feel good. And it made others feel good too. I could see the looks of pleasant surprise on the faces of harassed mothers when they came in to cook, expecting an unholy mess and not one clean saucepan.

Gradually I noticed a change in attitude towards me. Conversations didn't stop when I walked in. I was respected for the contribution I made. Because of that respect I started to feel better. Hope crept back into my heart. Suddenly it wasn't so bad being back in the Old Smoke. I knew London quite well, after all. I got income support and I had a few pounds to spare. There was no

three-week limit at Haven. You stayed until you were
housed by the council.

Time passed and I made my room into a little home with
a lamp, a rug and a radio/cassette player. A starter bed
was provided for Jack with a safety rail along the side. I
was glad about the safety rail.

Being at the refuge didn't seem to bother him. He was
just coming up to two when we arrived and I think he
was too young to be very aware of his surroundings or to
miss the people at the Priory. As long as he had me he was
all right and I protected him fiercely. I never let him out
of my sight – except once when I had to go upstairs
briefly and left him in the kitchen for a minute. It was just
one minute but it was long enough for him to cut his
eyebrow and for someone to wipe it with a filthy dish
cloth that gave him impetigo.

I was nervous when he played with the refuge children.
They all seemed hyperactive, always thumping each other
and crying or screaming. I recognised it and the insecurity
that drove it from my own childhood but I didn't want it
for my child so I took him to the playgroup at the main
house instead, where the atmosphere was decidedly calmer.
I watched him while he played, looking for signs of
disturbance after the Oliver episode, things like bullying
or shyness, but he was a joy – confident, gleeful and kind
to other children. How on earth had I done it, given the
circumstances? As I watched my beautiful happy son, I
felt that I'd pulled a rabbit out of a hat. It just goes to
show that if a child is in the care of someone who loves
them, they can weather most storms.

Bizarrely, amidst the squalor and chaos, Jack won a beautiful baby competition at the local branch of Boots. I was passing one day, entered him for fun and, with his blue eyes, blond curls and beaming smile, he won first prize. The winning portrait was displayed in the shop window for a week and the prize was a twenty-five pound gift voucher and a framed copy of the winning photo. I spent twenty pounds on nappies and the rest on a bright red lipstick called Empire of Fire, which came in a shiny black case and looked so stylish I thought I could build a life around it. I dreamt again of new horizons: a good man, a happy marriage, friends, dinner parties and nice clothes, with my Empire of Fire like a big red cherry on the top.

I joined the local library and borrowed tapes and books. I met up with Rose and we both tried to ignore the fact that Jack and I were living in a refuge. It must have been awful from her perspective – watching me taking Jack to Canada, getting married and coming back under a cloud. She couldn't be expected to know, as I knew, that we had our cosy little home within the refuge and we were safe.

One quiet Friday afternoon at the end of November, Kelly appeared. She seemed to come from nowhere and stood in the kitchen door asking me for the time.

"Ha ya go' the tame, hen?" said a squeaky little voice in a heavy Glaswegian accent. She reminded me of the woman in Canada who always scowled at me and hated Irish men. Like her, she was small and thin, with tufts of bleach-worn hair. She was cross-eyed and rather pathetic-looking but something about her frightened me and rather than feeling sympathy, my heart shrivelled up like a prune.

"Sorry?"

"HA YA GO' THE TAME?" she shouted, jabbing her finger at my watch and brushing past me to get at the pots and pans.

"Ten past two."

"I'm jus' gonna make masel somethan' ta eat, is that all reet?" she asked, pulling a packet of spaghetti and a tin of tuna out of a bag.

I left the room and went upstairs. Later when I returned I couldn't believe the mess. How could tuna and pasta cause such chaos? She'd tried to make cheese sauce and every saucepan had been pressed into service. The sink was full and onion peelings and shakings of flour were scattered everywhere.

She was drunk and greeted me like an old friend but I asked her coldly: "Are you going to clean this mess up?" My eyes murdered her for kicking my careful housework to the wind.

"Wo' mess?" and then she shouted drunkenly: "A COURSE AM GONNA CLEAN UP! AH NEVER LEAVE A MESS BEHIND ME! JUS LE ME FINISH MA CIGARETTE, WILL YA, HEN?"

With that she got up, staggered to the fridge and pulled out another can of Special Brew.

After Kelly came Suzanne, a frail little black woman with three children: a girl of ten, a boy of seven and a baby, all with big sad eyes. She was an alcoholic and at tea-time, when she was comatose, anyone who liked could feed her children. The little girl often made bread and butter for herself and her siblings and she regularly put the boy and the baby to bed. After Suzanne came Jennifer, the sort of drinker who kept a pint of vodka in her handbag.

This triumvirate – Kelly, Suzanne and Jennifer – brought out the worst in others. Unlike the refuge in Canada there was no night-time supervision and there were drinking sessions in the kitchen nearly every night. They drew the house in and nearly everyone was there. I could hear loud raucous laughter from upstairs and the ground floor became a no-go area for me in the evenings. I wouldn't have gone down to the kitchen at night when a session was in full swing for all the tea in China. I didn't trust anyone and I was afraid that the high opinion I'd been enjoying would be stripped away by the alcohol. I'd be laughed out of it for sure. I cringed in bed. In the morning, there'd be a dreadful mess: full ashtrays, spilled drinks, vomit in the sink. Once there was even a boot that I recognised as Kelly's, full of vomit.

Kelly was the driver, the cause of this ugly turnaround, and she loved it. She couldn't get pissed or stoned enough. Once, high on pills, she disappeared upstairs and returned with deep slash wounds to her neck and wrists. She was casual, resuming her seat and lighting a cigarette. At first, no one noticed but suddenly Angela, a big Cockney from Plaistow, stood up, her mouth open, and staggered back from the group. She pointed at Kelly and everyone looked and then they were all on their feet, backing away, hands to mouths, screaming and shouting: "JESUS CHRIST!" and "FUCKING HELL!" No one really knew what to do.

Kelly was sitting cross-legged, drinking her beer as if

nothing was wrong. Meanwhile blood was fanning out across her chest and soaking into her tee-shirt, dripping off her fingers, down the side of her beer can and onto the floor. The shocking sight registered with woman after woman and they clutched at each other for support. In a confused headless chicken way, they got tea towels, called an ambulance and pressed down hard on the wounds until the paramedics came.

The next morning it was the talk of the house. I got a blow-by-blow account from Michelle, who was in the room across the landing from me. She was breathless as she told me, reliving the horror. I was detached. My only thoughts were: *she wanted attention and now she's got it*; and: *hopefully that's put an end to the piss-ups*. Kelly came back that day, her neck in a brace with thick bandages around her wrists and she did get some sympathy. But by the time the bandages came off everyone had forgotten about her and she cut a lonely figure at the kitchen table, picking at the stitches and making them bleed. Soon after that she started bringing men back at night.

"WHAT? INTO A WOMEN'S REFUGE?!" I exclaimed angrily when I heard. I was fit to throttle her. Booze, drugs, men – the whole place was becoming a joke thanks to her. A French girl called Nadine shared her room and in a horrified French accent she recounted one morning how she'd just woken to the sight of a huge thrusting mound under Kelly's duvet and then the unmistakable sound of a man having an orgasm. The mound flopped to the side revealing a sweaty, flushed Kelly who lifted her head and called out cheerfully: "Mornin', hen!" I was worried about the types she was bringing back. If they were on her wavelength they could very well be disturbed and violent. Heaven knows what could have happened when we were asleep. Nadine wouldn't go back to the room and I realised that the only other free bed in the whole house was in my alcove. My stomach tightened.

My refuge within a refuge was disappearing. That night there'd be a complete stranger sleeping in our room. I wouldn't be able to close my door on the world any more. I'd no longer be able to say who came and went. And from what I'd heard, Nadine was far from normal, electing to sleep all day and wander around the house all night with a lighted candelabra. Oh God! We were sharing our room with a fire hazard. I already had a rope under my bed, just in case we had to escape out the window some night. My heart was throbbing with worry. I wouldn't be able to relax, uncertain that Jack and I were safe in our beds. Damn that Kelly! Nadine didn't waste any time. She moved in and went to bed in the alcove that very morning and stayed there for two days. I found myself tip-toeing around so as not to wake her and, catching myself, deliberately made a noise to wake her up.

By mid-December I'd had enough. I'd been at the refuge for three months. It was a wet, grey winter and we spent day after day cooped up indoors with nowhere to go and nothing to do. When the weather was bad, the house was crowded and the noise level was deafening. It was all I could do to keep Jack from being hurt by one of the older, boisterous children. More difficult women arrived and there was no privacy because the bed in the corner of my room was in constant use. Haven was no longer a safe place to be. Unstable women like Kelly could bring men in at night, others went round with lighted candles.

I spoke to a volunteer about the length of time I was likely to be there. She was an elderly Irish woman who answered in a slow, narcotic voice, as if she were on tranquilisers, that the average wait was about a year but that it would be longer for me because I didn't have any family connections in London. Her gaze sharpened briefly as she watched my reaction to this news. And she wasn't disappointed. My heart sank. We were in the lounge and the TV was blaring. I was wearing an old sweat suit from the bag under the stairs and my Empire of Fire. I looked pathetic and all wrong: with my saggy old sweats and my lips as intensely red as a 1940s film star. There was dirt everywhere. Kelly's stiletto boot was down the side of the sofa, vomit still stuck to the rim now hairy with mould. A child had pooed on the floor and other children were walking in it. There were little shitty footprints everywhere and I was doing my best to keep Jack away from it. It was pouring outside.

A year. Probably longer. Suddenly I burst into tears. The narco looked at me askance. I shouldn't have asked her. She didn't like me. She thought I was stuck up – always upstairs, always reading. The way I felt was beyond words. I simply had to get out of there. I clung to the memory of St Claude's and went to a nearby convent that had connections with the Priory. I was going to tell them about my circumstances and hoped they'd take us in as Ruth-Anne and Madeline had done. But this place was a different kettle of fish. It was a fortress-like building and when I rang the bell, no one answered. Eventually, the door opened a slice but I'd hardly said my name before a nun with cold blue eyes shut it in my face.

Desperately I tried another contact of Madeline's – a retired vicar in Dorset. One particularly bad day I rang him. My message was so garbled with stress that he couldn't understand what I was saying. He told me to slow down, "find my centre" and start again. So I took a deep breath and explained more calmly that I was in a battered wives refuge and it was terrible, that I'd come back from Canada in September and now it was December and I'd be there forever unless I could get myself out of it. I begged him to help me and he promised he would. Thanking him profusely, I put the phone down.

Two days later he rang back to say there was a woman in Poole who was looking for a lodger. Would I like to come and meet her? Yes. He said there was something I should know first. She was disabled and would need help in the house. I imagined a cottage and a little old lady in a wheelchair. Yes, yes, anything. Just get me out of here! Her name was Iris and we arranged that I'd get the train to Poole the following week to meet her. When I put the phone down, I realised I'd no idea where Poole was. I looked it up on a map. Dorset. On the south coast. About two hours from London.

I have always thought of coming to live in Poole as washing up on the beach in a storm. It could have been any beach. I'd never even have visited the place if dire circumstances hadn't taken me there. Dear old Poole, which opened its arms to me and my baby.

I remember the New Forest on the way down – what seemed like a million spectral tree trunks flickering by. Southampton, Bournemouth and then Poole. As the train pulled into the station, I was aghast at what I could see of the town. Planners had destroyed it with concrete monstrosities, arranged before me now along the railway track. I was met by a friend of the vicar called Francine, a fat woman with a crucifix around her neck, who took me to meet Iris. She wasn't there when we arrived so we waited outside the house. It was in fact a cottage, once part of a country estate now engulfed by suburbia. There was a driveway up to a ramshackle garage and a garden front and back. I hoped she wouldn't be long because Jack was getting restless in the buggy and Francine and I were running out of things to say. It was raining and the bungalows and semi-detached houses that stretched along the road in both directions looked drab under the grey sky.

I was biting my nails, wondering if I was doing the right thing in leaving London again. I thought back to the disaster with Arthur and felt that everything had happened because I left London. I was very unsure about the wisdom of burning my bridges again. On the other hand, I simply had to get out of Haven. I was driven to it. Jesus! Always driven to do things, never having the space to choose anything.

Brooding thus, I was startled by the sudden approach of a big gold Jaguar, a really beautiful old car that turned in and swept up the drive. It stopped and a pretty woman in a leather jacket got out and welcomed us with a broad grin. This must be Iris. But hang on, I thought she was disabled? The vicar had said so. I was expecting wheelchairs and walking sticks but the woman before me was most definitely able-bodied and, adding to the impression of rude good health, her constant laughter was loud and bawdy. She wore heavy mascara and had a kerchief tied jauntily around one boot. Introducing herself warmly, she shook hands with me and smiled at Jack. As we went indoors, I realised that I had little knowledge of English women and I'd certainly never lodged in the home of one before. I wondered what she'd make of the brogue.

Our room was tiny, just big enough for the two narrow beds and the wardrobe it contained, but of course I took it. I'd have lived in a tree house to get away from the refuge. There was a little sitting room as well with a television. It was arranged that we'd move in just after Christmas on December 30th. After a cup of coffee and more pleasantries we left.

When I asked Francine for details of Iris's disability, she was evasive: "Well . . . I don't know . . . she sometimes needs a walking stick."

I asked her what it was called.

"I don't know . . ." she repeated mysteriously, "I don't think it has a name."

We slept at Francine's that night, under layers of flowery nylon. Her house smelled of dogs. She and her husband took us on a tour of the area. I commented on how lovely the beach was.

"Yes, it's lovely here," her husband agreed, "and what's more, there aren't any blacks."

We stopped in Christchurch for chips and ate them in the car. Francine offered me a sausage.

"No, thank you," I replied from the back seat.

"No, thank you," she said to her husband, exactly as I had except in a high-pitched mewl. I was stunned to hear her mocking me right there under my nose.

I stared at the back of her head and the jaw working on the mouthfuls of chips and I felt as if I'd been slapped in the face.

I spent Christmas at the refuge. Rose came to see me with some presents and a card. She was going home for the holiday and we talked about the prospect of me joining her. She wanted me to but when I asked her if she thought I'd be welcome she chose her words carefully: "I don't think anyone would mind."

This euphemism convinced me to stay put. Anyway, it wasn't so bad. Most of the residents were going to be elsewhere. I bought extra oven chips and fish fingers, some chocolates and a bottle of gin and for a few glorious days the refuge was tidy and deliciously quiet.

On December 30th 1991 we were driven to Waterloo Station by a volunteer. Our belongings made a mound on the platform: suitcases, the rug, the lamp, the radio/cassette player, a tricycle I'd acquired, some books, with Jack's potty teetering on the top. My most treasured possession was really something of Jack's – a teddy bear that he'd been sent by Madeline and the rest of the community at St Claude's. He was knitted, brown and blue and had a name tag which read: "My name is Clive and I work for Amnesty International." Jack loved Clive and had him in a stranglehold in the buggy. I drank a cup of coffee and read *The Evening Standard* while I waited for the train and it was thus, so prosaically, that the turbulence of my younger years came to an end.

We were out of the storm, yes. On terra firma. But it was far from sunny skies. First there were obstacles to surmount. The first of these was Iris.

My initial impression of her as a warm, sunny woman was wrong. She wasn't like that at all. She was given to surges of bonhomie, which is what I got on that first day, followed by troughs of depression. The arrangement was that I'd pay for bed and board and also do the housework. This was on account of her disability. She couldn't muck in because of her dodgy muscles and had to have a nap every afternoon. She had a nine-year-old son called Reuben. When the day's chores were done and the children were in bed, I was to keep her company in her sitting room. As soon as I arrived with two mugs of coffee, she'd turn off the television and launch into an egocentric monologue that could last all evening. I wasn't to interrupt except perhaps with a question while she'd chain-smoke and had the demeanour of a celebrity being interviewed.

She was keen for me to know she was "an *it* girl". I didn't know what she meant.

"A what?" I asked.

"An *it* girl. You know . . . *It*. I have *it*. Sex appeal."

"Oh . . . right," I said, nonplussed, not knowing what to make of this blatant egotism.

"Yes. I never knew I had *it* until my mother told me. Like you, I said, 'What's that?' and she told me it was sex appeal and I said, 'Why didn't you tell me before?' and she said, 'Well, I thought you knew!'"

She was the only one of her friends who could pass the pencil test.

"What's that?" I asked.

"You know . . . you put a pencil under your boobs and if it falls they're still pert, like mine, but if it gets stuck you've had it." A great peal of laughter. "You'll have to do it. See which you are."

I cringed inside at her it-girl talk and her pencil test and I came to dread the moment when the television screen blacked out and I knew I'd be trapped for the next two or three hours in these strange one-sided conversations, feigning interest and wearing a false smile that made my face ache.

One evening she explained to me the full story of her disability and my ears pricked up. Lighting a cigarette to begin the narrative, she described the intermittent bloating and paralysis she experienced down her left side and battles with perfidious doctors who believed there was nothing wrong with her. She'd present herself at surgeries and stand before them with her left side drooping. They'd say that, yes, there was a slight droop but nothing out of the ordinary. She said she couldn't walk but when they checked her gait there was nothing wrong with it. Inwardly groaning, the doctors ran all the tests, which came back negative. Finally, because she wouldn't go away, they offered her an appointment with a consultant in London. She was thrilled – at long last, she crowed, she was going to see an expert, a man who knew what he was talking about. She'd get the correct diagnosis and go back to her GP vindicated. On the contrary and to her horror, he held her up in front of a roomful of students as a prime example of a certain psychosomatic disorder. In other words, it was all in her head, a phantom illness.

"Can you believe it? Psychosomatic indeed!" she interjected here.

I listened to the rest of the story: her undressing for the examination, the brush-off from the consultant, scuttling from the lecture room mortified. Throughout, I nodded my head and smiled, all the while realising, with mounting anger, that there was nothing wrong with her, that I was skivvying for a woman who was more than capable of doing her own housework and not only that, through my rent and housekeeping money I was paying her for the privilege.

And she did seem to think it was a privilege for me. Once, like Lady Muck, she "visited" me in the kitchen to discuss the menus for lunch and dinner. I looked up from the ironing, incredulous, and told her that lunch would be beans on toast and dinner would be egg and chips.

Living at the cottage was difficult. I'd never been a lodger before. Jack was two and getting into everything. I was ever-vigilant that he didn't twist the knobs off things or poo on the carpets. Iris didn't approve of the breakfasts I ate, which she said were too extravagant. I liked to start the day with a fried egg and some cheese between two slices of toast. It was something I picked up in the refuge in Canada. Angry and humiliated, I had to calculate the cost of a fried egg and a bowl of cereal. The difference was negligible.

Her friend came for coffee and brought her toddler. He was a biter and I wanted to strangle the stupid brat when Jack screamed in pain. Reuben, who was ten, didn't want us there. He scowled at us constantly and when Jack took one of his toys one day, he snatched it back from him, hissing: "I don't give my toys to paupers!"

Paupers.

The word hit me like a fist. I hadn't realised that that was how they viewed us. But, come to think of it, of course it was: I was a single parent coming from a refuge, living off the state with housing benefit paying the rent. I was glad that Jack was too young to understand.

I stayed out as much as possible and went back to what was practically our mobile home – me, Jack and the buggy with a bit of food in a bag, going clackety-clack along the roads. I accepted an invitation from the retired vicar to tea with him and his wife. When he drove us home, he kissed me hard on the lips in a quick snatching motion.

I dusted off my affirmations and repeated them desperately as I wheeled Jack around the town and then homewards in the twilight. "I am beautiful and everyone loves me," I affirmed over and over. I'd said it a zillion times by now but I still didn't believe it. As I neared the cottage, I sometimes stopped into a pub for a brandy. If that didn't work, I also recited the Lord's Prayer.

One night Iris told me that Francine had warned her about me.

"What do you mean . . . warned?" I asked, quaking in my boots, afraid that Francine had seen the badness behind my good manners.

"Well, she said to me, 'Be careful, you might get used'."

"What do you mean . . . used?" I asked faintly, the blood draining from my face.

"Well, I don't know . . . she's a funny old bird."

I couldn't sleep for thinking about it. I was a user. A sly, calculating type. Someone you get warned about. The sort who will take advantage of you as soon as your back is turned. But hang on. She didn't even know me, the judgemental old cow, with her crucifix hanging around her neck. All she knew was that I was a single parent. Was that it? Were single parents predisposed to taking advantage of people?

After sixteen months of life at the cottage I felt the way I had at the refuge – certain that I'd go mad if I didn't get away. And Jack was three then and needed a room of his own. I went to the council to see if they'd house us but the waiting time was in years, not months or weeks. And then, through word of mouth, I heard of a flat nearby that was empty.

It was an extension on the side of a house. Another small place. The kitchen was just a dark hole – a bit of converted garage with no windows, whose walls were raw breeze block. The lounge itself was long and narrow, like a hallway. If you stood in the middle and stretched out your arms you could almost touch the walls on either side. Upstairs was much better. It was light and airy with a spacious bedroom and bathroom. I loved the bathroom with its cork floor and big deep bath. I couldn't wait to get into it for my first soak in my own place. I took it all in, aware that the landlord, a divorcé called David who lived alone in the house, was at my side and watching us throughout. It made me nervous.

"Well Jack," I said, picking him up, "what do you think of your new hose?" Not *hose*, stupid! In my nervousness I'd run *house* and *home* together in my mind and it came out wrong.

"Steady on there," said David. "I haven't decided I'm giving it to you yet."

"Yes, of course, sorry," I apologised, suitably humbled. "Is it quiet?" I asked.

"Well, the last tenant, Wayne, could've been bangin' away in here all night and I never heard him," he said, grinning.

I blushed at such crudeness in front of my child. It was another thing I was glad Jack was too young to understand.

He wasn't sure about renting to a single parent. That's why he followed us around. He had to convince himself that I was a fit mother before he'd give it to me. I nodded in understanding. There were a lot of abused children about. But inwardly I was thinking: *Who made you an expert?* After cogitating he decided in my favour and I was overjoyed. At long last we had our own home again. It was a tiny flat but there was a kitchen, a lounge, a bedroom and a bathroom – in other words, somewhere to cook, sit, sleep and wash. Housing benefit would pay the rent. We didn't need any more.

There was a connecting door between the flat and the house and we went through to his lounge to sign the lease. The rooms I saw were sparsely furnished in the manner of a frugal bachelor. In the lounge, there was a television for sport, the fireplace he built himself, an armchair and a standard lamp for reading. The carpet was old and well worn. David was officious as a landlord. I watched him as he put on his reading glasses and got out a folder marked "flat". He was quite a good-looking man, bald with a silver beard and clear blue eyes, but his clothes were cheap and dirty. A red nylon jumper had grubby marks down the front as if he regularly wiped his hands on it and his tracksuit bottoms were full of holes. On his feet were an ancient pair of sandals whose soles were wafer-thin.

Horizons appeared again. He was a good deal older than me but never mind, I'd get him to buy himself some clothes, a leather jacket maybe and some jeans to knock the years off him and he'd be a sort of Hemingway lookalike who I'd fall in love with. He, on the other hand, hardly noticed me as he presented me with the contract of tenure and neatly wrote a receipt for the deposit and the first month's rent.

I left the cottage suddenly without giving notice and without a qualm of conscience. There'd be days when Iris would come down the stairs grim-faced and limping but I knew it was all in her mind.

I couldn't resist a visit to Francine. I rang the bell and when she answered I smiled sweetly. She invited me in and made a pot of tea. Trooping out the pleasantries, she sat down to pour and then I let her have it.

"Iris . . . says . . . you . . . warned . . . her . . . about . . . me," I said slowly and deliberately.

I watched her intently. The hand holding the teapot trembled.

"Why?" I asked.

She didn't say anything but made a surprised noise – "Ohh . . ." – and then back to the tea. "Would you like milk?"

"No."

"Sugar?"

"No."

She said nothing.

"Yes," I went on, "she said you warned her that she might be used . . ."

"Did I? What did I say that for? Used by who?"

"By me."

Knowing she would dissemble and that I'd never get the plain truth, I ploughed on for the sake of watching her squirm. "Why did you say that?"

"I . . ."

"You don't know me."

"No . . . I mean, yes, I don't."

"What did you mean exactly?"

"Well . . . I don't know . . . I . . . ehhmm . . ."

I waited.

"Oh . . . the blighter!" she announced finally, meaning Iris.

I stood up and said, "There was using done all right but it was *she* who used *me*."

And then I left her there in her stuffy front room with her undrunk tea.


David was a lonely man who was delighted that we'd come into his life. Sometimes he'd stand in the connecting doorway and throw us in confectionery – literally throw it in as if we were animals in a cage – and stand there, awkwardly grinning. Jack loved him instantly. For his fourth birthday David bought him his first proper toys: a go-kart, a play tent and an action man. When Jack was ill, he got him Lego, sweets and comics.

He wanted me to meet the neighbours. A lovely family, he said. I didn't want to. I was turned off people. One day, from upstairs, I heard their son baiting Jack in the garden: "Where's your Dad, Jack? Where's your Dad, Jack?" But when I got downstairs, the little bastard was gone.

David ate cheap, processed food. On top of the wonderful aroma of pipe tobacco and wood smoke, in the evenings there'd also be the greasy note of deep fried chips and beef burgers. So I cooked him some meals and before long we were eating together regularly. He shopped in economy stores and tried to get me to do the same but I refused. I'd been a devotee of Sainsbury's ever since that first day back from Canada when Adele had led me around like a zombie. I wouldn't budge on it, just as he wouldn't budge on the clothes. If he could get a pairs of trackies for £1.99, why should he pay thirty pounds for a pair of jeans. And as for a leather jacket. Forget it!

The evening came when David made a pass at me. I'd been waiting for it. I'd kept the Ernest Hemingway-in-a-leather-jacket image alive and daydreamed about it constantly. I turned to receive his kiss and was startled to find his mouth puckered up into a little hole as if he was sucking a lemon. I pecked the starfish that it made and pulled away, not realising until later that he was trying to hold his false teeth in. We went to bed together and it was awful. For a start, David had a secret: a very small penis, so small that penetration was almost impossible. He had no contingency plan and simply flopped about on top of me, trying to engage the unengageable, watching for my reaction. Once I'd seen it, he alluded to it constantly, hoping for reassurance I suppose, but I couldn't find the words. I was too shy to broach the subject of under-sized penises. And, in spite of myself, it disturbed me.

I fell asleep that first night and had a dream where I saw him naked with a black hole where his penis should have been, like a photograph in which someone had burnt a hole in the genital area with a cigarette. It woke me up in the small hours. I didn't know where I was at first but slowly recognised the outlines of his bare musty bedroom. I looked at him and was startled to see his head, face and all, wrapped tightly in the sheet, like a death mask. He said his bald head got cold in the night. Assuming he was asleep, I made to go to the toilet, but he wasn't asleep and as soon as I stood up, he whipped off the head dress and propped himself up on his elbow, all the better to cop a look at my naked body. I was startled by the sudden movement and the blatant voyeurism and after the bathroom I said good night and went back to my own bed in the flat. I needed to get back to Jack, who was sleeping peacefully in his little starter bed.

David may have taken my non-return that night as a judgement on his manhood and, sniffing rejection on the wind, he made a judgement of his own – it was better to go on the attack than to sit there and wait to be dumped. My dreams about Ernest Hemingway in blue jeans dissolved and as quickly as it had grown, the warmth I felt towards him drained away. This is why. One day not long after the bedroom fiasco, he asked me this question:

"Are you self-conscious about your height?"

My nerves reacted before my brain and I felt hot and uncomfortable. *Self-conscious*. The word ricocheted through me. It was what you said about a disfigurement. An ugly thing that you tried to hide. He thought I was ugly. Oh God!

Feeling knocked for six, my voice was shaky and lacked conviction but defiantly I answered, "No."

And it was true. I'd never thought about my height before. And no one had ever suggested it was an impediment. Until now. He looked at me for a long minute as if he found this hard to believe. My face was flushed with shame and I couldn't look at him but I managed to ask, "Why?"

He had his argument ready and waiting: "Well, I'm six foot and you're a good inch taller than me. That's way above average for a woman!"

Actually he was only five foot nine inches, but that didn't matter. Being a woman, I should have been shorter than him when, in fact, I was taller, and that made me somehow wrong. I dragged my gaze from the floor and I was startled by his eyes. They were ablaze with anger and his face and pate were mottled pink and white. He looked as if he hated me and I had no idea why. I didn't know what to say. His attack was so unexpected that it chased everything else out of my mind except the feeling of being too tall. Was I lanky? Lofty? Those playground taunts that I'd never been a victim of now occurred to me. Instinctively, I hunched my shoulders to make myself smaller and dreaded the moment when I'd have to stand up and expose my "wrongness".

Assured by my crouched posture that I was humbled, he continued: "It's all right though. You're tall, but you're quite attractive . . ."

I brightened.

". . . for your age."

I deflated again. Old. He'd brought me down with the

first comment and finished me off with this one. I was only thirty-four and he was fifty-six but that didn't seem to matter. In his opinion, I was getting on. In his eyes I was old and ugly. His ideal woman was much shorter and younger, sixteen or thereabouts. He made this clear by leering in an exaggerated way at such young women when we were out. Jesus, I thought, were all men paedophiles? Conversely, David liked other men to covet his woman. It made him feel like cock-of-the-walk. Thus I was on show when we were out and if I didn't get any attention, he was downcast and I blamed myself for not being more beautiful.

I twisted desperately on these humiliations and a series of violent images arose in my mind. I fantasised about killing him: strangling him, poisoning his food, burning his house down while he slept. I cried with the force of these murderous thoughts and I reached out to him for help in expunging them. I tried to talk to him about the height and age thing but he denied all knowledge of that conversation. I needed him to say: *No, you're not too tall. No, you're not too old.* But he wouldn't. I accused him of leering at other women but he denied that too. Clearly, he wasn't going to help me. Rather, he was leaving me alone with the bad feelings he'd engendered. Getting the boot in was all that mattered. Frustrated, I'd get drunk and start arguments with him but he'd just stare pointedly at my flat chest and those looks would undermine me more than anything he could have said. I threw drinks at him but he laughed. Once, I pulled his lighted pipe out of his mouth and threw it at him. Sparks flew everywhere. That got a reaction all right. He came at me, about to strike me with his fist, when Jack came in and ran at him, punching his legs with his little fists and shouting at David to get away from his mummy. That calmed us both down and we retreated. I wanted to quit the flat and I longed for the freedom I used to have in earlier times when I'd just end a relationship and move on. But things had changed. Now I had a child and it had been a long, difficult interlude since the last time I'd had a place of my own.

I tried to concentrate on the good things about David. Chief among these was the fact that he was good to Jack, kind and solid and generous. He trusted children, as we all do, because they couldn't hurt him. I thought of the jibes he might have suffered from women over the years because of his penis. With children, love seemed to flow out of him as naturally as breathing and Jack basked in it. I stifled my angry resentment for the sake of my child and Jack really benefitted from having David as a father figure. He played with him and read him bedtime stories every night, took him to football matches and Speedway and taught him to play cricket. There was never a repeat of the pipe incident. We ate together most evenings and David was the head of the "family", carving the joint, answering Jack's multitude of questions and teaching him table manners.

To the outside world I was completely transformed. I no longer wore old sweat suits or lurid red lipstick. I looked like any other respectable single parent, going about her business. I had a beautiful child, a nice little home, someone on hand to help me, who'd even marry me if I wanted it. But inside I was a devastated mess. Yes, the storm had truly ended but there was no peace, only a vacuum, and depression poured in. The adrenalin that had kept me going through countless dramas was gone. The words that described my state now were: flat, collapsed, empty, trapped, exhausted. I felt like I was in a hole, a million miles from home.

I became irritable and bad-tempered. I shouted at Jack and made him cry and when he whinged it made me worse. Once, I nearly kicked him, the toe of my shoe stopping inches from his little body. He saw the shoe and looked at me in horror. When our eyes met, the love that had always pulsed between us missed a beat. Jesus Christ! What am I doing?

I fell prey yet again to something that had plagued my whole life – abject loneliness. I didn't have any sense of belonging in Poole. My real life was somewhere else and I wanted to go and live it. I thought about Eamon Harris and howled bitter tears for the life I was sure I would have had as his wife and the mother of his children. Nostalgia eased my loneliness so I thought about home. I longed to be back there. I longed to be a child again, to go back to a time when innocence prevailed, in spite of my father. In my mind's eye, I wandered around the streets of Cobh. I preferred night time, after rain, with the deserted streets reflected in the wet, black tarmac. I'd sniff the many turf fires in the cosy sitting rooms as I wandered around the town. Up Harbour Hill to the Cathedral, along the Bishop's Road, past the convent where I went to school, through the Crescent, along West Beach then away from the lights of the town and out Ballywilliam into the sacred darkness of the countryside. Around the island and back home. Home. The word "home" would snap me out of my daydream and I'd open my eyes to the too-narrow lounge and realise that the only home I had was right there in that little flat. There was nowhere else.

David said I made everyone around me miserable and that I needed help. I resisted the idea of therapy fiercely, especially since he'd suggested it. Was this his latest insult? How dare he! It really was too much. I was old and ugly and now mental as well.

"HOW DARE YOU SUGGEST I'M INSANE!" I shouted at him.

I simply wouldn't consider it at all. He was just a stupid old man. What the hell did he know? I believed I was strong and that belief had been vital in my struggle to survive. I'd survived a hell of a lot after all. Without it I couldn't go on. Having therapy meant admitting I was weak and that I was failing in the challenges life set me. Furthermore I was sure none of the fragrant smiling mothers I met at playgroup ever went for therapy so obviously good people didn't need it. I was hostile and abusive whenever he mentioned it but he was so worried about my mental health – my constant crying and shouting and the effect on Jack – that he persisted.

And one day, I had to admit that he was right. I had to admit to myself that I wasn't happy and I wasn't the good mother that I thought I was. It was true; I *was* creating misery all around me with my black moods. I remembered that day with the pipe and little Jack defending his mother. He was so close to getting caught up between two warring adults and experiencing the kind of trauma that I'd experienced. But I'd rejected violence, hadn't I? I'd drawn a line under it for my child's sake. That was my guiding force. My basic principle was that Jack would not have the kind of childhood that I'd had. I'd promised him that in the womb, hadn't I? I'd promised him when he was born that I'd do my very best for him. I realised with a shock that an ugly force had come loose in me and was overriding my best intentions to be a good parent.

The danger of becoming a bad parent like my father and breaking my child's heart was so real now that I went straight to my GP for help. I didn't go into detail but told him that I couldn't stop crying and I felt so awful that I wanted to die. Rather than prescribing drugs, he referred me to a counsellor at the Alderney Community Hospital. A few days later I got the date and time of my first appointment in the post.

The morning arrived and I was nervous. A plethora of unknowns jangled in my head. Would the hospital be like the one my father had been at? Would there be tweedy old men with dirty minds? Women weeping hysterically? Would there be lunatics roaming around? Would I bump into anyone I knew? Believe it or not, in spite of my back catalogue of negative experiences, I didn't know what we'd talk about. What would the counsellor be like? All I knew about him was his name. Ian.

The block where I was to have my sessions was at the back of the hospital, farthest from the gate, and I had to run a gauntlet of eyes flicked in my direction before I got there. I cringed and hurried on to my destination. I sat in a foyer that was bright and sunny, with magazines on a coffee table. There were lots of plants and some books on shelves. There were other people waiting too but I stared fixedly out the window, avoiding eye contact.

Eventually I heard my name being called in a soft Australian accent and I looked around. A pleasant young man, thin and delicate with brown hair and eyes was coming towards me. I liked Ian immediately because he smiled so kindly at me. We went to a therapy room and sat opposite each other. He waited for me to speak. My eyes were locked onto his and he was very calm and in control. I just stared at him, my face sweating.

The trouble was, I couldn't talk at first. Although I had so much to say that it made me cry, I'd learnt as a child not to talk about the things that were hurting me. The more upsetting the experience, the less you talked about it. Ironically, in our house, it was not violence that was taboo but tenderness. We talked openly about my father's shortcomings. We denounced him regularly, calling him all sorts of names like madman, bastard, emotional cripple, sicko. But the feelings generated by his violence – fear, sadness and loneliness – and the language that described those feelings – I'm frightened, I don't feel safe, I want to die, I feel sick, I feel alone – were outlawed.

Eventually I said this: "I should be where you are!"

I just blurted it out and burst into tears. Ian wanted to know what I meant. Huge sobs shook me and I had my head in my hands as a torrent of pent-up feelings poured out. I couldn't speak. I just cried. But when the tears subsided, I was surprised to find that my reticence was gone and sentences vied to get out of my mouth.

Information tumbled out of me and I dumped it out in front of him, trusting that he'd be able to make sense of it all.

I told him that I'd studied psychology at university and might have been a therapist too if I hadn't had this awful life and made all these mistakes and dug myself into this deep pit that I couldn't get out of. I was a failure and living proof of that was the fact that I was there needing therapy.

"Oh, I see," he said gently.

I started crying again and my shoulders were heaving and the words were all coming out together as I told him my father was mad and my mother had abandoned me and my memories were terrible and I'd been badly beaten and I was ugly and I'd had three abortions. I could hardly get it all out.

To Ian, it was just a jumbled mass of distress, so he told me to stop, breathe deeply ten times and start again at the beginning. I did so and after the breaths I felt calmer and more in control. He, by comparison, was serene. As he listened, he took notes. That felt good. It made my pain more real somehow. It wasn't just in my head. It was down on paper as well. He went slowly through what I'd said, seeking details here, clarification there. Soon it was nearly the end of our hour and he put his notebook away and looked at me.

"You've certainly been in the wars," he said, his voice full of kindness and compassion. He told me we were going to finish with a visualisation exercise during which I'd make my way to a place where I felt safe and happy. Before he led me through it I'd have to relax more deeply.

He told me to close my eyes and breathe deeply. I had to imagine breathing into each part of my body in turn and telling it to relax. But when I closed my eyes and focused on my body that first time I had the strangest, jarring sensation that made me feel dizzy. Like a string puppet thrown in a chair, I felt that my limbs weren't in alignment, facing forward, but going off in different directions. I sensed my head angled to the left, my torso to the right, my arms to the left and my legs to the right. It was so bad that I had to stop and open my eyes to confirm that all my limbs were actually in line. They were, but when I closed my eyes again they weren't.

Ian began leading me along the path:

"There's a path before you. What's it like? Is it grassy or paved? You walk along this path. What can you see?"

I couldn't concentrate and my mind was whirring. He went on ahead and I lost track of the instructions. My eyes were closed but I wasn't seeing the path. Jack popped into my head. And then David. I was seeing Ian sitting opposite me, the room we were in, the hospital, even the plants on the window-sill behind his head. I went through the motions, his voice tuning in and out until finally he was saying: ". . . a place where you feel happy and safe".

But I couldn't see it. I'd lost the thread of the discourse.

"When you're ready, open your eyes."

Please don't ask me to describe my special place, I thought. And he didn't. I told him about the string puppet feeling and he said it was a symptom of stress and would pass eventually as I learnt to relax. He asked me how I felt and I said: "Much better." It was true. I felt that I'd found someone who understood me. I wasn't alone any more. We made an appointment for the following week. Then we both stood up smiling and said goodbye. I left the building and for a moment I stopped and looked back at the room I'd been in. I stared at the window with its venetian blind and had a wonderful sensation of lightness. I'd left my dirty foul baggage in there. It was in there, not in me. And Ian didn't mind. He knew what to do with it. He'd be happy for me to dump off more next week.

I was proud of myself for going. I marched out of the hospital with a bounce in my step, drinking in the sights and sounds and smells, revelling in the blue sky and the flowers that lined the avenue down to the main gate. I decided not to get the bus but walked home on a high. David had told me he was proud of me for going, so while I was at the hospital he'd gone out and bought the jeans I'd been trying to get him to wear. He was wearing them when I got home and I was touched by that. I picked Jack up and hugged him. We were all smiling and to celebrate we decided to go for a drive. David asked me where I'd like to go. The Purbecks, I answered without hesitation.

The Purbeck Hills lay west of Poole and I loved them because their high windswept fields and dry stone walls reminded me of Ireland. We stopped at an ivy-covered pub and sat in the garden, where Jack played with other children. David got him some chips and a bottle of pop while we adults had pints of shrimp and glasses of beer. The view was breathtaking. It swept down over a plain of farmland and water meadows and up again to Corfe Castle, a mighty fortress in its day, ruined by Cromwell. In the far distance, there was a silvery lick of Poole Harbour. We drove home through that beautiful landscape, singing "The Grand Old Duke of York" over and over for the benefit of Jack, who loved it.

At my next appointment with Ian I began to describe in detail my father's violent attacks on my mother, the awful physicality of the beatings, the fear that he'd kill her, the constant anxiety about the next assault, the foulness of his language, his hatred of us, the way he called us "swill", the isolation, and the shame of his attempted suicide. I cried copious amounts, really cried, storms of tears. For the first time in my life I was talking openly and at length about my childhood. It had never really happened before. Boyfriends didn't want to know, women friends were horrified and my siblings found it too painful. Now I had the opportunity to discuss my life at length with someone who understood these matters. Ian realised that I had been traumatised and without earlier intervention had carried that trauma with me all my life. Someone was listening to me and he was trained to help. The sense that I wasn't alone any more deepened. I felt validated. I'd presented myself with depression and, according to Ian, I had every right to feel depressed. Paradoxically, that made me feel better.

I saw Ian every week and we did a mixture of talking, relaxing and visualising. Eventually, with practice, I was able to relax enough to get to a special place. It was a sunny grove of tall pine trees by the sea. I felt happy and

peaceful there. Ian asked me to describe the beatings I'd
had. I did, but only up to a point. I didn't know what his
reaction would be if I admitted that I'd goaded men into
beating me. I skirted around this aspect of my relationships
with men. I didn't understand my experience of violence
well enough at the time to talk about my motivations. I
didn't understand then as I do now, that I'd internalised
violence as a result of my childhood. Awareness of violence
was part of my very being and, modelling myself on my
mother, I played the part of the victim.

People view domestic violence in a conventional way.
Men are the aggressors and women are the victims. For
instance, the woman who took me in when Nicholas
broke my nose cursed him for it. But, remembering all the
times I'd provoked him into violence, I'd said to her: "It
was my own fault."

She'd been appalled that I should think such a thing:
"Of course it wasn't, you poor girl. Stop blaming yourself."

"No! You don't understand! I *wanted* him to hit me!"

"Stop making excuses!"

"I'm not!"

"You're in denial."

"I'm NOT! I've never been more honest!" And I
hadn't.

But beating a woman is a social taboo. The idea of the
woman as the aggressor is an uncomfortable one.

Would Ian believe me? Would he think I was a bad
person, not worthy of his time? How would he compute
this information? I wasn't aware that such knowledge
would only help him to understand the depth of my
father's destructive influence. Far from thinking I was bad

he would have realised all the sooner how damaged I was.

We concentrated on visualisations and as time went on they became darker. In an effort to free me from my father's influence, Ian devised a visualisation in which my father was dead and I'm digging a deep hole and burying him in it, and another where I visualised myself as an adult, intervening during one of his attacks on my mother and stopping him. He made some recordings of visualisation exercises for me to do at home. I was deeply touched that he made such an effort on my behalf and I listened to them dutifully. Each time I did so the details of the scene became sharper. For example, I saw my father's immobile dead features, the colour and texture of the soil as I dug it, the depth of the hole I was digging.

I saw Ian for about six months and then he told me that he was going back to Australia and our sessions would have to end. I was dismayed. He was an excellent therapist and I felt the beginnings of change over the course of my weekly visits. The regular visualisations of my father dead and buried were helping me to emerge from his shadow. The visualisations of special places were helping me to relax and think positively. I really regretted that our relationship was ending but that first experience of therapy was my starting point. I was lucky to have had such a kind and sensitive man as my first counsellor. The crucial factor was that I *wanted* to talk to him. I *wanted* to hear what he had to say. That was my criterion in subsequent encounters with therapists. Did I feel comfortable with this person? Did I want to talk to him or her?

After Ian, I wanted more. Meeting him had put me on the road to recovery, albeit that road was long and bumpy. Before he left, he asked me if I'd be interested in group therapy. Of course I would. Now that I'd started, I jumped at the chance to continue counselling. So he referred me to a group run by two counsellors called Robert and Ellen.

The group sessions were right over on the other side of Bournemouth on Thursday evenings. I got Jack's tea early and David babysat. It took two buses in the rush-hour traffic and an hour and a half to get there. On that first evening there were eight of us and we sat in a circle. Those who knew each other were chatting and I sat there nervously waiting for the session to start. Ellen and Robert arrived and sat at opposite ends of the circle. They were striking-looking people. He was a handsome donnish man. She was elegantly dressed and doe-eyed, a beauty in her day, no doubt. She wore floaty dresses and beautiful jewellery. I felt ugly by comparison and drew my big clumpy trainers as far under the chair as I could get them. Ellen's elegance made me shy and I didn't want to speak but I knew that soon I'd be introduced as a new member and would have to say something about myself.

The moment came and, clenching my buttocks, I trotted out some details: "Hello. I'm Cora. I'm a mother. I'm Irish and I live in Poole."

No one said anything but I could feel a sort of psychic budging up to let me into the group. That felt good. Ellen turned her attention to the others with a fixed smile and enquired about the week: What had happened? What feelings came up? Any reflections? I studied those present from under my eyelashes. They were talking about ongoing situations in their lives, discussions that had started before I joined. There was Alan, whose wife had left him with the children; Sandra, whose father had beaten her; adopted Rachel, who was getting married – she was a size sixteen but wanted to be in a size twelve for the wedding; Mark, who couldn't get a girlfriend. Robert contributed a comment or two but was essentially a shy man. They were like parents to a family of waifs and strays.

After a few weeks I opened up a bit more and each week I told the group something new. First, that my parents had stolen so much from me and that I hated them for it. I was angry when I said this and I waited for the sky to fall down, but it didn't. Next, I admitted that I found motherhood hard at times. I'd always run away from difficulties before and now I couldn't. Again, I felt no disapproval. Then, the biggie:

"I've had three abortions."

Silence. The statement sailed out into the air and drifted away. It was all right. I'd said it to a roomful of people and I was still in one piece in my chair, with my coffee in my hand.

I was shocked to hear from Sandra, however, that Rachel disapproved of me. Being adopted, she was sensitive to maternity and thought it was disgraceful to have a child and not appreciate him. But I did appreciate Jack. She didn't understand. It was the circumstances of my parenting that I found hard, not my child, whom I loved deeply. I was shocked that in a therapeutic environment I should encounter someone who disliked me. It changed the whole tone of the experience for me. Now I was apprehensive about going, hoping she wouldn't be there and careful of what I said in front of her.

Suddenly Robert, the father-figure, left the group due to other commitments, and we all felt the sting of abandonment. One Thursday after his departure, I told Ellen about a dream I had where I was at a wonderful party and I was sitting on a bench talking to Robert. Suddenly he pushed me off onto the floor because he wanted to make room for someone else. Ellen's face hardened. She glared at me and ignored me for the rest of the session. I wished I hadn't mentioned my stupid dream. Perhaps I didn't appreciate the difficulties they had overcome to establish the group, the effort they put in or the strictures placed on them by the NHS. In any case, I was hurt by her exclusion and I cried miserably at the back of an empty bus all the way back to Poole.

Ellen and Robert's group was based on the writings of an American self-help guru called John Bradshaw. He had a twelve-step programme like Alcoholics Anonymous and had written four books on the theme of dysfunctional family life and the recovery process. The first book *The Family* was a wonderful read. It was so packed with insights and revelations about how dysfunction affects family members that my heart pounded as I read it. Over and over, I'd read something and respond, "Yes, yes, that's right! That's what I've got! I know how that feels!" I sat in the back garden with my book and cups of tea and I recognised all the features and symptoms of dysfunction. I had that feeling I'd had with Ian, that I wasn't alone.

The second book in the series, *Healing the Shame that Binds You*, describes shame as a master emotion in dysfunctional families, the underlying primary feeling that influences all other feelings. According to John Bradshaw, it is not the normal shame that we feel when we do something wrong but a toxic feeling of *being* shameful passed on to us by our parents. The difference was huge. We all do things that we're ashamed of. But we don't all feel that we *are* shameful. I did. I thought I was bad and ugly and from an early age longed for the dark of night or winter to cover me up. It didn't matter that I was a child and had never hurt a fly. I thought about the squalor we lived in: the piss bucket, my father's foul ranting, *swill*, the visits from the police, knowing people pitied us. But it wasn't just that. It was the shame that my parents had garnered in *their* sad childhoods and brought to our family. I was poisoned with it and it had destroyed my confidence and self-esteem.

I read these two books avidly, underlining something on nearly every page, and got what I needed from them – a bit more validation of what I'd suffered and why. And something else: the concept of the inner child. Bradshaw's theory suggested that my problems stemmed not from the fact that the child was gone, quite the contrary, they stemmed from the fact that the child was still there, unable to pass into memory because of unresolved issues.

Now, at the age of thirty-four, for the first time I looked back at myself as a child and I felt a lump in my throat. I'd grown up and stumbled from one bad experience to the next without ever pausing to take stock. I hadn't thought of myself as a child for a long time. Although I knew that my early experiences were at the root of my problems, I perceived my childhood as something that was gone. I was no longer a child. Therefore it was too late to help my childhood self. This was a big part of my problem. I felt as if there was a big piece of me missing which I'd never be able to retrieve. Therefore I'd never be whole.

But then I found an old picture of myself, aged about seven. It was an official photo, taken at my school on the morning of my First Communion. I'm smiling shyly at the camera, hair glossy and black, cheeks fat, skin glowing with health. I am a child of Christ, about to receive his body for the first time, so I'm dressed in a white lace frock, wearing a tiara and clutching a bunch of lily-of-the-valley with a candle stuck in the middle.

I vaguely remembered the chaos in the house that morning: everyone getting ready to go the Cathedral (all except my father of course, who stayed in bed), my mother shouting for someone to find the comb, pulling the curlers out of my hair and dousing me in hair spray. I remembered putting on the dress and feeling special, nervous about sticking out my tongue and then maybe biting the wafer and hurting Jesus.

I felt a graze of the intense heat I used to feel when my father was assaulting my mother. I remembered how I'd screamed and cried and tore at my hair and fingers in the throes of trauma. And yet my fat little face is smiling for the camera. Eyes crinkled up, lips together, not showing my uneven teeth – pleasing my grandmother. I am a picture of innocence and promise and the pathos of the greater context stabs me as I think of how my parents destroyed it all. I kissed the picture and held it close. I went inside, down into my stomach where I was most like a child and felt the fear and bewilderment of little Cora.

When Jack was in bed and I had time to myself, I'd sit quietly and imagine my young self on my lap, wrapped up safe and warm in my arms. I imagined I was her parent and I told her I loved her, cuddled her and rocked her. I switched roles and became the child and I could feel my young self receiving love for the very first time. I felt the warm arms around me. I felt the body of the loving adult. I knew that this adult would never abandon me. I felt her love as something solid and never-ending. I sat like this with my photograph many times and sometimes I cried. Eventually I had enough of it; I visualised putting her away in my heart and letting her go.

The group folded due to lack of funding. I wasn't sorry really. Group therapy wasn't for me. I couldn't take other people's problems on board. And I was upset to realise that at least one of the participants had judged me, rather harshly. I had so much to say but not in a public forum like a group, for the benefit of people who didn't understand me. I needed to talk in private to someone who could help me and give me guidance. Before the end, we went for an Indian meal with Ellen. She turned up kohl-eyed and expensively dressed and was the glowing focus of the evening. We vied to get her attention and I felt like a child again, vying with my siblings for a scrap from my mother. It made me feel bad.

After the group, I was alone again. As time passed, I slipped slowly back into depression. Daily life was a grind and everything seemed difficult. I cried a lot and lay on my bed, staring out the window. I didn't think of my feelings as an illness called depression because I'd had them most of my life. They just felt like me, but more so. I did my best to hide it from Jack. Gritting my teeth, I forced myself to be cheerful in his presence. I used visualisation to help me, seeing a knob, as on a TV, and turning off my low moods when I was with him. I saw a barrier, like a dam, between my child and my bad feelings, a wall keeping back the poison in me and stopping it from infecting him.

I made no such efforts with David. I hated him because I felt trapped in his flat and I picked at his insults so they never healed. How dare he say I'm too tall! How dare he say I'm too old! How dare he say I need help . . . etc., etc. When Jack was elsewhere, we bickered viciously about little things, which wore me down. He, on the other hand, enjoyed it because he saw our fighting as the scrapping of two of life's survivors. In his view we'd both survived by being hard-nosed: "When you bite, I bite back," he was fond of saying. One day he approached me tentatively and showed me an article he'd read in the *Daily Mail* about anti-depressants. Millions of people were taking them and feeling better. Why not try them? I was highly indignant at this suggestion. I didn't need drugs. I wasn't that bad, was I? Here he was, yet again, telling me there was something wrong with me. I was too tall, too old, mental and now sick as well.

"HOW DARE YOU SUGGEST THAT I NEED DRUGS!" I shouted, "*YOU* TAKE THEM IF YOU LIKE THEM SO MUCH!"

With that I scrunched the newspaper into a ball and threw it at him, whereupon he retreated and didn't mention the subject again. I fumed at the suggestion that I should be on prescription drugs. I was afraid of them. I associated them with my father, who kept a constant supply of pill bottles beside his bed and had emptied two of them *that night*.

After six months with Ian, I'd had my quota of NHS counselling and I couldn't afford a private therapist, so I cast around desperately for some other form of solace. Nostalgic for the community of St Claude's, I started going to the local Anglican church, St Luke's. The vicar, Charles Johnson, was a genuine man with the gift of oratory. What he said always touched me in some way and made me feel better. Once, he and his wife Karen invited Jack and I to Sunday lunch. I accepted the invitation in a dumbfounded way and squirmed with uncertainty for days afterwards. I couldn't go. What on earth would we talk about? We had nothing in common. They were so refined. Why had they invited me anyway? Did they feel sorry for me? Yes, probably. How dare they! No, I definitely wouldn't go. I wasn't a charity case. On the other hand, no one else in Poole had invited me to Sunday lunch so I changed my mind. In the end I went, armed with a bottle of wine and a bunch of flowers. I laughed nervously to myself on the way to the vicarage at what I'd have said ten years earlier at the thought of having dinner with a vicar.

The tablecloth was pristine white and there were crystal glasses into which Charles poured an inch of wine. I longed for more. Jack was three and a half and going through a fussy phase with food – he liked peas but not on Wednesdays, sausages were good but only cut up. We had potatoes, gammon and peas which was a relief because I knew he'd clear his plate. Portions were small, but beautifully cooked and presented. Their concept of a sufficiency of potatoes was very different to mine. One. Two perhaps, if you were still peckish. I could have eaten everything on the table by myself.

I'd listened to the news carefully during the week so I'd have something to say at the table. There'd recently been an IRA bombing in Warrington in which two children died. It caused outrage in the media and I alluded to      it now, inviting the scorn and contempt for the Irish that I was sure lurked beneath the polite exterior. Here it comes, I thought, as I sweated and shoved food into my dry mouth. But Charles astounded me. He laid his knife and fork gently on his plate, clasped his hands in his lap and fell silent. Then, addressing the middle distance, he said softly: "Everywhere we've been, we've caused trouble."

I looked at him and you could see it hurt him and he felt guilty for his race and for the sins of Empire. I couldn't think of anything ameliorating to say. And it wouldn't have been right anyway. He was an honest man who'd spoken the truth. The clock ticked loudly and then his wife moved the conversation on and slowly he resumed his meal. Jack chased peas around his plate with his fork and made us all laugh. After lunch we moved to the sitting room where Karen produced a box of chocolates and some toys for Jack to play with. Charles played Beethoven on the piano and each note seemed to caress my soul. I didn't want him to stop.

Thanks to his honesty, I left the vicarage with a positive sense of my Irishness. We weren't a murderous rabble as the gutter press were screaming, but a proud race forced to resist imperial abuse. And this was a fact underwritten by a dignified man of the cloth. I basked in the afterglow of that day, until I noticed the similarity among those who went to the vicarage for Sunday lunch – misfits and loners every one!

In spite of the kindness of the Johnsons, I never felt at ease at the church. I was sure the congregation looked down on me and I stopped going. But one day, not long after the Sunday lunch, I felt so bad that I ran up to the vicarage as if I were being chased by a monster and cried uncontrollably at the kitchen table. I told Karen I was so unhappy I wanted to kill myself. She comforted me as best she could and put me in touch with a counsellor whose name was Ralph. He was some sort of celebrant at St Luke's and I'd seen him at the church in his vestments giving out communion – a craggy, military type much older than Ian or Robert. I didn't inquire about his qualifications. I was happy with Karen's recommendation and the fact that his service was free and I wasted no time in seeing him.

Our sessions took place at a community centre on a vast housing estate. I went there by bus, often in the rain, and passed the journey looking out at the small uniform dwellings that covered the treeless hillsides. It was a depressing sight and although I was glad to be in therapy again, by the time I got to the clinic I'd feel worse than ever. During our first session, he told me that he was a counsellor first and a Christian second and I could tell him absolutely anything.

Painfully, I opened up and told him I wished I was dead, that I had an urge to kill Jack and then kill myself. I described in detail how I'd smother Jack, take his limp little body into my bed, settle him down beside me and then kill myself. Ralph was sitting facing me at close quarters and while I gave this account of my suicide fantasy, he ran his finger back and forth over my naked forearm. I was surprised by this action and felt confused. The sensation was startling and made me uncomfortable – yet he was helping me, wasn't he? A queasy, obsequious "that's nice" leaked out of my mouth and the guilty finger withdrew immediately.

Ralph dismissed my talk of suicide with a brusque rejoinder – "Now, now, there's no need for that" – focusing instead on my wedding ring and wanting to know why I wore it if I was a single parent.

"Because I'm married," I answered defensively.

"But you said you're a single parent."

"Yes, I am, but . . ." I was on the point of explaining that I'd got married in Canada when he interrupted me:

"Look dear," he pronounced emphatically, "if you're bringing your son up on your own, you are a single parent. You don't need that silly ring."

And, as if reading my mind, he added slowly and deliberately:

"You . . . have . . . nothing . . . to . . . be . . . ashamed . . . of."

So I took off my wedding ring and never wore it again.

One day I told Ralph about a dream I'd had where an angel is crucified on a tree trunk in a vast misty forest. I asked him what it meant. Did he think that the angel was me? Did the crucifixion represent my pain? Was the forest my life?

With a broad stroke, he swept aside all my introspections and answered with typical bluntness:

"Listen to me, dear, you are far too wrapped up in yourself. Never mind about angels and forests. You have to snap out of this morose thinking."

I was speechless at this reply. It stung that he'd summed me up so unflatteringly. I wasn't wrapped up in myself, was I? That was other people. I slunk out of the room at the end of the session, cross and vowing not to return, wanting vengefully to report him for the illicit caress I could still feel on my forearm.

However, when my pride recovered, I admitted to myself that it might be true. Maybe I did focus on myself too much. And at the expense of others. I had an awful image of myself wrapped up in the warm cloak of depression and victimhood while Jack and David shivered in the cold. I suddenly realised that I wasn't the only person in the world who was suffering. With shame now rather than anger, I remembered David braving my wrath and showing me the article about antidepressants. Maybe it wasn't such a bad idea. I asked Ralph for his opinion. He approved of medication in most cases and thought I could be trusted to take them sensibly – mentioning, by way of contrast, a woman who'd taken a whole month's supply of antidepressants in one night. He thought I should try them. And that's what I did. I went to my doctor and he prescribed Seroxat.

I didn't start taking them immediately. I studied them first. A month's supply on a card. Twenty-eight little blue diamond-shaped tablets, rather like the contraceptive pill.

Also targeting a hormone, the one that controlled mood – serotonin. I'd read all about how they worked – they'd boost my serotonin levels and I'd feel better. I knew that drug treatment was referred to in a derisory way. Terms like "happy pills" and books like *Prozac Nation* didn't help. I'd heard of people whose symptoms got worse and even people who'd killed themselves when they started anti-depressants, but I also knew that huge numbers of people took them without problems.

I'd had them in my bag for a few days when I went to meet Mark and Sandra, from the group, in Bournemouth one wet Friday evening. When I got to the restaurant Sandra was waiting outside – not directly outside, but across the road in a doorway. When she saw me coming she withdrew into the shadows. She didn't want me to see her. Why not? I thought. What have I done to her? Pretending I hadn't seen her, I went into the restaurant to wait. Rattled by this avoidance of me, I tore open my very first packet of Seroxat and took twice the recommended dose – forty milligrams instead of twenty – thinking they might act on me like valium. After about half an hour I felt sea-sick, with my head so heavy it was inches from the table. I left the restaurant early, pleading illness, and Mark and Sandra faded from my life. I never found out why she hid from me that night. I suppose she was just more comfortable with Mark than she was with me. Taking a double dose was a mistake and I felt terribly nauseous for the next twenty-four hours.

It was September 1994 and Jack had just started school. He was a week away from his fifth birthday. I'd gone back to teaching English as a foreign language. And on the Monday after the double-dose Friday, I went to work feeling sure everyone would know I was drugged up. But they didn't. Apart from the fact that I spoke more slowly, there were no outward signs. It was all inside. At first, I felt disorientated – sick and well, happy and sad at the same time. I felt strangely buoyant as if I was walking on the moon and I had no appetite.

Gradually, after about a week, the nausea passed and I was amazed at the change in my mood. It was like coming through clouds into sunshine, like a chemically induced miracle wherein my mind quietened right down. There was a sort of peaceful silence within me that I'd never felt before. All the anxious babbling voices were gone. It was wonderful. And so simple. I took one little tablet every day and I felt good, better than I'd ever done in my life.

David was impressed by the change in me. I wasn't nearly so bad-tempered and I smiled far more. I felt so good that I stopped seeing Ralph. Jack now had a room in the house. It was a beautiful autumn and in the evenings when he was asleep, I lay on my bed watching the sun go down and listening to music, particularly an album called *Deep Forest* – a mix of new age and ethnic instrumentals that suited my new-found peace of mind down to the last note. I thought about Jack asleep next door and my heart burst with love for him. I thought about the games we played together. Games that we made up ourselves and played every day – like Butcher Boy, where I mistakenly take the butcher's assistant (Jack) home instead of my meat; and Jack Cake where I buy the very last cake (Jack) in the shop and take it home for my tea. I thought about David and inwardly I thanked him for putting up with my problems and pointing me in the direction of antidepressants. I thought about the following day: getting Jack up and dressed for school, going to work, coming home, shopping, cooking and putting him to bed and I looked forward to it all.

There were stories about the difficulties of withdrawal. The information leaflets made clear that anti-depressants weren't addictive but that you shouldn't stop the medication suddenly. It should always be phased out. That sounded all right to me. In any case, I wasn't considering withdrawal. That would be at some distant point in the future. I felt great as a result of Seroxat. I had peace at last. So what if it was chemically induced, I argued. And there were other benefits. I slept well and when I woke up in the mornings I got up easily, and didn't cower under the covers for as long as possible as I used to. For the first time in my life, I could think and plan without being assailed by fear. The pit that I'd told Ian about was still there, but pharmacology had thrown me in a rope and I'd grabbed it with both hands.

I first learned about anger work from John Bradshaw's books. Most schools of thought agree that expressing anger is catalytic. Healing is not possible without getting it out of your system. You will never be happy unless you confront those who have hurt you and express your anger at them. As in my case, anger is often buried. As children, we suppress it in order to survive and it can stay like that for many years, lodged deep in the psyche, causing depression and other emotional problems. It takes time and commitment to access it and bring it to the surface.

Before I'd stopped seeing Ralph, I told him about my father and how much I hated him. Suddenly, he pulled up an empty chair and told me to imagine my father sitting there and to confront him with my feelings. I couldn't. I'd never done so before and I was far too inhibited for such an exercise. I looked at the empty chair and felt nothing. Ralph waited with his arms folded and part of me flew out of the therapy session and watched it from a distance. The whole thing seemed ridiculous. I felt like I was auditioning for a part in a play, the role of young-woman-gets-angry-with-father, a performance for the counsellor's benefit. I tried to push out some feeling but it wouldn't come. It was simply impossible for me to summon up powerful emotions on cue. Still he waited.

"I'm sorry. I can't," I admitted awkwardly.

"Maybe next time," he said curtly as he put the chair away.

Ellen had suggested smashing crockery to kick-start the anger. I couldn't do that because I didn't have any spare. I had just two of everything – two cups, two plates, two bowls – so I looked around for something else. I saw a tea towel, wet it, wrung it out and twisted it into a rope. Then I whacked it hard on the kitchen table.

THWOCK!

It made a loud noise that imprinted itself on the quiet morning air. It felt good. It had a force about it. I waited a few days and then I did it again and that felt good as well. The kitchen in the flat was very private. When the big heavy fire door was shut it was sound-proof, which was a great advantage. I went in there one day when Jack was at school and closed the door. I took the tea towel-rope once again and whacked it hard on the kitchen table. I picked up the pace and whacked it three or four times. My heart was racing but in a good way. The more I attacked the table, the more I wanted to attack it. I didn't address anyone, I just kept whacking and whacking. Thanks to the privacy, there was no restriction. I could beat the table as often and as hard and as long as I wanted. The thwocking of the tea towel and the energy required to do it summoned up deeper and deeper emotions. Sometimes, I felt electrified and I couldn't hit the table hard enough or fast enough. Sometimes I trembled as intense feelings coursed through me. Gradually I found my voice and I screamed and cried. Later, words came – three elemental words at first, that I screamed over and over:

"I . . . HATE . . . YOU! I . . . HATE YOU!!! I HATE YOU!!! I HATE YOU!!!"

I'd beat the table and scream as loud as I could until there was no more fire in me. The sheer force that I put into each whack and the savage thwocking sound shook me to my roots. After a few days I'd go back to it and soon I started to say more:

"I HATE YOU . . . YOU FUCKING BASTARD! YOU RUINED MY LIFE! YOU RUINED MY LIFE! I FUCKING WELL HATE YOU!"

I was beating my father hard with the tea towel as I roared these words. I was assaulting him as hard as I could. Afterwards I was always shaken and spent, so much so that I was sometimes reluctant to do the anger work. But I enforced a discipline on myself so that, doggedly, I'd pick up the tea towel, wet it, wring it out and begin. I always used the same tea towel and never used it for household chores. To me, it was full of poison and it lived on a shelf under the sink. When I hung it out to dry on the clothes line, I didn't put it near my washing. As I continued to connect with my feelings, I found that I was very angry indeed. Eventually I was crying out in accusation and beating the table every day and there seemed to be no end to it.

I went to see my father around this time. I wanted to accuse him directly of ruining my life. I wanted him to see my anger before he died. All the pus inside me was gathered together, ready for dumping, and I earnestly wanted to dump it on him. I'd vomit it up on him, as it were, and it would be a deeply cleansing experience. I walked purposefully to his house and knocked on the door. He opened it. Jesus, he was small now. He sensed trouble from the set of me and backed away into the house, shuffling rather than stomping as of old. I followed. The soles and the uppers of his shoes had come apart and socks with holes in them peeped out. There were food stains on his jumper, right on the apex of his bloated stomach. His eyes were wary but he made a play of putting the kettle on.

I suddenly remembered another kettle. The same thing for years in the old kitchen, heavy and silver, with a big thick flex. One Sunday when I was about twelve we were alone together and I was making him a cup of tea before he went to mass. The mood was bad and he was silent and as yet unshaven. The kettle made a strange rasping noise and he knew straight away what it was.

"You stupid fool," he growled, "you always have ta cover the element."

On the heel of these words he slapped me hard across the face. I was reaching for the switch to turn the kettle off just as he did so, and got a shock from the faulty wiring. Electric waves surged through me painfully. The slap and the shock happened at the same time and, to this day, in spite of myself, I have to check that I have covered the element whenever I fill a kettle. Curiously, for a man who expressed himself through violence, my father rarely beat us children. I think he preferred to ignore our existence and beating us would have required some level of engagement. Only once I remember he thrashed Joseph and me with a stick for staying out all day and that was only because his mother was watching. The fact that he never touched us but battered our mother so badly made me feel even more guilty. At least if he'd beat us as well we'd all have been in it together.

Now, the pathetic shuffling went on but I didn't care. What I had to say would upset him but what was a little discomfort over a few words to the decades of pain I'd endured? I declined the tea and got to the point:

"I've come here to say something to you and this is it . . ."

The eyes hardened up now. He looked as if, in another lifetime, he might have hit me.

"You ruined my life . . ." I paused for effect, ". . . and the lives of my mother and my brothers and sisters."

My heart was pounding but I went on:

"I've been in the gutter because of you. You frightened the life out of me when I was small and I'll never forgive you for that."

When I finished, I turned around and walked out.

Although I'd rehearsed my speech, I'd forgotten most of it through nerves. But it didn't matter. The fact that I'd done it was the important thing. The badness was back where it belonged.

I never saw my father again. He dropped dead in the street a few years later of a massive heart attack. The bull's heart had finally given out.

Rose was wonderful. Much more than a sister, she was a good friend and throughout the years she'd come to visit us, no matter where we were: Toulouse Avenue, Arthur's house, the room before Canada, the refuge in London, Iris's cottage, where she endured Iris mocking the way we said *Mammy* and not *Mum* or *Mummy*. Rose told her something about our mother and Iris brayed in her face like a donkey: "*Mammy* . . . ha ha ha . . . *Mammy* aah . . . ha ha ha ha."

And then David's flat. She was always there for me, no matter what the circumstances, and never once forgot Jack's birthday, which meant the world to me.

My mother once came to Poole with Rose. She didn't want to – Rose made her come. I knew she went back and forth regularly between Cork and London to see her more favoured children, and of course South Wales to see Grace. I used to imagine her in the sky above my head, to-ing and fro-ing between her home and those of my siblings. I knew as soon as they got off the train that my mother didn't want to be there. The belligerent acquiescence I remembered from the trip to my exhibition was written all over her face. Jack and I were on the platform with two bunches of flowers – one for each of them. Rose was all smiles, cracking jokes and making a fuss of Jack. We loved the way he insisted on calling her Rosa and not Rose. My mother's weak smile couldn't hide the fact that she was hating every minute of it. David was waiting for us in the car park. I introduced them and he was charm itself, but she barely acknowledged him. She didn't want to see me, never mind some old bloke I was living with.

I was nervous in the flat. What was she going to think of this – a bit of a garage for a kitchen and a lounge so small you literally couldn't swing a cat in it? I went to put the kettle on and she followed me into the kitchen. I pretended not to notice her looking around. Jesus Christ! She must be thinking: *a kitchen with no windows? And was that breeze block or some kind of paint effect?* She'd come down from Hannah and Peter's lovely London homes to this. And she hadn't even wanted to. Rose had frog-marched her to the train station. Under her cold gaze I felt stripped down to my ugly bad bones. Without realising it, I was clutching a drinking glass so tightly it broke. Pain stabbed my palm and blood oozed out over my claw-like grip. I hid the wound and carried on making the tea.

David had a stomach bug and spent most of the weekend in bed so we ate dinner without him, in his lounge. On the Sunday, he got up from his sick bed to drive us out to a country pub for lunch. He stayed in the car while we went inside. It was hot and noisy and we had a lasagne that was gone off. The conversation was strained and as always we avoided anything to do with feelings. There was no opportunity to speak to Rose alone because my mother was clinging to her like a limpet, but I sent her psychic messages to take her away and never bring her back.

My mother's visit got me down, in spite of my anti-depressants. I carried on with my anger work but it never touched on her. The guilt made anger taboo. I simply couldn't access my anger towards her. I was still very much in the land of guilt, which laid me out flat at her feet, not in the land of anger where I'd be upright and shouting my head off. I knew that she and Sarah rowed and that Sarah often let her have it with both barrels, shouting: "You and your husband fucked my life up", or words to that effect. I marvelled at Sarah's temerity and the emotional freedom which allowed her to say things like that. She always seemed to cut to the chase and what interested me was the fact that it seemed to bring them closer. She was able to do and say what she wanted and her relationship with our mother stayed firm.

In fact my mother's relationships with all her children were firm. I was the only one who was out in the cold and no one seemed to care except Rose. I slumped into self-pity and even my tea towel activities stopped. I still felt angry with my father and wondered if it would ever end. I felt pathetic, alone in a foreign country, a refugee from chaos. Once I put Jack to bed, I'd go back into the flat and watch television. I'd hear David moving about in the house and knew there was a roaring fire going in his lounge. How I wanted to sit in front of it! But I couldn't. Antipathy had grown between us to the point where we hardly spoke, except about Jack. There was an impasse.

He was always right and never wrong and I put up with it for Jack's sake.

Then something really good happened. In the summer of 1996, after three years in David's flat, Jack and I moved. Our new home was a charming old bungalow with a big, leafy garden and a pond full of frogs. David didn't want us to go. He'd redecorate, move even. Anything as long as we stayed. There was no biting now, only pleading, and suddenly I felt a touch of his pain. An illegitimate baby in war-time Kent. In the fields with his mother who was picking hops. Her death when he was fourteen. I assured him we'd only be a few streets away.

Apart from our beds, we had no furniture but it didn't matter because at long last we had a proper home of our own, a place that I loved, not another bolt-hole to get away from something awful. After the kitchen with no windows, this one had three, plus a glass door. It was bursting with light and I kept lots of plants there, which grew to profusion. There was an open fire in the living room which I lit in the winter and drew great solace from. Gradually I got all the things we needed, starting with a table and chairs, and David popped in regularly to see Jack.

Life was improving but still I felt great loneliness. It hurt so much. I dreaded the weekends, especially Sundays when the neighbourhood silence underlined my sense of desolation. Bank holidays were the worst because it was like two Sundays in a row.

Now that I wasn't under David's roof, I had several brief relationships with men. The first was a lonely heart, the second was a bus driver, and the third I met in a supermarket queue. He thought I'd engineered it to get near him, like some sort of grifter, but actually I'd stumbled into the queue just ahead of him in a state of premenstrual tension. They were all unsuitable, especially the last one, who beat me about the head one night when I was drunk and he was sober, putting his pipe down carefully to do it. It had been a long time since a man had attacked me like that, not since before Jack came along, but naturally I blamed myself. We carried on until one day he shouted at Jack loud enough to make him jump and I literally pushed him out of the house along with his wretched pipe and told him never to come back. Jack was about nine at the time and I drew a line under men and alcohol for good.

One afternoon in 1999 I met a work colleague in the Poole High Street. I was surprised to see him because he lived way over in Bournemouth. Shyly he admitted that he'd just been to see a therapist. I was surprised. He always seemed so happy – joking around and making people laugh. The therapist's name was Sue and instinct told me to get her phone number and ring her, which I did. Her voice resonated with kindness and we arranged an appointment for the following week. During our first session I took as a starting point the fact that I never went out. I didn't socialise. I worked and rested but I never played. I couldn't even imagine it. My idea of socialising had always been getting dead drunk. I couldn't enjoy life. Why not, I wanted to know. What was wrong with me? The people I worked with had social lives. The mothers of Jack's friends had social lives. Even my elderly neighbours had social lives.

Once, a mother came to collect Jack for a sleepover.

"Off out tonight?" she inquired pleasantly, since I wouldn't have Jack.

"No," I answered flatly with my poor social skills.

Her face fell as she moved away. I spent the rest of the evening angrily repeating her question to myself: *Off out tonight? Off out tonight?* I guiltily realised she was only being friendly and admitted reluctantly that I wasn't going out because I had nowhere to go and no one to see. Cora No Mates, I upbraided myself. But why? I'd had therapy. I'd chanted affirmations. I took antidepressants. I should be better now. But I wasn't. Whenever I made a friend I didn't know how to behave. My reaction was always one of two extremes: I either felt crowded by them and pushed them away, or I was insecure and clung to them, in which case *they* pushed *me* away.

I told Sue about my life, the impact that my childhood had had on me, the low self-esteem, the abortions and the violent relationships. She helped me to see that I hadn't escaped from it, in spite of my earlier therapy, because I still believed I was bad. She was right. Central to my being was the feeling of being bad. I was Bad Cora. My parents' treatment of me had always concurred with this, with the result that I didn't see Bad Cora as a belief but as an immutable fact. It was entrenched in my mind and my choices in adulthood bore it out.

Throughout our sessions she has given me various homework assignments and one of the first was based on this belief. I had to make out two columns headed "My good qualities" and "My bad qualities", and underneath list all the things about myself that I liked and all the things I didn't like. I spent ages on it but try as I might I couldn't think of anything good. There was virtually nothing in the good column while the bad column was as long as my arm. I took it to show her and she challenged my assessment of myself. Did I really believe I had practically no good qualities? What about my parenting skills? I batted this away as instinct. My artistic ability? Again, instinct, a gift. Did I really believe I had so many bad ones? Yes I did, I told her, my heart speeding up, getting panicky. I wanted to get up and walk out. She was challenging my view of myself, a view I based my whole life on. She told me to think about my good list again. I did so and added one or two things tentatively, but it felt hollow. I didn't believe the things I was writing down. Praise I'd had over the years had never registered. Only bad things got taken on board. This idea of seeing more good points wove like a golden thread throughout my therapy with Sue. It was reinforced by other homework I did; for example, writing down all the good things in my life and reading that list at least once every day. Or writing down bad feelings to externalise them and then destroying the paper, symbolically destroying the feeling in the process. I had to realise that I had positive qualities and that Bad Cora was a belief, not a fact. Once I'd accepted that this awful definition of myself was just a belief I could start working on changing it.

I told Sue that I couldn't deal with people. I felt that everyone looked down on me. I picked up crumbs of friendship wherever I could but I wanted to be like everyone else and choose whom I befriended, not wait like some sad mongrel for anyone at all to pat me on the head. If I had a difficult relationship with someone I assumed it was my fault. I was always wrong and they were always right. I couldn't see people as they really were – good and bad, fallible, with as many faults as I had.

I came to her with bad habits that were so long-established that they exercised a powerful hold over me. For example, I overreacted to every little problem. I catastrophised, imagining disaster around every corner; or the opposite, I idealised, imagining everything was absolutely wonderful. I yo-yoed constantly between these two feelings. I felt defeated easily. I was very negative and found it impossible to be positive for long. During therapy I reverted to those old habits time and time again. Sue described these habits as grooves in my mind that had indented themselves on me over the course of my life. I'd thought negatively for such a long time that these grooves were deep and worn well into me. It was like stopping a juggernaut at full throttle. It wouldn't happen suddenly. It would take time to change.

She introduced the idea of mind control to help me think more positively. Mind control sounds Orwellian but it simply means preventing negative thoughts from getting established, not allowing oneself to have them so that the mind gets used to a diet of more positive thoughts. Visualisations help. Ones that I used were: throwing negative thoughts on the fire, crumpling them up like pieces of paper and throwing them in the bin, flushing them down the toilet. It was a bit like kicking a habit, like an ex-smoker resisting a cigarette. Eventually the mind moulds itself to the new order.

We were working on my beliefs when suddenly I had a huge breakthrough. From deep inside me came an epiphany, a sort of awareness that was like a quantum leap in my recovery. It's hard to describe this exactly but I *felt* my childhood feelings – the ones that had been suppressed and outlawed, the ones that had been numbed out of place until I was like that alcoholic who set her bed on fire. Of course! They'd been under my nose all the time. The sadness, the shame, the loneliness and the feeling of exclusion that now made my life so bleak were all misplaced childhood feelings that had gone underground and erupted disastrously in my adulthood.

I was so excited at this discovery. Now that I could feel them, I could do a very important thing. I could work on putting them back where they belonged – in the past. I got out the picture I'd used before of my First Communion and stared hard at it, imagining the internal world of little Cora. I took some deep breaths and I visualised plugging the misplaced feelings into her heart. I did this visualisation many times and each time the sense of bad feelings being redirected away from me grew stronger. When I saw Sue after making this realisation I was fizzing with excitement, with an air of something truly amazing having happened. I described it to her as a seismic shift in my perceptions. I'd always known intellectually that my experiences in childhood were damaging my life but I'd never *felt* it before. Now I'd encountered my childhood emotions head on and started the work of consigning them to the past. After this revelation, things started moving. I gradually accepted that Bad Cora was only a belief. I got out my list of good and bad points, added to the good ones and scrubbed out some of the bad ones. Gradually, the good points I made lost their hollowness and began to feel true.

With Sue's encouragement I went back to my anger work. In the end I had to kill my father, symbolically, to get free of him. I'd read that some people can only recover from abuse by symbolically killing the abuser. I thought I'd try that.

In the days when Jack was a young child and money was tight I had only the bare essentials and I prized my few utensils. Chief among these was a little vegetable knife called a Kitchen Devil. I used it for everything. I loved to hold it in my hands knowing it could cut and slice just about anything. When you got it in a stabbing clutch, it looked deadly. I tried it out on a wooden chopping board one evening when Jack was in bed.

WHAM!

I jammed it hard into the wood. The tip got stuck and I had to yank it out. I did it again. Again I yanked it out. Once more I stabbed it in. A sleeping monster stirred inside me. It was anger, slow and dozy at first; I was out of practice. I made myself say some words, which came out flat and quiet.

"You fucking bastard. I hate you!"

I laughed a bit at the incongruity of the violent words and the timid self-conscious tone. I drove the knife into the chopping board again, this time with greater energy and shouted:

"YOU FUCKING BASTARD! I HATE YOU!!"

Shouting was good. It kick-started my energy.

I stabbed again and again, driving the knife into the

chopping board with greater and greater ferocity. Over and over it went in. And as it did so, I visualised sticking the knife into his belly and then going up inside his rib-cage. With the next jab I tore into his heart and gave the knife a good twist before pulling it out and jabbing it in again. I shouted this:

"HOW DOES THAT FEEL? HOW DOES IT FEEL TO BE DESTROYED, YOU FUCKING BASTARD? YOUR HOPE WIPED OUT. NOW – YOU – KNOW – HOW – IT – FEELS! I – HATE – YOU!! YOU – FUCKING – BASTARD. I HATE YOU!! I HATE YOU!! I HATE YOU!!"

I visualised the look on his face as he realised that he was done for. The eyes that had always shunned me were full of fear and then they closed as he slumped over the knife and died.

I killed him symbolically many times, jabbing the mortal blows up into his heart with great ferocity. I needed to be sure he was dead and that my anger was truly spent. In the end the chopping board was pitted with stab marks. When I was sure I wouldn't need them any more, I took the knife and the chopping board to the municipal dump and hurled them into the rubbish.

Therapy requires time and work and courage. Courage because you have to be honest. That can be quite frightening if you've built your life on lies and false beliefs as I had. My sessions with Sue are ongoing, though not as frequent. Now we meet once a month, with a view to phasing it out completely. That's eight years of unbroken therapy. The longevity of my counselling acts as a counterweight to the many years of dysfunction.

Sometimes I feel that the ghost of bad feelings is still there in spite of all the work I've done but Sue reminds me how long I'd spent feeling bad about myself – forty years. It's understandable to have those phantom feelings. Her willingness to work with me indefinitely and her patience with me when I lapse has helped me hugely to realise my own value as a human being.

At long last, I felt myself changing, lightening. Like a hot air balloon I was rising, bags of sand falling away from me. It was time to come off the anti-depressants. I'd been on them over six years. I started taking one every second night and did that for a fortnight, then every third night for a fortnight and so on until I was down to one a week. Sue pointed out that there was virtually none of the active agent, paroxetine, left in my system by then, so I came off them altogether. I had no withdrawal symptoms whatsoever.

It would be great if we could put our lives on hold while we deal with our issues but we can't. We have to deal with the present as well as the past. I was making great strides when, in 2003, David died at the age of sixty-six. Sadly, our relationship had never improved. He'd only come to the bungalow when he had to. Sometimes we had a drink in the kitchen but we'd sit there in awkward silence, the sipping and swallowing of tea the only sound. I was shocked by his death. He'd gone into hospital for tests, hoping the pains he was getting were just kidney stones, but it was pancreatic cancer, which was advanced and inoperable and two weeks later he was dead. I was sitting on the end of his bed when he told me it was terminal. He was going to die. Saying the words out loud frightened him and he bit his lip to stop himself from crying. I couldn't meet his eyes as he told me. I didn't know what to say. I was in shock. In spite of our ups and downs, he'd been my rock for the past ten years. I swallowed hard. I just couldn't believe it. He looked so healthy. I left the hospital in a daze. I had to find Jack, who was fourteen then, and break it to him. He didn't say anything but wanted to stay at his friend's house.

That night, I went back to the hospital and David was so glad to see me. We held hands and I told him I loved him. I don't know where that came from. He said he loved me too and then I started crying. I couldn't stop, even when I realised it was upsetting him. I held his hand more or less constantly until he died. The last day was terrible. He'd shrivelled up into a little leathery yellow creature whose last breaths were coming out as a black tarry spray. Everyone else had left the room when suddenly he seemed to wake from his morphine stupor, turned his head to me and opened his eyes. Did he see me? His eyes were unforgettably awful. Big black pools with red rims in whites gone ochre yellow. Then he closed them and exhaled his last.

Sometime after the first 'seismic shift', I went to Sue with another one. In my reading I came across an account of a girl who was socially phobic and I read it with great interest. This girl had had a childhood similar to mine, in that she was forced to witness her parents' violent marriage. Her therapist unearthed the connection between this girl's fear of people and childhood events. Her mother had blamed her for the fact that she was trapped in a bad marriage. She insisted repeatedly that if it wasn't for her daughter, she could leave. The child grew up feeling she had no right to exist. If she hadn't existed, her mother would have escaped. This assumption of guilt was reflected in a very poor social life. She thought she didn't deserve one. When I read this, the hairs stood up on my neck. She could have been describing me, my mother and what she used to say to us. Her exact words are etched on my mind:

"If it wasn't for you lot, I wouldn't be here."

These words were really painful because they were true. Why would she hang around to be savagely beaten if she didn't have to? She was stuck with us and that was a fact. Because of us, she was trapped, and in that entrapment she was horribly abused. I'd felt bad about that for as long as I could remember. I'd see her bruises and her puffy face and the guilt was annihilating. I didn't deserve to live, let alone enjoy life. What right did I have to enjoyment, when my mother had suffered so much? My life should be one of atonement and no more.

But that was all wrong and intellectually I knew it. What I was so excited about now was the fact that I *owned* the wrongness of it. I *felt* her inadequacy as a mother. I was her child; *she* should have protected *me*, not the other way round. She had the power to leave and she chose not to use it. Only recently I discovered that she regretted not staying in Midleton that time when we sheltered with the nuns. That means she must have had the choice. I'd always believed she was forced to go back. So, she could have saved us from the horrors that followed. It wouldn't have been easy. No doubt she'd have had to struggle and we might have been singled out in the playground because of our absent father, but that would have been so much better than going home.

I visualised hurling guilt at my mother and another great weight lifted off my shoulders. As I did so I shouted these words at her:

"HERE – THIS IS YOUR GUILT, NOT MINE!"

"I NEEDED YOU. SHAME ON YOU FOR PUSHING ME AWAY."

"SHAME ON YOU FOR NOT PROTECTING YOUR CHILDREN!"

I repeated this exercise many times and, as with my father, the buried anger rose up and bled into it. I shrugged off the guilt about the beatings she'd suffered and connected with the anger that was underneath and in the wake of expressing so many long-held resentments, I finally felt cleansed of the poison my parents had filled me with. I remain ambivalent about the concept of forgiveness. I no longer feel angry and I own the fact that they acted out of weakness rather than malice. That's the extent of my forgiveness.

The final and most important step for me in recovery was the development inside me of a parental voice, the voice that lucky children internalise as a result of having good role models. Well-adjusted people take this voice for granted and it's a natural part of their development. Growing up without love, as I did, means you develop slowly and face the world lost and raw. A few months ago, I noticed something new. Like a magical seed that had burst into life, there was a wise little voice in my head. I listened to it and it got stronger. It advises and guides me. I sometimes objectify this voice and call it *mother* because that word fills a hole in me. When I don't know what to do, *she* advises me. When I'm in trouble, *she* protects me. I'm not as hungry as I was because I can turn to *mother* for what I need. I'm not as insecure as I was because I can turn inwards for reassurance. This voice is my best friend and with its advent I can say unequivocally that I've finally grown up.

I never confronted my mother in person and she died this year, 2007. She was seventy-seven. I wasn't going to go to the funeral because I'd said a bitter goodbye to her a long time ago. I made excuses like: "I can't take the time off work" and "I can't afford to", but I changed my mind at the last minute and then it became hugely important to go. My heart was pounding as I booked the flight, nervous in case I wouldn't make it on time, afraid that I'd be cast out of the family forever due to my absence. Of course, that was all melodrama. Practically speaking, I've been out of the family loop for years. I went for the sake of my siblings. I didn't want people commenting about the missing daughter.

Grace and Peter met me at Cork Airport. We drove home to Cobh in semi-silence. It felt like a dream with the sunshine, the intense green of everything and the super new motorway that we were whizzing along. Grace said respectfully that my mother was in the house. I was surprised, having forgotten the Catholic rituals of laying out and removal. We arrived, and there she was – a tiny figure in a coffin surrounded by candles and flowers, the air charged with the solemn dignity of death. She was wearing a tweed coat under the satin folds of the coffin, which made her look even smaller. Hannah pointed out that she had that look on her face and I knew exactly what she meant. A disapproving set to the features, lips pressed together in a long thin line. I touched her face lightly but felt no stiffness. Her skin was cool and delicate. Her hands were hidden from view under the satin but looked as if they were clasped. I wanted to see them. I'd always loved her hands, with the long graceful fingernails so unlike my own bitten stumps.

I was startled when I looked out the kitchen window and saw a palm tree in the garden that must have been three metres tall. I didn't remember it from my last visit. Mind you, that was about seven years ago. I asked Hannah about it.

"Oh, Sarah gave it to Mammy to thank her for her help when, you know . . ."

Yes I knew – a difficult period for Sarah a few years earlier when her mettle had really been tested. My mother had been her stalwart helper and friend. I stared at it and my heart twisted. Where had my help been? Hannah knew what I was thinking and she changed the subject.

Five of us stayed in the house that night. Grace was in her room. Peter was in his. Rose was in Mammy's room and Hannah and I were in the Big Room, where we whispered late into the night, almost like children again in the bed settee. There were a lot of people at the funeral the next morning. They filed past the coffin and offered their condolences to us, shaking each of us in turn by hand. An old friend of my mother's peered at me sourly and passed me over. Another one thought I was her sister. There were whispers of wonderful woman, a lady, a kind lady, a good neighbour. I accepted their condolences and agreed. But even in death she divided us. You couldn't put your finger on it but Grace's grief was special, worse than ours.

Apparently my mother had wanted to be cremated but it didn't happen. Her final resting place was The Old Churchyard that lay in a dip behind the town. We used to go there when we were kids to see the skeleton in the one tomb and to laugh at the funny English names on the ancient crooked headstones: Araminta Ponsonby, 1795–1839. A retaining wall had crumbled once revealing packed earth full of yellowed skulls. The council eventually repaired it, but in the meantime, the ancient skulls grinned out at the townspeople as they came and went along the adjoining road.

There was a great spread at Sarah's afterwards and lots of photographs that I'd never seen: my mother as a young woman in Dublin, her first nephew on her knee, my father as a baby in a studio portrait. There was a portrait of my mother that I'd painted for her birthday once and she'd never displayed. It languished for years in a chest of drawers and now Sarah had it framed and on her kitchen wall. A cousin was telling us that the old farmhouse where my mother grew up was haunted. I was enthralled as he told the story of how one night as a child he stood at the gates and watched a light passing from window to window in the empty house. I remembered my mother's account of seeing an old man standing by the well.

My flight back to England was a couple of hours after the funeral and I had to drag myself away from the talk of ghosts and farmlands. I waited for the flight in the swish new terminal building, all glass and expensive little shops. I watched young Irish people coming and going, casual and confident, flying over and back to England as if it were a bus ride. I imagined Eamon appearing out of nowhere. It occurred to me that he must pass through here from time to time.

Finally the flight was called. On the way over, after a double dose of espresso, I'd been convinced the plane was going to crash. I'd squirmed in my seat like a nervous ferret, alert to every sound and fleeting expression on the faces of the crew. On the way back I didn't care. As the plane took off and we seemed to be at right angles to the earth I was too tired to be nervous.

Drowsiness set my mind wandering. I thought about Jack, who is seventeen now. I have learnt so much about life from him. He knows he is loved. He'd never even question it and because of that love he believes the world is a friendly place. He sees what is. Not a lot of bad things that he imagines to be there, like I did at his age. Watching him embrace the world and the world embrace him, I can see how wrong I'd always been about life. There had never been any rejection or humiliation waiting for me. I know that now. Regret squeezed my heart as I thought of all the time I'd wasted on being afraid. But no. I prized the witchy fingers of regret off my poor old heart and refused to fall into that groove. I chose to focus on all the life that is left. And the fun we have together. I laughed to myself, remembering things Jack has said or done, characters that we have created in play that I want to commit to the page in the form of children's stories.

We flew into the afternoon sun and I settled further

down in my seat. It was a comfortable journey. I'd done the right thing and gone to the funeral and now I was going home, to a house that I own thanks to an inheritance from David (and a hefty mortgage). I compared this flight with the one fifteen years ago when I'd come back from Canada. Jesus, I'd come a long way. Back then, Reuben's branding of us as paupers was unkind but accurate. We had nothing. We lived on state benefits and lodged in his mother's tiny spare room. The only place I'd really felt at home was on the streets where I trundled Jack and the buggy along the pavements of various towns and cities. And I'd felt so bad inside, like hell on earth. When I first came to Poole, I thought that getting onto terra firma was all that mattered. Now, after years of working hard on healing myself, I know that solid ground is not what really matters. On the contrary, it's all about knowing you can stay afloat when the boat is rocking. I look back at what I have been through and I own the fact that I weathered it all, and I'm proud of myself. I say affirmations every day, and now I believe them. You *have to* believe them. It's no good if you don't. You can say good things to yourself a million times, as I did at the refuge in London and at Iris's cottage, but if you don't think about what you're saying and *believe* it, it's just a waste of time.

A flight attendant progressed along the aisle with a clattering trolley. She thought I was asleep and didn't ask me if I wanted anything. I thought about how we'd all been together in our mother's honour and how, now that the lynch pin was gone, we'd all scatter. Jesus, what was I talking about? I had to stop thinking like that! We were already scattered and had been for years. It had been twenty-seven years since the last time we'd all been together like that. I can't remember the occasion, probably a Christmas.

We were cruising now, over Wales. Soon we'd be in London. I thought about my sisters and brothers. As far as I know, only Rose, I and possibly Grace have had therapy. I'm out of touch with all the others and don't know how they cope with the past. I assume they're strong people – none of them has gone completely off the rails. Apart from Rose, their lives are opaque to me. I thought about what I knew: Rose lives in Devon with her partner and two children. We speak on the phone and meet up regularly. She's soon to qualify as a psychotherapist. Grace is a teacher and lives in Wales with her partner. Joseph, a practising Catholic, inherited my father's house in Cobh and lives there with his two dogs. Hannah is a nurse and lives in London with her partner and three children. Sarah, an earthy, fun-loving woman, lives in Cobh with her children and new partner. Peter, hardly the baby now at thirty-nine, lives in London with his partner Leo. Ironically, I'm the only one who got married – and of course I'm divorced.

We landed smoothly at Heathrow and I got an early coach to Poole. This journey was going well. No bumps. No obstacles. No delays. I didn't want to think any more. There was no more to think about. I just wanted to enjoy the rhythm of the wheels on the road and let the coach take me home. I sat on a seat at the front having no more to say – knowing my story has been told. I made a pillow out of my jacket and very soon fell fast asleep.

THE END

Direct to your home!

If you enjoyed this book why not
visit our website:

# www.poolbeg.com

and get another book delivered straight to
your home or to a friend's home!

www.poolbeg.com

*All orders are despatched within 24 hours.*